# Japanese Tea Culture

## Art, history, and practice

**Edited by Morgan Pitelka**

RoutledgeCurzon
Taylor & Francis Group

LONDON AND NEW YORK

First published 2003 by RoutledgeCurzon
11 New Fetter Lane, London EC4P 4EE

Simultaneously published in the USA and Canada
by RoutledgeCurzon
29 West 35th Street, New York, NY 10001

*RoutledgeCurzon is an imprint of the Taylor & Francis Group*

"Shopping for Pots in Momoyama Japan" by Louise Allison Cort, is
reprinted with permission from Miyeko Murase and Judith G. Smith
(eds), *The Arts of Japan: An International Symposium* (New York:
The Metropolitan Museum of Art, 2000).

"Commerce, Politics, and Tea: The Career of Imai Sokyu" by
Andrew M. Watsky is reprinted with permission from *Monumenta
Nipponica*, 50:1, pp. 47–65.

Typeset in Sabon by Wearset Ltd, Boldon, Tyne and Wear
Printed and bound in Great Britain by MPG Books Ltd, Bodmin

*British Library Cataloguing in Publication Data*
A catalogue record for this book is available from the British Library

*Library of Congress Cataloging in Publication Data*
A catalog record for this book has been requested

ISBN 0-415-29687-0

The editor dedicates this book to Professors Ronald DiCenzo and Martin Collcutt, for inspiring so many in the study of Japanese history and culture.

# Japanese Tea Culture

From its origins as a distinct set of ritualized practices in the sixteenth century to its international expansion in the twentieth century, tea culture has had a major impact on artistic production, connoisseurship, etiquette, food, design and more recently, on notions of Japaneseness.

The authors use critical approaches and methods from the fields of anthropology, archaeology, history, art history, and film studies to dispel myths about the disputed development of rival branches of tea practice, to contradict the fiction of the dominance of aesthetics over politics in tea, and to demonstrate that writing history has always been an integral part of tea culture. *Japanese Tea Culture* is a fresh and stimulating study of a traditional art that continues to exert an influence on cultural practices inside and outside of Japan.

**Morgan Pitelka** is Assistant Professor of Asian Studies at Occidental College in Los Angeles, specializing in the cultural history of premodern Japan.

Of all non-alcoholic beverages, Tea claims the pre-eminence, being drank by near, if not quite, half the population of the world, and common alike to all climes and all nations.

In China it is the national beverage, and it is used not only as an ordinary drink, but it is the chief factor in visits of ceremony, and in hospitality. Japan, too, is a large consumer, and its houses of entertainment are "Tea" houses. In the wilds of Thibet its use is universal, and so it is on the steppes of Tartary, where, however, it is made as nauseous and repulsive a drink as possible. In Russia, it is the traveller's comfort, and every post house is bound by law to have its *samovar* hot and boiling, ready for the wayfarer. In Australia, New Zealand, and Tasmania, the "billy" of tea is familiar, and forms the only drink of the shepherd, the stockman, and the digger. All the British colonies and possessions are devotees to the "cup which cheers but not inebriates." Great Britain herself is a great tea drinker, whether it be the "five o'clock tea," which has developed into a cult, with vestments peculiar thereto; the poor seamstress, stitching for hard life, who takes it to keep herself awake for her task; or the labourer, who takes his tin bottle with him to the field. In fact, go where you will, in every civilized portion of the world (except Greece, where the consumption is merely nominal), and you will find drinkers of tea.

(James Mew and John Ashton, *Drinks of the World*, 1892)

The Philosophy of Tea is not mere aestheticism in the ordinary acceptance of the term, for it expresses conjointly with ethics and religion our whole point of view about man and nature. It is hygiene, for it enforces cleanliness; it is economics, for it shows comfort in simplicity rather than in the complex and costly; it is moral geometry, inasmuch as it defines our sense of proportion to the universe. It represents the true spirit of Eastern democracy by making all its votaries aristocrats in taste.

(Okakura Kakuzo, *The Book of Tea*, 1906)

# Contents

# Figures

# Contributors

**Louise Allison Cort** is the curator for ceramics at the Freer Gallery of Art and Arthur M. Sackler Galleries, which together form the national museum of Asian art at the Smithsonian Institution in Washington, DC. She received a Master of Letters from Oxford University. She specializes in historical and contemporary Asian craft traditions, especially ceramics, textiles, and baskets. She is the author of *Shigaraki, Potters' Valley* (1979; reprinted 2000), *A Basketmaker in Rural Japan* (1994), and *Seto and Mino Ceramics* (1992), as well as numerous articles on the topics of tea and ceramics.

**Tim Cross** is Associate Professor in the Department of English at Fukuoka University, Japan, and teaches tea- and noh-related courses at Kyushu University. He is currently researching differences in tea practice between the Nambō Ryū and the grand master model. His publications are listed at http://www.hum.fukuoka-u.ac.jp/~eng/cross.html.

**Patricia J. Graham** directs the Japan section of the Kansas Asia Scholars Program at the Center for East Asian Studies, University of Kansas, and serves as an appraiser and consultant on Asian art nationwide. She has taught at Cornell University, Hobart and William Smith Colleges, and the University of Kansas, served as a curator of Asian art at the Saint Louis Art Museum, and Consultant for Japanese art at the Nelson–Atkins Museum of Art. Her recent publications include *Tea of the Sages: the Art of Sencha* (University of Hawai'i Press, 1998) and "Early Modern Japanese Art History: An Overview of the State of the Field," *Early Modern Japan: An Interdisciplinary Journal*, Fall 2002 (10:2), 2–21. Her current research focuses on Japanese Buddhist art and architecture from the seventeenth to the twentieth century.

**James-Henry Holland** is Associate Professor of Japanese language and culture at Hobart and William Smith Colleges in Geneva, New York. His article, "A Public Tea Gathering: Theater and Ritual in the Japanese Tea Ceremony," *Journal of Ritual Studies* 14:1 (2000) argues that the creation of greater social density and of deeper initiation of novice practitioners distinguishes public gatherings from the exalted "high teas," yet serves to support them. In addition to tea, his research interests include gift exchange and material culture in Japan.

**Morgan Pitelka** is Assistant Professor of Asian Studies at Occidental College, Los Angeles, USA. His publications include "Sadō ni okeru 'tezukuri' no imi" [The Meaning of the "Handmade" in Tea Culture], in Kumakura Isao (ed.), *Nihonshi ni okeru yūgei no shosō* [The Diversity of the Arts of Play in Japanese History] (Yoshikawa Kobunkan, 2003); and "Kinsei ni okeru Rakuyaki dentō no keisei," [The Structure of Tradition in Early Modern Raku Ceramics], *Nomura Bijutsukan Kiyō* (Spring, 2000). He is currently rewriting his Ph.D. dissertation as a book, tentatively titled *First in the Realm: Raku Ceramics, the Raku House, and Japanese Tea Practice*.

**Dale Slusser** has practiced the Urasenke tradition of tea since 1983, including nearly four years of study at the Urasenke headquarters in Kyoto, Japan. He has been an instructor of tea, both privately and at the university level, since 1989. He is currently an associate of the Center for East Asian Studies at the University of Kansas. His chapter is based upon his master's thesis, "Collecting Power in the Field of Chanoyu: Tea, Art and Architecture in the Sengoku and Momoyama Periods" (UCLA, 1994). Recent publications include "The Katsura Basket and Rikyū's Tea" and "Flowers for Chanoyu," in *Japanese Bamboo Baskets* (Los Angeles: Cotsen Occasional Press, 1999).

**Tanimura Reiko** is a visiting scholar at the School of Oriental and African Studies (SOAS) at the University of London. Her publications include *Ii Naosuke kenkyū: shūyō to shite no chanoyu* [A Study of Ii Naosuke: Tea and the Cultivation of the Warrior in the Late Tokugawa Period] (Sobunsha, 2001), which was given an award by the Dai Nihon Sadō Gakkai in June, 2002; "Chanoyu ni okeru 'kaiseki' no keifu" [The Genealogy of "Kaiseki" in Tea Culture], *Shūkyū to geijutsu* 52; and "Chanoyu to seiji: Ii Naosuke no chakai" [Tea and politics: Ii Naosuke's tea gatherings] in Kumakura Isao (ed.), *Nihonshi ni okeru yūgei no shosō* [The Diversity of the Arts of Play in Japanese History] (Yoshikawa Kobunkan, 2003).

**Andrew M. Watsky** is Associate Professor of Art History at Vassar College, New York. His publications on Japanese art include "Floral Motifs and Mortality: Restoring Numinous Meaning to a Momoyama Building," *Archives of Asian Art 50* (1997–1998): 62–92. His forthcoming book on the sacred island of Chikubushima in the Momoyama period will be published by the University of Washington Press. He is presently working on an annotated translation and analysis of the *Yamanoue no Sōji ki*, a sixteenth-century text on *chanoyu* and *chanoyu*-related objects.

# Acknowledgments

Louise Allison Cort thanks Nagata Shinichi and Kyoto-shi Maizô Bunkazai Kenkyûjo for enabling her to see the Sanjô sites. This article is reprinted here, slightly revised, with the generous permission of Miyeko Murase and Judith G. Smith of the Metropolitan Museum of Art. Tim Cross thanks Sogetsu Kai, Gretchen Mittwer at Chadô Urasenke Tankôai and Ms. Watanabe at Kyoto Shinbun for assistance locating resources. This research was funded with grants from the Australia-Japan Cultural, Economic and Legal Studies Academic Research Group of Fukuoka University. Earlier versions benefited from readings by (in alphabetical order) David Griffiths, Jeff Isaacs, Tom Looser, Jefferson Peters, Dale Slusser, and Stephen Timson. Thanks also for the patient tearoom encouragement of Omori Sôetsu and Tokushige Sôki.

Patricia Graham thanks Ogawa Kôraku for invting her to present an early version of this essay at a tea conference in Shizuoka, Japan, in October 2001

James-Henry Holland wishes to thank his informants: Their names are obscured here, but their generosity is deeply appreciated.

Morgan Pitelka thanks Kumakura Isao, Tani Akira, and Sen Sôin for their advice and encouragement, and Omotesenke for the invitation to the opening ceremonies and exhibition marking the release of *Kôshin Sôsa chasho* in 1998. David Howell and Ted Demura-Devore read drafts of the Kôshin Sôsa essay, while James-Henry Holland, Dale Slusser, and Laura Nasrallah read drafts of the introduction. This project was begun with the generous support of the Robert and Lisa Sainsbury Fellowship, the Sainsbury Institute for the Study of Japanese Arts and Cultures, England, and Nicole Rousmaniere, Timon Screech, and John Carpenter.

Dale Slusser thanks Herman Ooms and Andrew M. Watsky.

Tanimura Reiko thanks Minamoto Ryoen, Kumakura Isao, M. William Steele and Richard Wilson. Thanks also to Lesley Fraser.

Andrew M. Watsky thanks Martin Collcut, Lousie Cort, Christine Guth, and Dale Slusser for reading drafts and his research assistant, Danielle Fisk, for helping to prepare the article for re-publication. this article is reprinted here, slightly revised, with the generous permission of *Monumenta Nipponica*.

# Introduction to Japanese tea culture

*Morgan Pitelka*

The image of a mysterious, ossified cultural practice that the phrase "tea ceremony" conjures up does not do justice to the vibrant and contested tea traditions in either contemporary or historical Japan. Likewise, the term *"chanoyu"* (literally, "hot water for tea") with its close connections to the powerful tea schools that dominate Japanese tea discourse today, does not adequately represent the great diversity of practices attached to and influenced by tea consumption. The chapters in this book examine Japanese tea culture, the set of cultural practices that revolve around tea consumption in Japan. It is by no means a comprehensive volume, and in fact focuses in large part on one segment of tea culture, the ritualized, performative forms of tea practice that have been popular among elites in Japan since the sixteenth century. The authors attempt to avoid perpetuation of the linear, totalizing conception of tea that has come to dominate modern discussions of Japanese culture, and instead apply critical methods from a range of academic disciplines to situate tea in a broader hermeneutic context.

Why tea? Historically, tea played a central role in political and social life beginning in the sixteenth century, and deserves our attention for its great influence on varied forms of cultural production. Tea remains the non-alcoholic drink of choice for most Japanese despite the twin challenges of commodification and globalization. Historically foreign products such as coffee, cocoa, milk, soda, juice, and flavored and "enhanced" waters have flooded into the domestic marketplace, but tea endures.

The simplest and most common form of contemporary tea culture is the canned beverage available hot or cold from vending machines or "convenience stores" on any street corner. Such vending machines contain far more variety than similar machines in other countries. According to a 1997 study, for example, most vending machines in the United States averaged six available beverages, while in one small area of Hokkaidō, Japan, more than 140 separate drinks were available from vending machines. These included five types of oolong tea, eight types of "Western style" (black) tea, and two types of "traditional" (green) tea.[1] These distinctly modern beverages are usually consumed alone, on the way home from the train station or during a brief break from work. By contrast, the most rarefied form of tea culture is the powdered green tea drunk in ritualized contexts by devoted students of the art of *chanoyu*. These practitioners host and attend highly choreographed gatherings at which art objects and tea utensils (ranging from priceless treasures to improvised stand-ins) are displayed and used. This form of tea practice has had a profound impact on social etiquette, notions of hospitality, art production and connoisseurship, architecture and landscape design, and more recently, understandings of "Japaneseness" and the value of tradition. For these reasons, *chanoyu* and its rival tradition, *sencha* (steeped tea), are the primary focus of this volume.

This Introduction will begin by examining the practice of tea culture in Japan today, focusing in particular on beverage consumption, etiquette, ritual, performance, devotion, and narrative. The second section looks at the way in which we read tea culture, literally embodied in the state of academic scholarship on tea in Japan. The third section examines the process of writing about tea culture, and suggests a number of issues that are in need of further attention. The concluding section of the Introduction considers the experience of tea culture, and asks how we can represent the lived experience of tea practice. These varied approaches to thinking about tea culture in Japan set the framework for the chapters that follow.

Before turning to the practice of tea, we should address the mundane but salient question: What is tea? In popular usage around the world, the term tea can refer to any kind of infusion. A Japanese grandmother once confided that her only remaining means of feeling healthy and vital was to drink "carrot tea" (*ninjin cha*), which she made by boiling grated carrots to create a watery, orange-colored concoction. In contemporary Europe and North America, it is a simple matter to purchase and consume similar "herbal infusions," ranging from old favorites in Western cupboards like peppermint and chamomile, to more recent imports such as rooibos (a South African legume, *Aspalathus linearis*), maté (leaves from the South American *Ilex paraguariensis*), and yoco (bark from the South American plant *Paullinia yoco*).

The drink of concern in this book, however, is not the "all-natural" herbal infusion, but processed and fully caffeinated tea. In its wild form, tea is an evergreen, flowering bush or tree of the order Ericales, family Theaceae, and genus Camellia, known as *Camellia sinensis*. A range of varieties are grown today, including *Camellia sinensis* var. *sinensis* ("China tea") and *Camellia sinensis* var. *assamica* ("Assam tea"). Cultivators usually keep the plant pruned to a height of not more than 6 feet (2 meters) to encourage a "flush" of growth, the soft, young leaves and buds from which tea is made. In some locales, particularly Japan, they also partially cover the plant just as the buds begin to emerge, to encourage larger and longer growths in increased numbers. The next stage in tea production is the processing of the flush; different methods result in different types of tea. To make green tea, for example, the flush is picked, heated to prevent fermentation, crushed, and dried. Chinese oolong or jasmine tea, by contrast, is partially fermented. The buds are picked, allowed to rest, crushed, and then partially fermented before being heated to halt the fermentation process. The tea commonly drunk in Europe and North America ("black tea") is produced by yet a different method. The tea leaves are picked, allowed to wither, crushed, and then left to ferment entirely before being heated and dried.[2]

Like drinkers and distributors of herbal infusions, present-day tea producers and consumers vociferously make health claims for their prized beverage, much as they have for millennia. Tea seems to have various antioxidant and antibacterial properties, the latter enhanced by the fact that the beverage is made using boiled water. Tea has also been identified as a stimulant from the very beginning of its use in China. The primary source of tea's stimulating effect is now known to be caffeine, which is found in large quantity in tea leaves and buds: 3.5 percent by weight compared to 1.1 to 2.2 percent for coffee beans.[3] Critics have historically leveled a range of condemnations at tea as well, and in the modern era caffeine itself has been the source of some controversy as "the world's most popular drug." Tea and coffee are, after all, the two most commonly consumed beverages on the planet; one estimate claims that we drink 700 billion cups of tea and 600 billion cups of coffee per year.[4] Carbonated, caffeinated beverages such as cola are not far behind, making the impact of caffeine on our bodies a public health issue of vital concern.[5]

Tea therefore exists within a larger global market of non-alcoholic, caffeinated beverages that seems to be growing yearly under the control of large, multinational corporations. The survival of so many forms of tea practice in Japan would thus seem to be a somewhat surprising event. Similarly complex beverage cultures have disappeared or been homogenized as the victims of new trends or mass-produced competitors. The practice of crushing cocoa seeds to make a beverage, for example, has largely disappeared from the northern hemisphere. When the Spanish arrived in the Americas, they encountered cocoa for the first time; natives alternately used the beans as currency or crushed them and combined them with water and a variety of spices.[6] The Spanish soon added cinnamon or vanilla to their own mixtures, as well as a dollop of cane sugar. By the eighteenth century, this was one of the most popular beverages in Baroque Europe. In the 1870s, however, the Swiss developed milk chocolate, forever changing the nature of chocolate consumption north of the Equator. Today chocolate is inextricably linked to milk, and it is difficult to find the old form of the beverage outside of South America.[7] Other beverage practices such as drinking a mixture made from the dried, roasted, and ground root of the chicory plant, or the imbibing of salep (also saloop; made from the dried, ground tubers of orchid roots) have similarly faded from widespread, popular practice.

How did tea survive in Japan in its many forms? Although it is impossible to answer this question definitively, the chapters in this volume sift through tea culture's textual and material traces to highlight some key trends from four hundred years of heterogeneous practice. The two chapters by Watsky and Slusser, for example, focus on the alchemy of politics, social status, and cultural production that placed tea culture and the rhetoric of tea aesthetics in such a prominent position in the sixteenth century. Chapter 3 by Cort on the ceramics of late sixteenth- and early seventeenth-century Japan points to the great diversity in material culture of that period's urban marketplaces, and the facility of tea practitioners and utensil dealers at producing new cultural trends. My own chapter on the seventeenth-century tea master Sen Kōshin Sōsa illustrates the mediating role tea masters played at the intersection of politics and culture, and also points to the growing prominence of the Sen house of tea masters as the authors of orthodoxy in the tea world. Chapter 5 by Graham on the art of *chanoyu*'s counterpart, *sencha* (steeped tea), illustrates how collecting objects to use for drinking tea could function as a form of personal narrative in which the collection metonymically represents the collector and a set of (in this case Sinocentric) ideals. In Chapter 6 Tanimura's study of the warrior politician and tea practitioner Ii Naosuke likewise reveals that tea practice was for many an arena in which struggles over moral behavior, social status, and idealized cultural values could be waged. Chapter 7 by Cross deals with three cinematic representations of the life of *chanoyu*'s mythologized founder, Sen no Rikyū, and deconstructs the manner in which tea has simultaneously been situated as a global, peace-producing cultural practice and a uniquely Japanese tradition. Holland's chapter concludes the book with an ethnography of the use of written records and memoranda in contemporary tea gatherings, and the playful contrast between public and private narratives they create.

## Practicing tea

Tea first arrived in Japan as a component of a larger package of imported Chinese culture and technology. Writing, literature, architectural methods, music, dance, political ideology, and visual and material objects traveled to the Japanese archipelago from China – often by way of the Korean peninsula – on the vehicles of trade, diplomacy, and Buddhism. Tea carried associations of the exotic and advanced continental societies, making its consumption an inherently performative act. Members of the Japanese elite could symbolically imbibe the Chinese "empire of things" in a cup of tea.[8] Early drinkers also understood tea to be a medicinal brew, and drank it to increase health and vigor. Buddhist monks in particular relied on tea to keep them awake during the long hours of meditation. Symbolic and practical functions were juxtaposed in tea consumption from the start.

The combination of varied meanings and purposes in Japanese tea culture is by no means unique. In past and present societies around the world, beverage consumption manifests in myriad structures ranging from highly visible social practices to private forms of succor or devotion. Drinking, like eating, is above all a basic corporeal function. As the authors of an 1892 guide to drinks of the world noted,

> From the Cradle to the Grave we need DRINK, and we have not far to look for the reason, when we consider that at least seventy percent of the human body is composed of water, to compensate the perpetual waste of which, a fresh supply is, of course, absolutely necessary.

We drink, then, to subsist and survive, and yet the act of drinking is also a source of enjoyment:

> Thirst is the notice given by Nature that liquid aliment is required to repair the waste of the body; and, as in the case of Hunger, she has kindly provided that supplying the deficiency shall be a pleasant sensation, and one calculated to call up a feeling of gratitude for the means of allying the want.[9]

The individual practice of beverage consumption often manifests in particular and idiosyncratic rituals that vary from person to person: coffee drunk from purpose-built, insulated cups during the morning commute; a glass of purchased or squeezed juice swallowed as much for health as for pleasure; a sports drink consumed for extra energy during a run or hike; and a glass of water, or perhaps whisky, sipped before bed. The act of imbibing liquid can be a particularly private act.

For some time, however, collective beverage consumption has been understood as socially (though not always morally) normative. The practice of drinking feels most "natural"[10] in a group context, and likewise is thought of as promoting sociability. Coffeehouses, for example, spread throughout the Arab world in the sixteenth century, much as the practice of holding social tea gatherings spread among elite urban merchants and warriors in the same period in Japan. Taking a trip to the coffeehouse was an innovative act, a departure from the solitary and familiar domain of the home into the social world of interaction, discussion, and sociability.[11] The pioneering sociologist Georg Simmel referred to such sociability as "the *play-form* of association," an artificial world of staged interaction that simultaneously produces feelings of emancipation and conventionalism.[12] This concept of the dialectic relationship between "play" and "form" is quite useful for understanding the particular combination of opportunities for staged creativity with ruthless enforcement of individual and group norms produced within Japanese tea culture. The manner in which the gradual institutionalization of tea both restricted tea practice and created new spaces for creative cultural production will be explored further in the chapters in this volume.

How, then, is tea practiced in Japan today? The tapestry of tea culture is woven of many complex strands that defy easy untangling, but at a general level most Japanese encounter tea on a daily basis as a simple beverage. In specialty tea shops or in the average supermarket, a shopper can expect to find a startling variety of tea products. Steeped green tea (*sencha*) is perhaps most common, and available in many forms ranging from high quality "jeweled dewdrop" (*gyokuro*) tea to the rough, leafy "coarse tea" (*bancha*). "Roasted tea" (*hōjicha*) and "stem tea" (*kukicha*) are popular as well, often drunk cold in the hot summer months. Also common is "whole rice tea" (*genmaicha*), made of an equal mixture of roasted low-grade green tea and toasted whole rice. Chinese-style teas are also quite popular in Japan, particularly the semi-fermented oolong tea. Though harder to find, novelty teas such as "go-stone tea" (*gosekicha*), which consists of green tea molded into small spheres, are still produced and consumed. As mentioned above, many of these teas are available in cans from vending machines or markets, allowing the consumer to participate in the "complex cultural conversation" woven by the interplay of commodities in society.[13]

When served in social situations, tea also manifests as a key element in etiquette. Visits to shops, offices, or residences frequently result in the serving of green or black tea, a trend that goes back to the merchant shops of sixteenth- and seventeenth-century Kyoto. In contemporary situations that are more self-consciously constructed as "traditional," such as when visiting the workshop of a traditional craftsperson or performing artist, powdered green tea (*matcha*) might be served in a tea bowl, usually preceded by a sweet of some kind. The carefully choreographed movements of serving tea, which are themselves seen as physical manifestations of respect, have developed under the influence of *chanoyu*'s attention to walking, posture, and breathing in the context of the tea gathering.[14]

Tea practice continues to thrive in ritualized formats such as *chanoyu* and *sencha*, preserved and disseminated by the large, corporate schools that dominate the tea landscape. At the central headquarters, at regional branches, or in small local classrooms, students acquire specialized training in tea procedures, tea art connoisseurship, manners and decorum, and the school's version of tea history. Though the tea schools do not to my knowledge release official counts of their students, the guesses of observers range as high as four to five million total practitioners. Urasenke, the largest and most financially successful school, was reported in 1997 to have 300,000 members in the Tankōkai association of its organization, the majority of which are official teachers and instructors.[15] The number today is likely higher, implying a total population of well over one million students in Urasenke alone. Each member student pays a monthly fee, as well as a special license fee that is required each time a new course of techniques is begun. The costs of licenses are set by the schools with prices rising for more advanced licenses. Informants indicate that profit for one's immediate teacher is built into the price, although the majority of the fee is sent back to the headquarters of the organization. Moreover, tradition often dictates that a gift of cash up to the fee for the license be given to one's teacher at the time the license is received. Additional fees apply when a student has earned the right to purchase a "tea name" or attends special events and gatherings.

Membership in a tea school opens many doors in Japan. Students become affiliates of an imagined cultural community as well as a real network of teachers, craftspeople, art dealers, academics, and fellow learners that extends to every corner of Japanese society. The discourse and curriculum of the schools additionally serve to construct a temporal matrix within which the majority of official (i.e. school-sanctioned) tea practice occurs. Classes are held on a weekly or monthly basis, creating a phenomenological rhythm of lived tea experiences. Regularly occurring seasonal gatherings mark important aesthetic/symbolic moments in the annual calendar superimposed on the longer narrative of the school's linear development. Furthermore, the constant striving for higher licenses and greater access to the core of the school creates an imaginary temporal narrative of progress that is always approaching, but never reaching, a conclusion of complete mastery, acceptance, and access. Students can and do take part in tea activities outside of the school network, particularly gatherings hosted by or sponsored by tea dealers, who stand to profit from business with as many tea practitioners as possible, regardless of affiliation.[16] Access to these "informal networks" is often introduced or mediated by tea school membership.

*Chanoyu* is very much a performative ritual as well. The small, private gatherings that typify *chanoyu* meetings are intrinsically performative, with the host and guest(s) playing roles and speaking from a learned script in order to create, observe, and participate in a symbolically rich routine.[17] For ambitious tea practitioners, more conspicuous public gatherings that are staged for strangers and outsiders also represent opportunities to engage in mutual performance, but with the additional element of a non-participating audience.[18]

For some individuals who count themselves tea practitioners (and perhaps members of official tea schools), preparing and drinking tea is also understood as a form of personal spiritual devotion. Tea devotees often refer to their practice as "the way of tea" (*chadō* or *sadō*), a term that appropriates the Chinese religio-philosophical notion of the path or "way" (Chinese: *dao*; Japanese *dō* or *michi*) to legitimatize an increasingly popular (and increasingly contested) form of cultural production.[19] Like dozens of similar cultural practices that were reinvented as consumable paths in the lively urban marketplaces of Kyoto, Osaka, and Edo, tea was simultaneously popularized and systematized in this period. The association with religion was not, however, merely a seventeenth-century construct. As mentioned above, Buddhist monks drank tea in China, Korea, and Japan as a stimulant, and eventually tea consumption was incorporated into the definition of a healthy Buddhist life.[20] Furthermore, many of the sixteenth-century Japanese pioneers in the development of new designs in tea architecture and material culture were associated with Zen Buddhist temples in the cities of Kyoto and Sakai. Mythologized founding figures such as Murata Shukō, Takeno Jōō, and Sen no Rikyū all were either patrons of Zen or held Zen titles. Rikyū's descendants in particular continued his close affiliation with certain powerful Zen institutions, and in modern hagiographies of Rikyū, tea and Zen have been inextricably linked as a result. For the purposes of this section, the historicity of this correlation is irrelevant; it is enough that some contemporary practitioners believe that tea practice is a form of Zen-like meditation, and seek personal spiritual salvation in the processes and atmosphere of the tea gathering.

A final strand in this cultural tapestry is tea practice as a form of narrative. Tea practitioners constantly reiterate famous tea gatherings of the past. They also strive to re-enact the perceived aesthetic decisions (the "taste" or *suki*) of tea luminaries such as Rikyū. The major tea schools, for example, routinely stage private and public tea gatherings that mark important events in the lineage's history, often using the tea utensils that were selected for the original gathering. These are nostalgic acts that constantly seek to embrace the phantasm of tea's mythic past.[21] At the popular level within tea culture, the act of selecting and arranging tea utensils for a gathering is explicitly acknowledged as a form of constructing private and public narratives, as Holland explores in the final chapter in this volume. Tea practitioners collect and use tea utensils to display wealth and taste, to demonstrate personal connections, and to engage in non-verbal conversations with other tea practitioner *cognoscenti*.

## Reading tea

For many students of Japanese culture and history, tea is accessed first and foremost through scholarship. The vision of tea presented in academic writing in Japan reflects many of the trends seen in the practice of tea as described above, but also represents a more controlled, ideological form of cultural production. Since the seventeenth century, writing about tea has been incorporated into the assemblage of skills of the elite tea master, with the result that struggles between teachers and schools have occurred as much on the written page as they have in the classroom and the marketplace.

Post-war tea historiography has been dominated by scholarship written by a small and elite group of tea practitioners, or sponsored by the most influential tea schools. The three Sen family tea schools – Omotesenke, Urasenke, and Mushanokōji Senke – have been particularly vigorous in their promotion of research on tea history and culture. Urasenke, for example, runs a "research center" in Kyoto (the Chadō Shiryōkan) that holds exhibitions and conferences and includes a library staffed with full-time researchers. Urasenke also has an affiliated publishing house

(Tankōsha) through which it publishes two monthly journals (*Tankō* and *Nagomi*) and dozens of tea-related monographs.

The influence of the tea schools on research, publishing, and access to and dissemination of primary sources has serious ramifications for tea scholarship. Editors in the affiliated publishing houses are themselves members of the sponsor tea school, and it goes without saying that scholarship that is highly critical of the school or the school's vision of tea history is not likely to be accepted. Furthermore, because substantial rivalry exists between tea schools, affiliation with one school limits a researcher's access to the sources of other schools. Studies of important individuals or events in tea history based entirely on the documents and objects in the collection of a single school are common. Many important primary sources have been published during the post-war period, removing them from the confines of restricted access and making them available to all researchers. Even in this area, however, the influence of the tea schools has been unduly great, because the documents are preselected by tea school insiders before being published.

As a result of these trends, post-war Japanese tea scholarship has tended to privilege one individual – the founder of the Sen lineage, Sen no Rikyū – as the progenitor of Japanese tea culture, while largely ignoring the larger social, economic, and political context for his and other tea practitioners' activities. This vision of tea culture has gone mostly uncontested, and today is accepted in the general population as the only authentic version of tea's past. In this sense, the Sen tea schools have enjoyed overwhelming success in shaping the horizon of expectations of readers and practitioners.

In the past two decades, however, academic historians who specialize in research on tea history but are not necessarily affiliated with tea schools have begun to emerge, and they have moved away from a monolithic conception of tea culture. Archeologists have also become increasingly active in the study of tea's material culture, radically changing many long-standing assumptions about the history of tea utensil development. In 1993, the Society for the Study of Tea Culture (Chanoyu Bunka Gakkai) was founded, the first independent academic organization devoted to tea culture. In 1994 the Society began publication of an annual journal of tea research.

These developments have begun to affect publishing by the major tea houses. In 2000, Tankōsha began publication of an eleven-volume series of monographs devoted to every aspect of tea culture.[22] It included numerous essays by non-affiliated scholars, and generally approached themes such as "the art of tea" in a fresh manner. Perhaps most remarkable have been a number of symposia held in recent years that bring together traditional, tea school-sponsored scholars with archeologists and historians who do not share the orthodox vision of tea's development. In 1999, for example, Urasenke sponsored an exhibition and symposium titled "Famous Tea Bowls of Chanoyu: Domestic Tea Bowls [*Chanoyu no meiwan: wamono chawan*]." On the surface, this event was just another canonical display of the key objects that are said to reverberate with the rustic spirit of Rikyū. The symposium and accompanying catalog, however, revealed a far more contested field. Archeologists who increasingly believe that many of the ceramics associated today with Rikyū were in fact produced after his death spoke alongside some of Urasenke's most respected and knowledgeable proponents. A historian of ceramics who had previously been ostracized from the clique of school-sponsored scholars (as well as from the key resources they control) was suddenly presented with the opportunity to present her insightful yet unorthodox research. If such occasions for open dialogue continue, tea scholarship seems likely to diversify further in the future, which hopefully will lead to the much needed problematization of the ideological shibboleths found at the intersection of tea practice and scholarship.

A scattered but useful literature on tea has emerged in English over the course of the twentieth century, often following the trends in Japanese tea practice and tea scholarship.[23] In 1906, the "internationally minded Japanese intellectual and globe-trotting Zen priest"[24] Okakura Kakuzo described *chanoyu* as "the true spirit of Eastern democracy," in his book on "the tea cult," a cultural practice represented as at once utterly alien and seductively intuitive. A.L. Sadler remedied Okakura's vague, aphoristic account with a deceptively encyclopedic volume on the treasures, heroes, and history of the "tea ceremony" in Japan.[25] In the post-war years, as Urasenke in particular became progressively more internationalist, increasing numbers of Japanologists studied tea and wrote about its history, usually in the mode established by Japanese practitioners and scholars. Translations of works by Japanese scholars also became increasingly available.[26]

Certain studies broke the mold of Japanese tea scholarship, such as Louise Cort's ground-breaking 1979 study of the long history of a rural pottery community, which paid significant attention to interactions with tea practitioner consumers.[27] Robert Kramer's insightful (but unfortunately unpublished) 1985 University of Chicago dissertation went even further in its critical application of post-structuralist theory to the early modern and modern history of tea.[28] More recently, the art historian Christine Guth has insightfully examined the interest among Japan's first modern industrialists in collecting tea utensils and other genres of "traditional" Japanese art.[29] The historian Mary Elizabeth Berry discusses tea practitioners in her well-written account of social and political turmoil in sixteenth-century Kyoto.[30] Most recent is art historian Patricia Graham's study of Chinese-style steeped tea (*sencha*) and its associated arts, a project that she develops further in her chapter in this volume.[31]

## Writing tea

In writing about the history and contemporary practice of tea culture in Japan, we participate in a tradition of commentary and critique that extends back to the sixteenth century. Recording our hermeneutic encounters with textual and material remnants of tea's past and fading present is in and of itself a form of tea practice, though the extension of this process outside of the dominion of tea adherents and into the field of academia is a relatively new phenomenon. In writing, though, we participate in the ongoing cultural production of tea. To borrow a paradigm from Bernard Faure, previous writings affect our understanding of tea, and our understanding of tea in turn affects the type of scholarship we produce. This "circular causality" has rarely been acknowledged in tea historiography.[32]

The authors in this volume emerge from a broad range of backgrounds and professions that inform the manner in which each writes about tea culture. We include academic historians and art historians; current and former members of tea schools; museum curators; and an academic anthropologist. Our personal and professional identities inform the manner in which we have encountered and experienced tea, and also influence our practical and methodological responses. It goes without saying that the problems and concerns of one author are not necessarily those of the next, and that the range of approaches and interpretations presented in this book is in no way representative of a new school or movement of tea scholarship.

Working on this volume has raised a number of issues that this author believes deserve further concerted consideration. The historical and contemporary relationship between tea and Zen, for example, is in dire need of critical appraisal. As mentioned above, many of the iconic figures of tea history were closely affiliated with Zen Buddhism, the most prominent being Sen no Rikyū. Emerging from the institutionalized hagiography of Rikyū is an orthodox rhetoric of tea practice that is filled with discursively irrational aphorisms of the sort common to the Chan/Zen tradition. These pronouncements have all too often been given too much importance, particularly the notion that "tea and Zen have the same flavor" (*chazen ichimi*). Christians, Shinto priests, Confucianists, and members of other Buddhist schools have also practiced tea throughout its history, often making major contributions to tea's development. More importantly, the ideological functions of tea practitioners' appropriation of Zen hierarchy, Zen notions of lineage, Zen naming terminology, and the language of Zen enlightenment have been completely ignored in the secondary literature. We need to reconsider the historical relationship between Zen and tea as an alliance between two corporate entities, a bond that held as much for political and economic reasons as for spiritual or aesthetic ones.[33] We need to pay particular attention to the essentialist and nationalist reverberations in modern writings on tea and Zen, and be wary of the simplistic conflation of the complex religious practice that is Zen Buddhism and the equally convoluted cultural practice that is *chanoyu*.

Another issue that needs further consideration, not only in the study of tea but in the larger field of "traditional" culture, is the historical and contemporary role of the *iemoto* system in shaping practice and discourse. "*Iemoto*" is sometimes translated into English as "family head" or "grand master," though these phrases do not adequately capture the flavor of the Japanese term, which literally translates as "origin/source of the house." This *iemoto* system of social and cultural organization, though seen in elemental form before the early modern period, emerged as a dominant force in the late seventeenth and early eighteenth centuries. In this period, the male heads/grand masters of schools instituted new standards for training, accreditation, membership, practice, and even aesthetic taste. The *iemoto* defined the terms of practice for all members of the school. The claim of belonging to a familial group and the acquisition of skills offered by *iemoto* organizations proved extremely popular, and many existing tea schools saw their memberships rise dramatically. By the end of the eighteenth century, some had expanded throughout the Japanese archipelago, regulating large populations of amateur tea practitioners through a unified curriculum and system of licensing.[34] The *iemoto*-led tea schools proved remarkably adaptable, and managed to survive the ruptures of the Meiji Restoration and World War II. Their impact on the formation of cultural structures historically, and their role in both limiting and preserving myriad cultural practices over time are topics in need of focused research.

Also related is the difficulty of studying culture through documents, visual sources, material objects, and architecture. Most scholars of tea, both inside and outside of Japan, tend to approach their research from a single academic discipline such as history (with its focus on documents) or art history (with its focus on stylistic analysis and connoisseurship). This approach is at odds with the inherent interdisciplinarity of tea practice, which demands close interaction with written records and memoranda (as described by Holland), ceramics and other utensils (as described by Cort), visual and textual materials such as inscribed paintings or calligraphies (mentioned in Graham's chapter), and the symbolically constructed spaces of tea gardens and tea houses. Although it is near impossible to be fluent in all of these fields of study, ignoring whole categories of historical evidence produces a narrow and uninformed vision of tea practitioners and tea culture.

## Experiencing tea

The relationship of language to experience lies at the heart of the study of culture. It inspires simple but thorny questions such as those posed by Susan Stewart in her influential book, *On Longing*: "How can we describe something? What relationship does description bear to ideology and the very invention of that 'something'?"[35] This issue seems particularly problematic in the case of tea practice, which for most people is a non-rational, non-discursive experience. Spoken language is abolished from certain portions of the tea gathering, replaced by focused and choreographed interactions that constitute a shared performance. The movements of preparing, serving, and drinking tea are physically internalized as forms (*kata*) by rote repetition rather than through lecture, dialogue, or interrogation. The hostility to rhetoric in tea culture – borrowed perhaps from Zen – partially explains why tea practitioners' attempts to compose written histories have tended to reveal more about their absorption of modern paradigms of culture and history than about their subject matter.

In light of the danger of reproducing tea's ideological structures in scholarship, reflexive ethnography emerges as a particularly appealing approach to studying tea practice. I do not mean to imply that ethnographers translate the experience of tea into words more truthfully or objectively; rather, on the whole, experience has not "fallen in value" for the ethnographer who still appreciates the power of storytelling, both on the part of the informant and the anthropologist.[36] A number of recent (and as yet unpublished) studies have attempted to investigate the contemporary practice and meaning of Japanese tea culture without becoming imbricated in the legitimating strategies of the tea schools.[37] A diverse picture of the "tea life" of Japanese tea practitioners emerges from this still growing literature.[38] Holland, for example, fashions affecting biographical sketches of his informants, and then engages in thick description of their associations inside and outside the tea room. His analysis of non-elite tea gatherings as instances of "ritual performance" in which complex communicative allusions are made through the selection of utensils (*toriawase*) reveals tea society to be diversely stratified and rich in opportunities for creativity. These aspects are all too often overlooked in scholarly accounts of tea culture.

It is inevitable, perhaps, that countless aspects of the historical and contemporary experience of Japanese tea culture are missing from this volume. The central importance of the tea garden or "dew-covered path" (*roji*) as a liminal and transitory margin between everyday and ritual space, for example, is hinted at in Slusser's chapter, but not addressed directly in any of the other chapters. Likewise, tea practitioners' many innovations in architectural design – beginning in the sixteenth century and continuing to the present – unfortunately are not attended to in these pages. Perhaps most importantly, the tactile, non-discursive moments of tea practice have not been captured in the chapters contained herein. The sounds, smells, and sights of the tea room, not to mention the close proximity of bodies and art objects, combine to form an unspoken grammar of sensation and awareness. Like historical pasts that can never be fully recovered, these experiences lie suspended between the poles of encounter and representation. The following chapters record our own encounters with tea practice and its historical traces, selected and arranged (*toriawase*), carefully prepared, and ritually offered up for readers' consumption.

## Notes

1 Michael Ashkenazi, "The Can-nonization of Nature in Japanese Culture," in Pamela J. Asquith and Arne Kalland (eds), *Japanese Images of Nature: Cultural Perspectives* (Curzon, 1997), pp. 207–212.
2 For more information on the science and cultivation of tea, see Bennett Alan Weinberg and Bonnie K. Bealer, *The World of Caffeine: The Science and Culture of the World's Most Popular Drug* (Routledge, 2001), pp. 246–251.
3 These figures are somewhat deceiving, however, because the caffeine levels in the final beverage are generally lower for tea than for coffee. Bennett and Bealer, *The World of Caffeine*, pp. 236 and 327.
4 Ibid., p. 236.
5 It is clear that caffeine consumed in extremely large quantities can be dangerous, particularly because it can inhibit iron intake. In regular doses of the sort seen in popular beverage consumption, however, adverse effects are not immediately apparent. At present we find no consensus among scientists on whether or not caffeine poses a health risk. See Weinberg and Bealer, *The World of Caffeine*, for summaries of recent research.
6 Ibid., pp. 47–49.
7 William Gervase Clarence-Smith, *Cocoa and Chocolate, 1765–1914* (Routledge, 2000), pp. 10–32.
8 This term emerges in Simon Schama's reading of Roland Barthes' 1953 text, "Le monde-objet." Though Schama's subject matter – Dutch still life paintings – seems far removed from early Japanese tea consumption, the manner in which both forms of cultural production point to "the fateful connection between 'the domestic empire of things' and the global empire of commerce" is instructive. Simon Schama, "Perishable Commodities: Dutch Still-life Painting and the 'Empire of Things,'" in John Brewer and Roy Porter (eds), *Consumption and the World of Goods* (Routledge, 1993), pp. 478–479.
9 James Mew and John Ashton, *Drinks of the World* (Charles Scribner's Sons, 1892), pp. 7–8.
10 Ralph S. Hattox, *Coffee and Coffeehouses: The Origins of a Social Beverage in the Medieval Near East* (University of Washington Press, 1985), p. 127.
11 Ibid., pp. 87–91. It should be noted that coffeehouses were also sources of controversy among religious and political authorities in the Islamic world. Opposition to coffee consumption was argued on the grounds that drinkers "behaved in a reprehensible way." Of particular concern was the fact that social gatherings organized around coffee consumption often consisted of "clandestine nocturnal gatherings." See ibid., pp. 29–45.
12 Georg Simmel, *On Individuality and Social Forms* (The University of Chicago Press, 1971), pp. 127–140.
13 This phrase comes from T.H. Breen, "The Meanings of Things: Interpreting the Consumer Economy in the Eighteenth Century," in Brewer and Porter (eds), *Consumption and the World of Goods*, p. 250.
14 See Kumakura Isao, *Bunka to shite no manaa* (Iwanami Shoten, 2000).
15 Anonymous, "Kessoku 'ichimai iwa' e fushin," *Kyoto Shinbun* (29 September 1997).
16 See James-Henry Holland, "Allusion, Performance, and Status: The Social and Aesthetic World of Elite Practitioners of the Japanese Tea Ceremony," (Ph.D.

diss., Cornell University, 1997), particularly the section on informal networks: pp. 133–153.

17 Herbert Plutschow suggestively applies Emile Durkheim's theory that ritualistic rules of conduct invoke the sacred to the case of tea culture, arguing that for tea practitioners the sacred is not any identifiable deity but rather "the entire *communitas* assembled in the sacred space" of the tea room. "An Anthropological Perspective on the Japanese Tea Ceremony," *Anthropoetics* 1:5 (Spring/Summer 1999). See also Richard Schechner, *Between Theater and Anthropology* (University of Pennsylvania Press, 1985), pp. 138–144, on the mutual creation of performance. I am grateful to James-Henry Holland for this second reference.

18 Public gatherings of this sort are sponsored by tea schools, by tea utensil dealers, by individual practitioners, and by associations of tea and flower arrangement practitioners. As public performances, they serve both as opportunities to display wealth (in the form of tea utensils) and power (in the form of participants and attending audience members) and as chances to display technical mastery of the routines of being a host or guest. See Holland, "Allusion, Performance, and Status," pp. 148–153.

19 See Slusser's discussion of the conception of tea practice as a path or "way" in Chapter 2.

20 See, for example, *Kissa yōjōki* by the monk Eisai (1141–1215), founder of the Rinzai school of Zen Buddhism in Japan.

21 Marilyn Ivy uses the term "phantasm" to indicate how nostalgia for something absent is neither an exercise in complete imaginary construction nor an attempt to recover something authentic, but "an epistemological object whose presence or absence cannot be definitively located." *Discourses of the Vanishing: Modernity, Phantasm, Japan* (The University of Chicago Press, 1995), p. 22.

22 *Sadōgaku taikei*. Even this series, however, has Sen Sōshitsu, the head of Urasenke, listed as the supervisory editor.

23 I focus in this Introduction on English language research, but there is a lively literature on Japanese tea culture in other European languages. Recent works in German, French, Italian, and Russian, for example, include the following: Norbert R. Adami, "Tee-Zeremonie in Japan oder Form und Inhalt," in *Münchner japanischer Anzeiger: Eine Vierteljahrsschrift* 4 (1993), pp. 8–33; Franziska Ehmcke, *Der japanische Tee-Weg: Bewusstseinsschulung und Gesamtkunstwerk* (Cologne: DuMont, 1991); Nicolas Fieve, Sylvie Guichard-Anguis, Michèle Pirazzoli-t'Serstevens, *et al.*, *Les arts de la cérémonie du thé* (Dijon: Faton, 1996); Manar Hammad, *L'architecture du thé* (Paris: Groupe de recherches semio-linguistiques, École des hautes études en sciences sociales, Centre nationale de la recherche scientifique, 1987); Horst Siegfried Hennemann, *Chasho: Geist und Geschichte der Theorien japanischer Teekunst* (Wiesbaden: Harrassowitz, 1994); Horst Siegfried Hennemann, *Cha-no-yu: die Tee-Kultur Japans* (Nachrichten der Gesellschaft für Natur- und Völkerkunde Ostasiens, Hamburg: Otto Harrassowitz, 1980); Aleksandr Nikolaevich Ignatovich, *Filosofskie, istoricheskie i esteticheskie aspekty sinkretizma* (Moskva: Russkoe fenomenologicheskoe obshchestvo, 1997); Christlieb Jobst, "Befriedigung aus Tee und Blumen: Traditionelle Formen der Selbstverwirklichung," in Gebhard Hielscher (ed.), *Die Frau in Japan* (OAG-Reihe Japan modern, vol. 1, 1984); Dani Karavan, *Tè: la cerimonia del tè* (Gliori-Fattoria di Celle, 2000); Brigitte Kita, *Tee und Zen – der gleiche Weg* (Munich: Erd, 1993); Bernadette Raab, *Das Wunder der Teestunde: Teegeniesser erzählen eigene Erlebnisse* (Aufl.-Ottensheim: Lilanitya, 1997); Hans Schwalbe, *Die Teezeremonie* (Munich, 1979). I am grateful to Michael Wachutka and Hideyuki Morimoto for assistance in compiling these references.

24 Robert Sharf, "The Zen of Japanese Nationalism," *History of Religions* 33:1 (August, 1993), p. 3.

25 A.L. Sadler, *Cha-no-yu: The Japanese Tea Ceremony* (J.L. Thompson & Co., 1934).

26 Some admirable studies include Rand Castile, *The Way of Tea* (Weatherhill, 1971); Ryoichi Fujioka, *Tea Ceremony Utensils* (Weatherhill, 1973); Sen'o Tanaka, *The Tea Ceremony* (Kodansha International Ltd, 1973); T. Hayashiya, M. Nakamura and S. Hayashiya, *Japanese Arts and the Tea Ceremony* (Weatherhill, 1974); Henry Mittwer, *The Art of Chabana: Flowers for the Tea Ceremony* (Charles E. Tuttle Company, 1974); Theodore Ludwig, "The Way of Tea: A Religio-Aesthetic Mode of Life," *History of Religions* 14 (1974); Beatrice M. Bodart, "Tea and Counsel: The Political Role of Sen Rikyū," *Monumenta Nipponica* 32 (1977); H. Paul Varley and George Elison, "The Culture of Tea; From its Origins to Sen no Rikyū," in George Elison and Bardwell L. Smith (eds), *Warlords, Artist and Commoners: Japan in the Sixteenth Century* (University of Hawai'i Press, 1981); Theodore M. Ludwig, "Before Rikyū: Religious and Aesthetic Influences in the Early History of the Tea Ceremony," *Monumenta Nipponica* 36 (1981); Shigemori Chikamatsu, *Stories from a Tearoom Window* (Charles E. Tuttle Company, 1982, trans. Kozaburo Mori); Dorinne Kondo, "The Way of Tea: A Symbolic Analysis," *Man* 20 (1985); Herbert E. Plutschow, *Historical Chanoyu* (The Japan Times Ltd, 1986); Jennifer Anderson, "Japanese Tea Ritual: Religion in Practice," *Man* 22:3 (1987); the essential multi-author volume, Paul Varley and Kumakura Isao (eds), *Tea in Japan: Essays in the History of Chanoyu* (University of Hawai'i Press, 1989); Richard Wilson, "The Tea Ceremony: Art and Etiquette for the Tokugawa Era," in *The Japan of the Shoguns* (The Montreal Museum of Fine Arts, 1989); the Urasenke-centered but very helpful ethnography by Jennifer Anderson, *An Introduction to the Japanese Way of Tea* (State University of New York Press, 1991); Barbara Lynne Rowland Mori, "The Tea Ceremony: A Transformed Japanese Ritual," *Gender and Society* 5 (1991); Barbara Lynne Rowland Mori, *Americans Studying the Traditional Japanese Art of the Tea Ceremony: The Internationalizing of a Traditional Art* (Mellen Research University Press, 1992); Julia Nakano-Holmes, "Furuta Oribe: Iconoclastic Guardian of Chanoyu Tradition," (Ph.D. diss., University of Hawai'i Press, 1995); Dennis Hirota, *Wind in the Pines: Classic Writings of the Way of Tea as a Buddhist Path* (Asian Humanities Press, 1995); Sen Sōshitsu XV, *The Japanese Way of Tea from its Origins in China to Sen Rikyū* (University of Hawai'i Press, 1998); and of course the many translated and original essays in Urasenke's English-language journal, *Chanoyu Quarterly*, which consists of eighty-eight issues published between 1970 and 1999. A number of anthropologists have also conducted research on tea culture in recent years. See n. 37.

27 Louise Cort, *Shigaraki, Potters' Valley* (Kodasha, 1979).

28 Robert Kramer, "The Tea Cult in History" (Ph.D. diss., University of Chicago, 1985).

29 Christine M.E. Guth, *Art, Tea, and Industry: Masuda Takashi and the Mitsui Circle* (Princeton University Press, 1993).

30 See Chapter 7 of Mary Elizabeth Berry, *The Culture of Civil War in Kyoto* (University of California Press, 1994).

31 Patricia Graham, *Tea of the Sages: The Art of Sencha* (University of Hawai'i Press, 1998).

32 Bernard Faure, *Chan Insight and Oversight: An Epistemological Critique of the Chan Tradition* (Princeton University Press, 1993), p. 145.

33 Greg Levine's attention to Rikyū's patronage of the powerful Zen temple Daitokuji is particularly instructive. See "Jukōin: Art, Architecture, and Mortu-

ary Culture at a Japanese Zen Buddhist Temple" (Ph.D. diss., Princeton University, 1997) and his work-in-progress, tentatively entitled, *Daitokuji: Visual Cultures at a Japanese Zen Buddhist Monastery.*

34  See Chapter 4, "The Raku House and the Iemoto System," in Morgan Pitelka, "Raku Ceramics: Tradition and Cultural Reproduction in Japanese Tea Practice, 1574–1942," (Ph.D. diss., Princeton University, 2001) for more on the history of the *iemoto* system in tea.

35  Susan Stewart, *On Longing: Narratives of the Miniature, the Gigantic, the Souvenir, the Collection* (Duke University Press, NC, 1993), p. ix.

36  This interpretation is inspired by Walter Benjamin, "The Storyteller," in Walter Benjamin, *Illuminations* (Schocken Books, 1968), p. 83.

37  Authors are of course reflexive to different degrees. Holland, "Allusion, Performance, and Status," is a particularly notable example of an ethnographer critically examining his position *vis-à-vis* his informants, and taking into account the manner in which his presence impacts their practice. Also interesting is Melissa Marie Kane's work, "Communicating Tea: An Ethnography of Social Interaction and Relationship Construction in the Japanese Tea Ritual," (Ph.D. diss., University of Washington, 1998). She applies speech communication theory and the insights of Mikhail Bakhtin on speech as a social event to the communication that occurs in the tea gathering. As is the case with the scholarship of Barbara Mori (1991; 1992), Kane conducted much of her research among tea practitioners outside of Japan, illuminating the transnational character of Japanese tea culture in the post-war years. The most recent ethnography as of 2002 is Etsuko Kato, "Bodies Representing the Past: Japanese Women and the Tea Ceremony after World War II," (Ph.D. diss., University of Toronto, 2001). Kato interprets the study of the procedures of preparing, serving, and drinking tea (*temae*) as an act of oppositional empowerment on the part of socially "nondominant" groups, such as commoners in the early modern period, and urban housewives in the post-war period.

38  Holland, "Allusion, Performance, and Status," p. 29.

# 1 Commerce, politics, and tea
## The career of Imai Sōkyū (1520–1593)

*Andrew M. Watsky*

## Introduction

The ritual preparing and drinking of powdered green tea was significant in sixteenth-century Japan for more than its contribution to a still-reverberating and distinctly Japanese aesthetic. Of equal, if not greater, importance was the role it played as a widely accepted forum for men of different social strata. Tea allowed warriors and merchants to make formal contacts and eased their communications regarding the many concerns they shared. These intertwined aspects of tea – the aesthetic and political – have often been commented on. Sen no Rikyū (1522–1591) in particular has been the subject of countless scholarly writings, for his crucial role in developing the aesthetics of tea in the late sixteenth century and for his politically colored activities as tea master to Toyotomi Hideyoshi.[1] The attention accorded Rikyū has had the unfortunate consequence, however, of overshadowing other tea men of the time and thus obscuring some of the rich complexities of the period.

This chapter aims to shed light on one of these marginalized figures, Imai Sōkyū (1520–1593). Throughout the rule of Oda Nobunaga (1534–1582), Sōkyū was pre-eminent among the merchant tea men of the flourishing port city of Sakai. His central role in the rapidly developing tea aesthetic is manifest in his connoisseurship and acquisition of tea utensils that were widely commented on by fellow tea men as the finest in Japan.[2] During this period, moreover, no one was so skilled as he in using aesthetic means to achieve decidedly non-aesthetic ends. With Nobunaga's backing, Sōkyū garnered numerous lucrative appointments and privileges that made him one of the most successful participants in the conflux of art and power that was sixteenth-century tea. Sōkyū should, indeed, be recognized as a model for Rikyū, who enjoyed his most successful years under Hideyoshi, only after the death of Nobunaga and the waning of Sōkyū's fortunes.

To begin, it is instructive to follow Sōkyū's account of a Sakai tea gathering held in 1554. The host was the leading tea master of the day, Takeno Jōō (1502–1555). The only two guests were Sōkyū and Matsunaga

Hisahide (1510–1577), one of the most powerful warriors in the city. Sōkyū describes the proceedings in his tea diary, first listing the utensils used according to their relative placement within the tea room.[3] Among them were a large jar for tea leaves and a small container for powdered tea, identified respectively as the Matsushima jar (*tsubo*) and the "eggplant" tea caddy (*nasu chaire*).

Sōkyū lingers in his discussion of these two objects. He notes, "The jar is not very large; there are holes on the front near the base. It is a particularly fine jar." For the small tea caddy, he provides four precise measurements and comments, "The overall shape is excellent. On the bottom is written in Jōō's brush the name [of the tea caddy] 'Miotsukushi,' and [Jōō's] cipher." In this, the opening entry of his tea diary, Sōkyū exercises his considerable powers of connoisseurship and political acumen. He locks his gaze on two utensils that, as will be seen below, captured the attention of the most influential mercantile and political figures of his age, including Nobunaga. Sōkyū used the Matsushima jar and the eggplant tea caddy – and tea culture as a whole – to help further his remarkable career.

Sōkyū's career can be traced in considerable detail, through a wealth of contemporary materials, including tea diaries and letters, many of which invoke Nobunaga's name and authority. In this chapter, I begin with the years leading up to his initial contact with Nobunaga, and then focus on the period during which his interactions with the ruler brought him to the height of political influence and commercial success.

## Sōkyū's early years

Sōkyū's ancestry and early years prior to the 1550s must be pieced together, primarily from retrospective accounts.[4] Claiming warrior ancestry for the Imai, an eighteenth-century family lineage states that the clan descended from the Sasaki of Ōmi province and that during the Bunmei era (1469–1487) Sōkyū's grandfather was castellan in the town of Imai, in Takashima county, from which the family name was taken.[5] Sōkyū later moved to Sakai, and retrospective accounts consistently note his association with the tea master Takeno Jōō.[6]

The earliest known contemporary reference to Sōkyū dates to 1551, and is found in the tea journal of the prominent Sakai merchant and tea man Tsuda Sōtatsu (1504–1566).[7] Recording a gathering he had hosted, Sōtatsu lists Sōkyū as one of seven guests. But to be invited to a gathering hosted by Sōtatsu is evidence of Sōkyū's entrée into the rarefied circle of Sakai's tea society that he would eventually come to dominate. Within three years of Sōtatsu's gathering, Sōkyū was invited to share tea with Takeno Jōō, as mentioned above. In 1554 he returned the invitation to Jōō, to whom he refers with the respectful suffix of "elder" (*rō*), inviting the master to his residence for a private tea.[8] By the mid-1550s Sōkyū had also attained a measure of success in his commercial career, as reflected in a 1554 document that records his substantial cash donation of 170 *kan*[9] to Daisen'in, a sub-temple of Daitokuji.[10]

In the following year Sōkyū with Jōō and two others attended a gathering hosted by Sen no Rikyū, who thus makes his first appearance in Sōkyū's extant diary; he is called by the name he then used, Sōeki.[11] Sōeki would eventually eclipse Sōkyū in the favor of the ruling elite and in his importance within the historical tea hierarchy. At this time, however, Sōeki was a junior member of the trio of rising merchant tea men that also included Sōkyū and Tsuda Sōtatsu's son, Sōgyū. The material wealth of Sōeki, also born of a merchant house, may be ascertained by Sōkyū's account, which notes that on display at the 1555 gathering was a self-inscribed painting by the Southern Song master Muqi, a painter whose works had been treasured and collected in Japan from at least as early as the fourteenth century.[12]

Sōkyū's chronicle of successive tea gatherings is interrupted late in 1555 by an entry that records an event of major importance: the death of Takeno Jōō.[13] Although he thus lost his father-in-law and tea mentor, Sōkyū apparently gained much from Jōō's passing. In an account of a gathering he hosted in 1556, Sōkyū notes that he placed on display the Matsushima jar that was once owned by Jōō; the same object that he had two years earlier described with such admiration had apparently passed into his hands.[14] Another account of this gathering, described as hosted by "Naya Sōkyū," may be found in Tsuda Sōtatsu's diary.[15] After providing a comprehensive listing of the objects used, he selects and describes individual pieces in greater detail, including the Matsushima jar. He describes the jar in terms that echo Sōkyū's earlier comments: "On the bottom of the front, there are small holes in the earth. It is not a very large jar, and the shoulder is not broad. The shape is especially fine."[16]

Sōkyū's professional status may be at least partly understood from the reference to him in this entry as "Naya Sōkyū." *Naya* refers to a building used for the storage of commercial goods. During the period of Sōkyū's activity, men engaged in the warehousing business were among the wealthiest of merchants. When Sōkyū first arrived in Sakai, he stayed with a man involved in this business, and from that time presumably took up the trade as well.[17] We will see that warehousing was only one of several profitable ventures that Sōkyū was involved in, but it is by this trade name that he is often mentioned in contemporary tea diaries.

One tea diary records a gathering hosted by Sakai Naya Sōkyū in 1559.[18] The careful description of the utensils notes that certain tea bowls, the bamboo scoop, and many of the other items used during the preparation of tea had been owned formerly by Jōō. After the tea portion of the gathering had been completed, the Matsushima jar was brought for the guests to inspect, and it was then placed on display in the alcove. The sons of Jōō and Sōkyū, respectively Shingorō (1550–1614) and Sōkun (1552–1627), then served the meal.[19] By obtaining a substantial cache of tea utensils that were formerly Jōō's treasures, Sōkyū acquired the symbolic mantle of the late master's prestige; he apparently even had become the guardian of Shingorō, then about 9 years old.

Throughout the late 1550s and 1560s tea diaries record Sōkyū's increasingly prominent role in a full calendar of gatherings. In the tea setting he met time and again with figures of political stature in Sakai, including important warriors such as Matsunaga Hisahide[20] and numerous merchant tea men.[21] The diaries that record these gatherings rarely provide more than a list of the host and guests, a catalog of the utensils used, perhaps an aesthetic evaluation of these utensils, and the menu of the meal that followed the serving of tea. If discussions at the gatherings of matters not related to tea did take place, they are not recorded. During the first fifteen or so years from the first instance of Sōkyū's name in a tea diary in 1551, we may understand at the very least that he rose to a position of prominence within the tea world and that this afforded him opportunities to meet with men of equally high position both within and beyond his social class. Whatever substantive benefits may have resulted from these encounters cannot be judged from the content of the tea diaries. After 1568, however, increased documentation of Sōkyū's actions outside the tea room improves our ability to evaluate his stature and breadth of activities. Many of the documents speak of his association with Nobunaga, illustrating his shrewdness in judging the latter's potential.

## Nobunaga and Sakai

In 9/1568 Nobunaga entered Kyoto, completing a military advance begun less than three weeks earlier. He was accompanied by Ashikaga Yoshiaki (1537–1597), pretender to the office of Shogun, whose cause Nobunaga ostensibly supported.[22] Nobunaga wasted little time in maximizing his own prospects. Yoshiaki was soon installed as Shogun, and he then offered Nobunaga the post of deputy shogun (*kanrei*).[23] Nobunaga refused, requesting instead the right to place deputies (*daikan*) in Ōtsu and Kusatsu in Ōmi and in Sakai in Izumi.[24] He astutely recognized that to realize his own ambitions to power, he needed access to the rich and well-established commercial structure in Sakai.

Nobunaga moved rapidly to assert his authority on the cities and establishments in the region near the capital. Early in the tenth month he assessed "arrow tax" (*yazeni*) on both Settsu and Izumi provinces.[25] He directed Hōryūji to make immediate payment of 150 pieces of silver.[26] He also demanded and received 5,000 *kan* from Ishiyama Honganji. Two months later Hōryūji paid 600 *kan* as proclamation tax (*satsuzeni*). Knowing of the great wealth concentrated in Sakai, Nobunaga levied an arrow tax of 20,000 *kan* upon the city. Sakai's elite group of commercial administrators (*egōshū*), initially rebuffed this order.[27] The city was encouraged to give this response because of support offered by the

Miyoshi warrior clan.[28] The administrators even sent a letter to the leaders of neighboring Hirano inviting them to join Sakai in resisting Nobunaga.[29]

Nobunaga's directive also served notice to the traditional warrior-class holders of power in Sakai and its surrounding area.[30] In the late fifteenth century, Sakai had been controlled by the Hosokawa clan, although their authority there was eventually undermined by ambitious retainers, the Miyoshi. The Miyoshi assumed control of the city, reaching their apex under the determined rule of Miyoshi Nagayoshi (1523–1564). From the late 1560s, after Nagayoshi's death, the Miyoshi clan was led by a group of his former vassals consisting of the self-serving Matsunaga Hisahide and three other men.[31] Although this group engineered the demise of the Shogun Ashikaga Yoshiteru, their collaboration soon ended in armed conflict. Hisahide capitulated to Nobunaga in 1568; the other three were staunchly opposed to Nobunaga's intervention in Kyoto and chose temporary retreat over submission.

Early in 1569 the Miyoshi forces set out from an encampment in Sakai, entered Kyoto and attacked Yoshiaki. The ensuing events are related by Tsuda Sōgyū in his diary, in an entry from slightly later in that same year, "On the sixth day [of this month] there was a battle at the mountain castle by the Katsura River between Yoshiaki's forces and those of the Miyoshi. The Miyoshi were crushed and they withdrew from Sakai."[32] Nobunaga then sent envoys to convey his threat of retaliation for Sakai's support of the Miyoshi.[33] Sōgyū's diary account continues in an understandably agitated manner:

> Since the twelfth, all of Sakai has been in an uproar. From the tenth month of last year, moats have been dug and turrets have been raised. . . . The tea utensils and women and children were removed to Osaka and Hirano.[34]

Three months later Sakai still had not paid the arrow tax demanded by Nobunaga. On the first day of the fourth month, a letter jointly signed by five of his military commanders was sent to Sakai.[35] A deadline was set for payment – the fifteenth of that month – and the city was told that Nobunaga was greatly upset. Precedent must have given the residents of Sakai pause when they considered the possible consequences of continued resistance. Two months earlier, Nobunaga had sent a force of three thousand men to the port city of Amagazaki, which had refused to pay his requested arrow tax. While his initial attack was repulsed, a subsequent thrust left thirty men and women dead and four areas completely destroyed.[36]

It is unlikely that Nobunaga desired to carry out destructive military action against Sakai. From the fifteenth century a burgeoning merchant establishment had built the port into a prosperous commercial center. The city had managed to escape the war ravaging much of the country in that period. By the sixteenth century Sakai was one of the largest urban communities in Japan and arguably the leading commercial center. According to the Portuguese missionary Luis Frois (1532–1597):

> No other place apart from Kyoto is as important as the city of Sakai. The Venice of Japan, it is not only large, wealthy, and full of commerce, but it is also like a central market for all the other provinces, and people from different regions are continually flocking there.[37]

Whatever desire Nobunaga may have had to exact retribution on Sakai for its support of the Miyoshi and for its resistance to his overtures was mitigated by his understanding that the city was useful to him only with its commercial base intact.

The situation was eventually resolved to Nobunaga's liking when Sakai paid the arrow tax and offered proper apologies. Even while Nobunaga was posturing and making threats against the city, however, it is likely that he was engaged simultaneously in private negotiations in an effort to gain the commercial center by peaceful means. Such a policy required the cooperation of people of influence within the city. One such collaborator was Imai Sōkyū.

## Sōkyū's early successes under Nobunaga

Nobunaga encouraged collaboration by showing Sōkyū favor in matters that fell within the warlord's purview. Late in 1568, at a time when Sakai had not yet submitted to the ruler, a terse letter jointly signed by four vassals of Nobunaga – including Kinoshita Tōkichirō (later, Toyotomi Hideyoshi) – was sent to Matsunaga Hisahide. The letter concerned a dispute between Sōkyū and Takeno Jōō's son, Shingorō. The body of the text reads, "Despite Nobunaga's remonstrations, Shingorō has protested [Nobunaga's decision] regarding the litigation between Imai Sōkyū and Takeno Shingorō. The entire amount [*ichien*] is to be given to Sōkyū. . . . We thus give notice."[38] On his father's death, Shingorō was apparently placed in Sōkyū's care, as were also Jōō's famous collection of tea utensils. The "entire amount" mentioned in the letter is not explained, but likely included the tea utensils, if not more.[39] Shingorō, now in his late twenties, was agitating to recover the prestigious heirlooms he had been unable to inherit as a child. Matsunaga Hisahide, a frequent participant at Sakai tea gatherings and obviously well known to both men, was chosen to convey the decision. The adjudicator was none other than Nobunaga, in whose name a decision favorable to Sōkyū was made.

Nobunaga's support of Sōkyū's claim to the property – the earliest secure documentation of an exchange between the two men – has several possible interpretations. With Sakai still holding out against him, Nobunaga may have identified Sōkyū as an individual of sufficient influence within the city's commercial establishment to swing local opinion in his favor. Earlier contacts between the two men resulting in an alliance cannot be ruled out.[40] Nobunaga also surely recognized that it was prudent for his future success to cultivate a relationship with Sōkyū in order to tap the merchant's professional abilities. He recognized the importance of Jōō's renowned tea treasures, and the decision to grant them to Sōkyū was surely made with full expectation that it would work to his favor both in the difficult confrontation with Sakai and in the future.

Extant letters show that Sakai's capitulation to Nobunaga in 4/1569 was followed by a rapid rise in Sōkyū's professional fortunes. A letter from the sixth month reads, "Imai Nyūdō Sōkyū often travels to the capital on official business [*kōgi goyō*]. Nobunaga has ordered that [Sōkyū] encounter no problems shipping goods and be allowed to proceed freely."[41] The letter is addressed to the owners of licensed cargo vessels that plied the Yodo River, the primary transportation route between Sakai and Fushimi and part of the network linking the Inland Sea and Lake Biwa. The letter was issued by the shogunal official responsible for regulating the boats and is backed by an invocation of Nobunaga's authority.[42]

The special right of unimpeded passage on the waterways was of critical importance for any merchant. While the business that required Sōkyū's frequent journeys to Kyoto is not specified here, later letters document a wide range of commercial activities that involved the movement of goods. Additionally, Sōkyū mentions in his diary several tea gatherings with Nobunaga in the capital; these gatherings required the transportation of people. Another letter indicates that Sōkyū was fortunate to receive confirmation of this privilege in the following year as well.[43]

In 8/1569, Sōkyū was allowed to view Nobunaga's castle at Gifu. The occasion is recorded in the diary of a courtier, who refers to a companion as Kusuriya Sōkyū from Sakai.[44] Letters from the Imai family archives place Sōkyū in Gifu at this time, and so it is reasonable to assume that this "Kusuriya Sōkyū" was in fact Imai Sōkyū.[45] It is also likely that the name Kusuriya refers not to a merchant of medicine (the common meaning of the term), but to another usage of the word *kusuri*: gunpowder. It is fitting that this, the earliest recorded visit of any Sakai townsman to the castle at Gifu, would be by a merchant of such modern military supplies.

Sōkyū's involvement in the trade of such supplies is confirmed in a letter from the following year, 1570.[46] While fighting for Nobunaga against the Asai clan, Hideyoshi wrote to Sōkyū, "I have urgent business for you. Send gunpowder of the highest possible quality, about thirty *kin*; also send thirty *kin* of niter."[47] The writer continued by assuring Sōkyū that the route to his position had been secured so that shipment might be made without worry, and that payment in rice was waiting for Sōkyū in Osaka. In another letter from this period, Sōkyū complained to a customer about non-payment for a shipment of gunpowder. He had been promised payment in silver, which was never delivered, and then rice, also not forthcoming. Sōkyū was waiting, he wrote, impatiently for the matter to be resolved.[48]

The relationship between Sōkyū and Nobunaga involved more than trade in goods and privileged passage on the Yodo River. A group of letters from 1569 details Sōkyū's acquisition of several financially rewarding proprietorships. In each letter Nobunaga's name appears to legitimate the specific claim. Sōkyū addressed the following letter to the salt and preserved fish guilds, both presumably of Sakai, and also to the Yodo salt guild:

> The portion of supplementary income for salt and preserved fish previously stipended [*zonchi*] to Sogō Dono has been awarded to me by Nobunaga. You should be aware of this. If this decision has not yet been reported, it is an oversight.[49]

Sōkyū thus assumed control of stipended rights, privileges formerly held by Sogō Kazumasa (d. 1561), youngest of the three brothers of Miyoshi Nagayoshi and a member of the ousted Miyoshi clan.[50] Access to these rights was no small matter in the sixteenth century, as salt and preserved fish were essential parts of the diet.[51] The recipients of the letter are informed, if they had not been already, of a change in the previously existing state of affairs. Payments forthwith would be made to Sōkyū, in accordance with Nobunaga's wishes.

Shortly thereafter, Sōkyū wrote another letter of similar content. The first part reads, "Herein reported is the matter of the income for preserved goods previously stipended to Sogō Dono. The rights to this income were awarded to me last year by the Shogun and Nobunaga's finance office [*ryōsho*]."[52] The recipient of the letter was Mitsubuchi Fujihide (d. 1574), a life-long vassal of the Ashikaga shogunate, serving first Yoshiteru and then Yoshiaki, whom he had defended against the Miyoshi forces earlier that year in Kyoto. Even when addressing Fujihide, whose primary allegiance was to the Shogun, Sōkyū indicates that his claim to these rights derived not only from Yoshiaki but also from Nobunaga. It is of interest that in the previous letter, to parties without such a connection to the shogunate, Sōkyū felt compelled to invoke only one authority, that is, Nobunaga, to establish these rights. The letters raise two important points. First, they reflect the authority commanded by Nobunaga less than one year after his entry in Kyoto; and second, they show that Sōkyū's own relationship to the loci of power was weighted toward Nobunaga.

Even with the backing of Nobunaga's authority, the transfer of property rights was not necessarily uncontested. More than once, repeated threats from above were required for Sōkyū to secure the rights he had been granted. Another letter from this time "concerns the matter of the Zenjuan portion that is part of Sōkyū's Sakai Gokanoshō domain. Although [Zenjuan] is part of Tennōji, Nobunaga wants it to be given to

Imai. The matter will be investigated and resolved."[53] The letter implies that the rights to a domain in or near Sakai had already been given to Sōkyū.[54] In dispute were the rights to a portion of the domain, rights that overlapped those claimed by Zenjuan, a subtemple of the famous Settsu temple Tennōji.

The letter was written by a warrior from Owari who had long served Nobunaga and was addressed to Ikeda Katsumasa. Katsumasa, a native of Settsu, had at first staunchly resisted Nobunaga's forays into the area. He eventually became his supporter and was confirmed as lord (*shugo*) of Settsu. Because Tennōji was located in Settsu, it is reasonable to speculate that this letter was meant to inform the locally influential Katsumasa of the situation. Implied is the threat that activities counter to Nobunaga's order – that the rights be transferred to Sōkyū – would not be tolerated.[55]

Near the end of 1569 Sōkyū sent a letter regarding an area that had been forfeited to his ownership:

> I write regarding the debt of Nojiri Bingo no Kami Dono. Despite repeated demands, the matter has not been resolved. I have received Nobunaga's opinion, which is that Nojiri's fief should pass to me. To that end, the envoys of Sakai Ukon and Kinoshita Tōkichirō issued a letter. Moreover, other payments should be double.[56]

The letter is directed to the elite "named" farmers of Makinogō in Kawachi. It declares that because Sōkyū now controlled the lands formerly held by another man, he would be recipient of subsequent taxes. Sōkyū concludes the letter by informing the farmers that other unspecified, perhaps auxiliary, payments would forthwith be doubled. Once again, the content of the letter is backed by the word of Nobunaga, as conveyed by his vassal Hideyoshi.[57]

## Sōkyū, Nobunaga, and the province of Tajima

During this period, one of the most financially rewarding activities Sōkyū engaged in under the banner of Nobunaga took place in the province of Tajima, in present-day Hyōgo prefecture. Nobunaga turned his attention to Tajima in the second half of 1569. The province had long been controlled by the Yamana clan and held enormously rich reserves of silver at the Ikuno silver mine, as well as other metals.[58] In 8/1569 Nobunaga sent troops into the province and quickly ousted its nominal ruler, Lord Yamana Suketoyo (1511–1580). Remaining in place, however, were men of the rank of local lord (*shugodai*) and lower, the true holders of local power. Suketoyo submitted to Nobunaga and then requested that he be reinstated to his former domain. Sōkyū supported his cause.

Late in 1569 Nobunaga granted Suketoyo his wish, and he in return promised a gift of 1,000 *kan*. Another letter tells us, however, that Suketoyo actually paid only half this sum with money borrowed from Sōkyū.[59] By the beginning of 1570 Suketoyo was back in Tajima.[60]

Nobunaga and Sōkyū treated Suketoyo as merely a puppet. It is clear that their efforts on his behalf were motivated only by a desire for access to Tajima's natural resources. In 1570 a letter from Nobunaga was sent to four troublesome local agitators:

> Last winter, Tsuguhiro [Yamana Suketoyo] went to Tajima province and reported on the situation there. The matters of the disposition of the Ōtagaki brothers and the decision regarding their domain were put in writing. The portion of the income of the mine opened last year should not be any different [from that agreement]. There are presently delays [in payment]. The matter will be investigated. To this end, Imai Sōkyū and Hasegawa Sōnin are being sent. If there are still problems, they will be reported immediately. This intention is made known to each of you.[61]

In understated fashion, the four men are accused of not obeying an earlier agreement. In particular, the Otagaki are singled out; it is no coincidence that the Ikuno mine was located precisely in their area of influence. The problem mentioned in the letter concerned the payment of fees associated with the operation of a newly opened mine, presumably the Ikuno mine. Suketoyo here plays a parenthetical role, as the eyes of Nobunaga. His weakness provides another opportunity for the ruler to warn the offenders that behind Suketoyo is the warlord himself; an offense against Suketoyo would be interpreted as an offense against Nobunaga. Sōkyū is Nobunaga's representative sent to investigate the problem.

By no later than the seventh month of that year, Sōkyū had assumed the important responsibility of placing the deputy at the Ikuno mine. In a letter from this time, he politely thanks the three recipients for kindnesses they had recently shown his representative.[62] He then informs them of Nobunaga's most recent military exploit, a crushing victory over the Asai and Echizen forces in the previous month. The letter continues, in a more aggravated tone:

> The agreed official blacksmith tax[63] should be paid directly by Shimo-sai. My deputy has reported that, in fact, this has not been done. Previously, we had a firm agreement that, as silver is found, it should be reported and given to the representative. A copy of this agreement was presented to you. As commanded, this agreement should be observed without any deviance. But you have not followed it, and I am quite annoyed.

The letter proceeds in this accusatory manner, harshly rebuking the men for not observing the agreement, reiterating the severity of the breach, and demanding that a letter of apology be sent after proper payment is made. It ends with the pointed threat, "Nobunaga will soon be coming to the capital." The three men, probably Tajima locals associated with the mines, were being warned that if Sōkyū's authority was not enough to make them cooperate with his efforts to collect his just rewards, they should remember that Nobunaga would be duly informed.

Another of Tajima's desirable resources was iron, found in the district of Yabu.[64] Iron was required for the manufacture of firearms, the weapons then transforming warfare and determining the balance of power in Japan. Sōkyū wrote two letters in early 1570 that suggest he was actively involved in this industry as well. The first is addressed to the community of Minatomura: "The blacksmiths in this village of ancient lineage shall, as before, serve in Abiko, Gokanoshō. This order should be obeyed without delay."[65] The second letter follows the first by only two days and assumes a more urgent tone:

> The other day a letter was sent regarding the matter of the blacksmiths, and still there is no response. . . . I was ordered to the capital for a day or two to meet with Nobunaga, and he very much wanted to be informed of the situation. The blacksmiths should be dispatched without delay. An envoy shall inform you of the details.[66]

The blacksmiths were to be employed in the manufacture of firearms. Sōkyū sought to make Abiko a center for firearms production, and also summoned craftsmen from Kawachi.[67]

Nobunaga's personal interest in the Minatomura blacksmiths indicates the value he placed on these weapons. The ruler used firearms, first introduced into Japan in the 1540s, to great effect in his military campaigns.[68] Sakai was not the only source he tapped to acquire them. In the mid-1570s he increased production in Kunitomo, a center of firearms manufacture that had previously supplied the weapons for the defenders of Otani Castle, which fell to Nobunaga's forces in 1572.[69] It was to the merchant Sōkyū's advantage to maximize production in Sakai. These letters reflect his desire to see the enterprise succeed. To this end, and for all of his activities in areas of Nobunaga's influence, Sōkyū used his renowned skills in the tea room to cultivate his relationship with the hegemon.

## Sōkyū, Nobunaga, and tea

Throughout this period of Sōkyū's intensive mercantile and political maneuverings under the banner of Nobunaga, tea gatherings continued to play as significant a part of his routine as they had done earlier. While letters detailing Sōkyū's activities post-dating the documents examined above are no longer extant, tea diaries record his interactions with significant people and suggest the continuing success of his career. Indeed, it is only when the gatherings and other tea-related activities are placed in such a context that their full significance can be appreciated.

In 4/1570, shortly after his letters regarding the blacksmiths of Minato-mura and a little more than two weeks before Nobunaga's letter about non-payment of taxes in Tajima, an entry in Sōkyū's tea diary reads as follows:

> It was announced by the Elder Matsui Yūkan that Nobunaga would examine the many famous utensils in this port [Sakai]. Today we went to his house and the viewing took place. I presented the Matsushima jar and the painting of Sweets [to Nobunaga] from my collection of tea objects.[70]

The Matsushima jar, as we have seen, was one of the utensils that Sōkyū treasured above all others, an object lauded in his earliest extant writing. Once acquired, it was often displayed and guests recognized its importance. It represented the finest of the widely famous Sakai utensils, so distinguished that it made an appropriate gift to Nobunaga, who was behind Sōkyū's recent success.[71]

Matsui Yūkan served Nobunaga closely, especially as his administrator (*mandokoro*) of Sakai. He held this position from around the time of the above event until he was dismissed in 1586, some sixteen years later.[72] Yūkan was responsible for supervising and implementing Nobunaga's policies in the city, and this included the assessment of taxes and organizing events such as the one mentioned above.[73] Sōkyū first met Yūkan around the eighth month 1569, when he began a letter to him by acknowledging that a recent meeting was their first.[74] From late 1569 Yūkan's presence is ubiquitous at Sakai tea gatherings and at the increasingly frequent events that were attended or hosted by Nobunaga himself.

One of the most significant gatherings of the early 1570s took place in the eleventh month of 1573, when Nobunaga hosted a tea gathering at Myōkakuji in Kyoto.[75] Sōkyū records in his diary that he was accompanied by two other guests: Yamanoue Sōji (1544–1590), a resident of Sakai and a disciple of Sōeki, and Matsui Yūkan. Sōeki was also present. He is described not as a guest, however, but as the man who prepared the tea, the same role he played in the 1570 Sakai event during which Nobunaga was presented with tea objects. Sōeki was assuming an increasingly significant role in the context of tea, as Nobunaga's chief tea master.

Indeed, it is important to note that while Sōkyū was the earliest to jockey himself into an advantageous position with Nobunaga – and received commensurate rewards – other Sakai merchant tea men soon sided with the warlord. Sōeki is today best remembered as an innovator of the rustic *wabi* tea aesthetic, but he did not win Nobunaga's favor only with his aesthetic acuity. He was also a reliable merchant of arms, as reflected in a 1575 letter in which Nobunaga personally thanks him for sending 1,000 bullets during a campaign in Echizen.[76]

Tsuda Sōgyū initially misjudged Nobunaga's potential. From around 1565 Sōgyū had commercial dealings with the religious establishment of Ishiyama Honganji, Nobunaga's arch-enemy, and even supported the Miyoshi effort against Nobunaga.[77] One event from this period is particularly informative in this regard. Early in 1569, before Sakai had submitted to Nobunaga, a large contingent of the warlord's vassals journeyed to the port and gathered at Sōgyū's residence.[78] In his diary, Sōgyū lists the names of some of the notable individuals in attendance, including ranking military leaders in Nobunaga's service, and estimates that the group numbered "about one hundred." Given Sōgyū's recalcitrant position about this time, it may be suggested that Nobunaga's men were there as a show of force, to persuade Sōgyū and others in Sakai who were still resisting that continued rejection of the ruler's demands was not advisable.

Sōgyū eventually capitulated to Nobunaga. He achieved a position of sufficient status to be invited, on the day prior to Sōkyū's gathering with Nobunaga at Myōkakuji, to a similar affair with two other tea men of Sakai.[79] Two weeks later Sōgyū invited Yūkan to his residence for a private tea. This was only one of many gatherings he would share with the Sakai administrator, reflecting his attempt to insinuate himself with the people he had come to recognize as the holders of power and opportunity.[80] The peak of Sōgyū's career came in 1574 when he was honored with an invitation to a private viewing of Nobunaga's utensils.[81] Included in the display were the Matsushima jar as well as Jōō's eggplant tea caddy, which Sōkyū had apparently given to Nobunaga.[82]

Despite their success in the tea context, there is no secure evidence that either Sōeki or Sōgyū received the kind of influential and lucrative administrative appointments that Sōkyū did. Although the possibility cannot be discounted that documents recording such rewards are now lost, it is doubtful whether either man was ever able to usurp Sōkyū's high position while Nobunaga was alive. Precisely because of Sōgyū's early leanings away from Nobunaga, he is unlikely to have ever gained the ruler's full trust. Although Sōeki played a conspicuous role in Sakai tea gatherings from an early date, there is no record that he gave desirable gifts to Nobunaga nor of other early contacts with the warlord.

It was, however, to Nobunaga's advantage to favor all three men – and others in Sakai – to foster good relations with the various mercantile interests they represented. Nobunaga had not exercised such restraint in his initial approach to Sakai without good reason. The commercial well-being of his administration was tied to a cooperative Sakai. To elicit this cooperation, Nobunaga formed social bonds within the tea room and through other activities such, as Noh drama. Especially prominent in these activities were Sōkyū, Sōgyū, and Sōeki.

The pre-eminence of this trio of Sakai merchants is clear in a gathering at Shōkokuji in Kyoto in the third month of 1574, hosted by Nobunaga and attended by people from Sakai.[83] Sōkyū notes that the guests included himself, Sōeki, Yamanoue Sōji, and several other men, all from Sakai.[84] Nobunaga first prepared and served tea to his guests. He was followed by Yūkan, who served thin tea. Sōgyū, joining the tea mid-way, writes, "In the shoin room, Sōkyū, Sōeki, and I were allowed to view the plover (*chidori*) incense burner."[85] Significantly, Sōkyū's name is listed first, an indication of his relative standing among the three. Less than two weeks later, they were again received by Nobunaga at Shōkokuji, along with Yūkan.[86] Sōgyū and Sōeki – but apparently not Sōkyū – were further favored by Nobunaga in receiving a piece of the famous Ranjatai incense from the Shōsōin.[87] Sōkyū reports that in 1578 Nobunaga gave Sōgyū water from a famous Kyoto well.[88] These acts of showing and giving objects of widely accepted cultural significance were the signals of political favor, the mediating tools that facilitated exchange between warrior and merchant.

Nonetheless, Sōkyū maintained his position of superiority within the trio. In 1578 he hosted a tea at his residence that was attended by arguably the most impressive group of cultural and military elite to participate in a gathering – excluding those given by Nobunaga himself – until perhaps Hideyoshi's great tea event at Kitano Shrine in 1587.[89] Nobunaga was present, as were Hosokawa Yūsai and Tsutsui Junkei, both famous for their martial and literary activities. A contemporary diary notes that Nobunaga came to Sakai at another time in 1578 to see iron-clad ships that he had ordered.[90] On this occasion, "Nobunaga stopped at Sōkyū's house – [the visit] would be a source of pride for Sōkyū's descendants – and they shared tea. On his return, [Nobunaga] paid visits to the homes of Sōeki and Sōgyū."[91] The order of Nobunaga's rounds matches the hierarchy that is recorded in the tea diaries.

## Sōkyū in the post-Nobunaga era

During the first half of 1582 Nobunaga continued, and perhaps even increased, his frequent meetings with the Sakai merchant tea men. As before, Sōkyū occupied the pre-eminent position among his peers. Sōgyū writes that on the first day of the year, he and others from Sakai, including Sōkyū – conspicuously noted in first place – and Sōeki, went to pay their respects to Nobunaga at Azuchi; Yūkan was also present.[92] Sōkyū stayed on for several days. Sōgyū reports that in the fifth month, ten men from Sakai joined other guests and Nobunaga at Azuchi to view performances of Noh; we may assume that among the ten was included Sōkyū.[93]

Shortly thereafter, Sōkyū reports in his diary that Tokugawa Ieyasu traveled to Sakai, came to his house, and shared tea. Ieyasu informed him that on the third day of the following month, Sōkyū should be prepared to serve tea at his house to, the language suggests, Nobunaga.[94] On the same day, Sōgyū wrote that Ieyasu visited him and many others to discuss the planning of a party at Sakai.[95] Nobunaga would soon be coming to town.

Nobunaga never made that journey to Sakai, for Akechi Mitsuhide's attack on Honnōji intervened. On the evening of the second day of the sixth month Sōkyū recorded in his diary: "The Elder Yūkan came and announced that in Kyoto this morning, [Nobunaga] took his own life because of [Akechi Mitsuhide's attack]."[96] Sōgyū provides a more complete account of the event and its effect:

> [Nobunaga] committed suicide. [Mitsuhide] had him cut his stomach at Honnōji. Ieyasu left Sakai [today] to return [to Mikawa]. We were off to Kyoto and already well into the journey when, near Tennōji, we learned of the incident [and returned to Sakai]. [Yūkan] also turned back midway.[97]

Nobunaga's death instilled in the travelers fear that the country would lapse again into a state of violent anarchy. But within two weeks of the Honnōji attack, a fleeing Mitsuhide met his death at the hands of peasants. Hideyoshi soon attained the position of national hegemony formerly held by Nobunaga and successfully repulsed challenges to his authority until his death in 1598.[98]

During Hideyoshi's rule, Sōkyū did not maintain a position as favorable as he had enjoyed under Nobunaga. His successful career stemmed from his personal relationship with Nobunaga. This relationship was formed on the basis of his early recognition of the warlord's authority and potential, and the help he gave Nobunaga in securing the submission of Sakai. Although long acquainted with Sōkyū, Hideyoshi owed him no such debt.[99] Indeed, there were others in Sakai whose assistance commanded Hideyoshi's loyalty, such as Konishi Ryūsa (d. 1593). Konishi was a wealthy Christian merchant who supplied Hideyoshi during the Kyushu and Korean campaigns, and served as his deputy in Sakai. Although Sōkyū continued to participate in tea gatherings of the elite, Sōeki succeeded him to the top position. Sōeki played the central role at Hideyoshi's most important tea events, including an imperial gathering in 1585 – at which he was designated "foremost tea master in the realm" – and the Grand Tea at Kitano Shrine in 1587.[100] He served in an active political capacity, becoming involved in the conduct of sensitive administrative policy and even serving as overseer of Osaka Castle when Hideyoshi was absent.[101]

During the Nobunaga era, however, Sōkyū's career was the measure of success.[102] It highlights the critical role that tea culture played in the development of alliances between the mutually dependent sectors of Japanese society. In part, Nobunaga engaged in tea and other artistic pursuits because he, like other military men turned political leaders, understood that cultural erudition was expected of the legitimate Japanese ruler. The participants in tea culture, including Nobunaga and Sōkyū, created a common aesthetic language and system of aesthetic evaluation. Sōkyū's gift of the Matsushima jar to Nobunaga was meaningful because both the giver and the receiver recognized its relative worth within the tea context. Such understanding, in turn, encouraged cooperation between the two men in the political and mercantile spheres. Sōkyū's remarkable achievements under Nobunaga were realized because of his combined talents in tea, politics, and commerce. With the Honnōji incident and the rise of Hideyoshi, Sōkyū was eclipsed by Sōeki. His career thus also reflects the vicissitudes of that turbulent time, and how one man's achievement was ultimately bound to the fortunes of a powerful but vulnerable patron.

## Notes

1 For recent discussions of Rikyū in English, see Kumakura Isao, "Sen no Rikyū: Inquiries into his Life and Tea," and Theodore M. Ludwig, "*Chanoyu* and Momoyama: Conflict and Transformation in Rikyū's Art," in Paul Varley and Kumakura Isao (eds), *Tea in Japan: Essays on the History of Chanoyu* (University of Hawai'i Press, 1989), pp. 33–69 and 71–100. For Rikyū's political role, see Beatrice M. Bodart, "Tea and Counsel: The Political Role of Sen Rikyū," *Monumenta Nipponica* 32 (Spring 1977): 47–74; and for politics and tea in general, Beatrice M. Bodart-Bailey, "Tea and Politics in Late-Sixteenth-Century Japan," *Chanoyu Quarterly* 41 (1985): 25–34.

2 Unlike the case of Rikyū, there is no account written by a devoted tea disciple that details Sōkyū's thoughts regarding tea practice. We are left to interpret his tea activities through contemporary diaries, which record patterns of activity rather than explain the thinking behind those activities. In this chapter, I begin an interpretation of Sōkyū's contributions to the then rapidly evolving tea culture by focusing on the links among tea, commerce, and politics. There remains room for more focused examination of Sōkyū's contributions to the aesthetics of tea, a study which would benefit from further examination of the tea diaries.

3 *Imai Sōkyū chanoyu nikki nukigaki* (also known as *Imai Sōkyū chanoyu nikki kakinuki*) is a compilation of extracts from Sōkyū's tea diary. It is transcribed in Nagashima Fukutarō (ed.), *Imai Sōkyū chanoyu nikki nukigaki*, [hereafter cited as *NN*], in Sen Sōshitsu *et al.* (eds), *Chadō koten zenshū*, vol. 10 (Tankō Shinsha, Kyoto, 1961), pp. 3–64. This entry is dated Tenbun 23/1/23 and is found on pp. 3–4. Selections from this and other important tea diaries of this period are examined in Kumakura Isao (ed.), *Shidai chakaiki*, vol. 3 of *Chanoyu no koten* (Sekai Bunkasha, 1984). See pp. 40–41 for a discussion of this particular entry.

4 Miura Hiroyuki (ed.), *Sakai-shi shi*, 8 vols (Sakai Shiyakusho, Sakai, 1929–1931), is the key secondary source for material related to Sōkyū and Sakai. Many of the important primary documents cited in the text are transcribed in vol. 4. Sōkyū's early biographical information is collated and presented in vol. 7, pp. 126–127, and appears to be the work from which many other secondary accounts are derived.

5 The lineage is titled *Imai shi shichi sekihimei narabini keizu*, and is transcribed in Miura, vol. 4, pp. 365–366.

6 A lengthy entry in the eighteenth-century *Sukisha meishōshū* indicates that Sōkyū was a direct disciple of Takeno Jōō as well as his son-in-law. *Sukisha meishōshū*, an annotated lineage of famous tea masters, was written by the Sakai resident Tani Ninsai (d. 1744), and is reproduced in its entirety in Miura, vol. 4, pp. 324–366. The section regarding Sōkyū is on pp. 331–332. The brief entry for Jōō's daughter in *Takeno ke keizu* does not identify her by

name, but notes that she was Sōkyū's wife. The lineage is reproduced in Miura, vol. 4, pp. 353–356.

 7 The tea journals of Tsuda Sōtatsu, his son Sōgyū, and his grandson Sōbon, are collectively called *Tennōjiya kaiki*. All are published and extensively discussed in Nagashima Fukutarō (ed.), *Tennōjiya kaiki*, [hereafter cited as *TK*], in Sen, vols 7–8. The entry discussed above, dated Tenbun 20 (1551)/12/3, morning, is in vol. 8, p. 23.

 8 Tenbun 23 (1554)/10/7, morning: *NN*, p. 4.

 9 *Kan* (short for *kanmon*) was a cash unit equivalent to 1,000 copper coins.

10 This document, dated Tenbun 23 (1554)/6/26, is cited in Toyoda Takeshi, *Sakai: Shōnin no shinshutsu to toshi no jiyū* (Shibundō, 1957), pp. 80–81.

11 Tenbun 24 (1555)/4/1, morning: *NN*, pp. 5–6. I give the name Sōeki instead of Rikyū in this article, because this is the name used in most of the contemporary documents.

12 For the importance of Muqi's paintings for Japanese artists and collectors, see Richard Stanley-Baker, "Mid-Muromachi Paintings of the Eight Views of Hsiao and Hsiang" (Ph.D. diss., Princeton University, 1979), pp. 22–27.

13 Tenbun 24 (1555)/10/29: *NN*, p. 6.

14 Kōji 2 (1556)/11/8, morning: *NN*, p. 7.

15 Kōji 2 (1556)/11/8, morning: *TK*, 7, pp. 45–46.

16 Sōtatsu attended another tea hosted by Sōkyū on the morning of Eiroku 6 (1563)/1/21, in which the Matsushima jar was displayed. The gathering is noted in Sōkyū's diary (*NN*, p. 12) as well as in Sōtatsu's diary (*TK*, 7, p. 102).

17 The man with whom Sōkyū stayed was Naya Sōji. Toyoda, pp. 80–81.

18 This gathering, in the morning of Eiroku 2 (1559)/4/19, is recorded in *Matsuya kaiki*, the diary begun by Matsuya Hisamasa (d.1598). See Nagashima Fukutarō, *Matsuya kaiki*, in Sen, vol. 9, pp. 31–32. Also Kumakura, *Shidai chakaiki*, pp. 46–47.

19 Shingorō is also often referred to as Sōga.

20 Kōji 4 (1558)/9/9, afternoon, in *NN*, p. 9. Also, Eiroku 6 (1563)/11/4, morning, in *NN*, p. 13. Also, Eiroku 10 (1567)/8/27, morning, in *NN*, p. 18.

21 Considering the pre-eminence of commercial interests in Sakai, it is not surprising that merchants form the largest single group of participants in tea gatherings. Sheer volume prohibits a comprehensive accounting of the names and the dates of the meetings.

22 Ōta Gyūichi, *Shinchō Kō ki*, in Kuwata Tadachika (ed.), *Sengoku shiryō sōsho*, vol. 2 (Jinbutsu Ōraisha, 1965), pp. 84–86. For Nobunaga's entrance into Kyoto with Yoshiaki and a discussion of the ensuing power struggle, see Hisashi Fujiki with George Elison, "The Political Posture of Oda Nobunaga," in John Whitney Hall *et al.* (eds), *Japan Before Tokugawa: Political Consolidation and Economic Growth, 1500–1650* (Princeton University Press, 1981), pp. 149–193.

23 Fujiki logically posits that Yoshiaki's offer was an attempt to place Nobunaga within the existing shogunal structure, and in a position subservient to him, and that Nobunaga's refusal of this appointment, even after subsequent urging by the emperor, was motivated by his own designs on power.

24 Discussed in Asao Naohiro, "Shokuhōki no Sakai daikan," in *Akamatsu Toshihide kyōju taikan kinen kokushi ronshū* (Bunkōsha, 1972), p. 798.

25 An overview of the impositions can be found in Okuno Takahiro (ed.), *Zōtei Oda Nobunaga monjo no kenkyū* (Yoshikawa, 1988), addendum and index volume, p. 22. See also V. Dixon Morris, "The City of Sakai and Urban Autonomy," in George Elison and Bardwell L. Smith (eds), *Warlords, Artists, and Commoners: Japan in the Sixteenth Century* (University of Hawai'i Press, 1981), pp. 52, 292–293, n. 75.

26  Okuno, vol. 1, pp. 207–211.
27  For the commercial administrators in Sakai, see Morris, pp. 36–39.
28  Toyoda, p. 74.
29  Toyoda, p. 74; see also Okuno, vol. 1, pp. 154–155.
30  For a review of warrior control over Sakai, see Morris, pp. 39–54.
31  The other three were Iwanari Tomomichi, Miyoshi Nagayuki, and Miyoshi Masayasu.
32  Eiroku 12 (1569)/1/11: *TK*, vol. 7, p. 148. Also discussed in Kumakura, *Shidai chakaiki*, pp. 56–57.
33  Toyoda, p. 75.
34  This entry appears to have been written after 1/12, as Sōgyū discusses these events in the past tense, but before 2/28, the date of the following entry. Luis Frois corroborates the panic felt in the city:

> Nobunaga has received some trouble from the city of Sakai, and the citizens feared that he would order it to be destroyed. Great was their fear as it is one of the finest cities in Japan, as well as being the richest and with the greatest nobility and commerce. Everyone, as best he could, left his house and fled with his wife, children, and wealth, some in this direction, others in that.
>
> (Luis Frois, *Historia de Japam*, vol. 2, Biblioteca Nacional, Lisbon, 1976–1983, p. 259)

35  [Eiroku 12 (1569)] 4/1: Okuno, addendum and index volume, pp. 20–22, supplementary document 18.
36  Toyoda, pp. 77–78.
37  Frois, 1, p. 234. Frois spent four years in Sakai, 1565–1569, and so knew the place well. His text is rich in references to the city.
38  [Eiroku 11 (1568)] 12/16: Okuno, vol. 1, pp. 234–235, document 138. This document and many others collected in Okuno that I discuss in this article are also examined in Sakaguchi Yoshiyasu, "Oda Nobunaga no jōraku to Sakaishū, 2: Nobunaga to Seishō Imai Sōkyū," in *Shōkei Daigaku kenkyū kiyō* 7 (1984): 27–42.
39  *Ichien* often refers, in conjunction with the term *chigyō*, to land. In this case, the context justifies the interpretation that the tea utensils are included as part of the *ichien*.
40  The retrospective *Shinchō Kō ki*, pp. 86–87, claims that two months earlier, on the second day of the tenth month of 1568, Sōkyū visited Nobunaga at his battlefield encampment at Akutagawa in Settsu, and presented him with the Matsushima jar. While the possibility of the meeting taking place is not denied, it is unlikely that on this occasion Sōkyū gave Nobunaga the vessel. See below, n. 71.
41  [Eiroku 12 (1569)] 6/8: Okuno, vol. 1, p. 309, document 186.
42  The use of the term *kōgi*, especially in conjunction with the explicit statement of Nobunaga's support, indicates that the official business concerned Nobunaga. The term *kōgi* is discussed at length in Hall *et al.* (1981), especially pp. 120–124 and 257–261.
43  Okuno, vol. 1, p. 309. Additionally, an Imai family document records that Yoshiaki ordered the establishment of a passenger boat for the Yodo River, and this became known as the "Imaibune." Toyoda, p. 85.
44  The diary of Yamashina Tokitsugu (1507–1579), a courtier with warrior contacts, is called *Tokitsugu Kyō ki*. See the entries for Eiroku 12 (1569)/7/22 and 8/1. Hayakawa Junzaburō (ed.), *Tokitsugu Kyō ki*, vol. 4 (Kokusho Kankōkai, 1914–1915), pp. 360–362.

45  Toyoda, pp. 82–83.
46  [Genki 1 (1570)] 6/4; paraphrased in Toyoda, p. 86.
47  Translation from Mary Elizabeth Berry, *Hideyoshi*, Harvard University Press, 1982, p. 45.
48  [Eiroku 12 (1569)] 11/9: paraphrased in Toyoda, p. 86. Okuno, vol. 1, pp. 351–352, dates the letter to Eiroku 12.
49  [Eiroku 12 (1569)] 8/12: Okuno, vol. 1, pp. 316–317, document 193.
50  Asao, pp. 804–805.
51  An indication of the importance of salt in Japanese commerce during the pre-modern era is reflected in a statistic from an earlier period than that under discussion here, but still relevant. As recorded in *Hyōgo Kita no Seki nyūsen nōchō*, 1445, about 40 percent of the boats that passed through Hyōgo Kita no Seki in that year were involved in the transportation of salt. Cited by Watanabe Norifumi in *Kokushi daijiten*, vol. 6 (Yoshikawa 1979–), p. 649.
52  [Eiroku 12 (1569)] 8/17: Okuno, vol. 1, pp. 319–320, document 195.
53  [Eiroku 12 (1569)] 8/8: Okuno, vol. 1, pp. 315–316, document 192.
54  The exact location of this domain is unknown.
55  Okuno, vol. 1, p. 316, states that Katsumasa himself was the root of the problem, although the letter itself does not seem to indicate this. Rather, the threats are meant to be directed against anyone, including Katsumasa, who impeded the implementation of the decision. Three months later, a letter involving the same parties indicates that the matter had still not been brought to a conclusion.

> The Tennōji Zenjuan portion of the Sakai Gokanoshō domain of Imai Sōkyū was recently discussed in a letter. The portion has not yet been handed over. It is desirable to give it to Imai quickly and without equivocation, as Nobunaga is aware of the matter.
> ([Eiroku, 12 (1569)] 12/27: Okuno, vol. 1, p. 323, document 199)

56  [Eiroku 12 (1569)] 9/16: Okuno, vol. 1, p. 322, document 198.
57  A slightly later letter notes Sōkyū's assumption of *daikan* rights to another area ([Eiroku 12 (1569)] 12/27: Okuno, vol. 1, pp. 340–341, document 207.

> Regarding the Financial Bureau [*ryōsho*] portion within the Nishi Kujō area, the *chigyō* rights to the *nengu* [annual tax], *jishisen* [land rent], and various goods formerly held by Sogō Minbu Daifu Dono and listed in the vermilion seal [document] have been awarded to me. As before, submit them to the appropriate office. With regard to other payments, they shall be double.

In this letter, directed to the "named" farmers of the Nishi Kujō area of Kyoto, Sōkyū informs them of his assumption of rights held formerly by the ousted Miyoshi clansman.

58  A discussion of these events is found in Nagashima Fukutarō, "Oda Nobunaga no Tajima keiryaku to Imai Sōkyū: Tsuketari Ikuno Ginzan no keiei," in *Kansei Gakuin shigaku*, vol. 5 (1959): 100–120.
59  The letter, dated [Eiroku 12 (1569)] 12/12, is quoted in Nagashima, "Oda Nobunaga no Tajima keiryaku to Imai Sōkyu," p. 110.
60  Nagashima, "Oda Nobunaga no Tajima keiryaku to Imai Sōkyu," p. 111. This information is contained in a New Year's letter from Sōkyū to Suketoyo's wife.
61  [Genki 1 (1570)] 4/19: Okuno, vol. 1, pp. 373–374, document 224. The four

addressees are Ōtagaki Tosa no Kami [Terunobu], Yagi Tanba no Kami [Toyonobu], Kakiya Harima no Kami, and Tainoshō Hidari no Uma no Suke.

62 [Genki 1(1570)] 7/3: Okuno, vol. 1, pp. 404–406, supplementary document 242.

63 *Fukiyazeni*. The meaning of this term is not known, although Nagashima "Oda Nobunaga no Tajima keiryaku to Imai Sōkyu," p. 119, suggests that it was a tax levied on production at the mine.

64 Nagashima, "Oda Nobunaga no Tajima keiryaku to Imai Sōkyu," p. 109.

65 [Genki 1 (1570)] 2/17: Okuno, vol. 1, p. 350, document 212. The location of Minatomura is not known, although Okuno, vol. 1, p. 351, suggests that it may have been west of Sōkyū's Northern Estate of Sakai.

66 [Genki 1 (1570)] 2/19: Okuno, vol. 1, pp. 351–352, supplementary document 212.

67 Okuno, vol. 1, p. 351.

68 There is much scholarly literature on the introduction and dissemination of Western firearms in Japan. One useful study for the period under consideration here is Hora Tomio, *Teppō denrai to sono eikyō: Tanegashimajū zōhoban* (Azekura, 1959), particularly Chapters 1 and 2.

69 Berry, pp. 54 and 252, n. 26.

70 Eiroku 13 (1570)/4/1: *NN*, p. 21. There is room for interpretation whether it was Sōkyū or Sōeki who received the gifts from Nobunaga; I agree with the reading suggested in Komatsu Shigemi, *Rikyū no tegami* (Shōgakukan, 1985), p. 286.

71 The retrospective *Shinchō Kō Ki*, p. 87, incorrectly states that Sōkyū gave the Matsushima jar to Nobunaga on Eiroku 11 (1568)/10/2. See n. 40, above.

72 For a comprehensive study of Yūkan and his service to Nobunaga in Sakai, see Kawasaki Kikuko, "Oda seikenka no Sakai: Matsui Yūkan no yakuwari ni tsuite," *Hisutoria* 92 (1981): 39–56. Kawasaki, p. 50, points out that Yūkan was one of Nobunaga's two representatives through whom Kennyo (1543–1592) sued for peace in the tenth month 1575.

73 Kawasaki, pp. 45–47.

74 [Eiroku 12 (1569)] 8/22; Kawasaki, p. 50.

75 Tenshō 1 (1573)/11/24, morning: *NN*, pp. 24–25.

76 [Tenshō 3 (1575)] 9/16: Okuno, 2, pp. 82–83, document 545.

77 Toyoda, p. 79.

78 Eiroku 12 (1569)/2/11: *TK*, 8, p. 140.

79 Tenshō 1 (1573)/11/23: *TK*, 7, pp. 187–188.

80 Genki 4 (1573)/3/4, morning: *TK*, 8, p. 188.

81 Tenshō 1 (1573)/1/24: *TK*, 7, pp. 191–193. See also Kumakura, *Shidai chakaiki*, pp. 60–61. Sōgyū goes into great detail describing this important event. Members of Nobunaga's family served the meal at the gathering. Sōgyū's second portion of rice was offered by Nobunaga himself.

82 What is likely the last documentary notation of the Matsushima jar is a reference in Ōta's *Shinchō Kōki*, pp. 217–218, to an object referred to simply as "Matsushima" at a tea gathering hosted by Nobunaga on Tenshō 1 (1578)/1/1. The Matsushima jar is believed to have been lost during the attack on Nobunaga at Honnōji in 1582.

83 Asao, p. 812, n. 38, suggests that the Sakai people in attendance were members of the commercial administration (*egōshū*).

84 Tenshō 2 (1574)/3/24, afternoon: *NN*, pp. 25–26.

85 Tenshō 2 (1574)/3/24, afternoon: *TK*, 7, pp. 195–196. See also Kumakura, *Shidai chakaiki*, pp. 63–65.

86 Tenshō 2 (1574)/4/3, afternoon: *NN*, p. 16, and *TK*, 7, pp. 196–197.

87 Sōgyū tells the story of Nobunaga's acquisition of the incense in an entry dated Tenshō 2 (1574)/3/27: *TK*, 7, p. 196. See also Kumakura, *Shidai chakaiki*, p. 65.

88 Tenshō 6 (1578)/10/28: *NN*, p. 30.

89 Tenshō 6 (1578)/9/15: *NN*, p. 30.

90 Tenshō 6 (1578)/9, last day; the diary is the *Tamon'in nikki*, cited in Miura, vol. 4, p. 125.

91 Ōta, *Shinchō Kōki*, pp. 231–232.

92 Tenshō 10 (1582)/1/1: *TK*, vol. 7, pp. 355–356.

93 Tenshō 10 (1582)/5/19: *TK*, vol. 7, p. 363. As noted above, it is possible that these ten men represented the Sakai commercial administration (*egōshū*).

94 Tenshō 10 (1582)/5/29: *NN*, p. 34.

95 Tenshō 10 (1582)/5/29: *TK*, vol. 7, p. 364.

96 Tenshō 10 (1582)/6/2: *NN*, p. 34.

97 Tenshō 10 (1582)/6/2: *TK*, vol. 7, p. 364. See also Kumakura, *Shidai chakaiki*, pp. 71–72.

98 For a review of the events following the Honnōji incident, see Berry, pp. 71–80.

99 While Nobunaga was still alive, in the early 1570s, Hideyoshi sent a letter to Sōkyū politely expressing his gratitude for being shown Sōkyū's tea utensils. Toyoda, pp. 88–89.

100 For the Kitano gathering, see Louise Allison Cort, "The Grand Kitano Tea Gathering," *Chanoyu Quarterly* 31 (1982): 15–44.

101 Sōeki's political involvement under Hideyoshi is examined by Bodart, "Tea and Counsel," pp. 49–74.

102 The date of Sōkyū's death, unrecorded in extant tea diaries, is given in the eighteenth-century *Imai shi nana sekihimei narabini keizu* as Bunroku 2 (1593)/8/5. Miura, vol. 4, p. 367.

# 2 The transformation of tea practice in sixteenth-century Japan

*Dale Slusser*

## The field of tea culture

The drinking of powdered green tea (*matcha*) became popular in the beginning of the fifteenth century as one element of opulent social gatherings held at the residences of the military elite. The Ashikaga Shogun and other high-ranking military lords, who had established Kyoto as their headquarters, did not limit the scope of their activities to politics, but soon began to display their power and riches in the cultural life of the capital as well. By the middle of the Sengoku period (1467–1568), tea had emerged within the sphere of warrior cultural pursuits as an elaborate ritual art that came to be practiced by a significant number of merchants, warriors, and noblemen over the course of the following century.

The development of tea culture is generally seen as a consonant progression toward a more spiritually profound practice, inspired by Zen Buddhism. This trend is often attributed to the "enlightened vision" of certain key figures. In contrast to the traditional interpretation, this chapter will propose an alternative thesis to explain the manner in which new aesthetic ideals developed.[1] Some studies have noted the political function of tea masters as messengers or even negotiators during the intimate atmosphere of a tea gathering and the advantages of social cohesiveness to be gained by such participation.[2] However, scholars have tended to ignore tea as a ritualized system of disciplined behavior in which the actions and beliefs of practitioners could be manipulated. In the following pages we will examine the early history of tea culture from its inception as a ritual art in the fifteenth century to its expansion in the late sixteenth century. The focus is on the complex relationships between the entrance of rich merchants into the field of tea, earlier the exclusive domain of military lords; struggles to define the legitimate practice of the art and the new modes of practice which were thus created; and, the shifting value of specific forms of capital, beginning with tea utensils and later including the ability to judge the quality of objects and skill in their ritual manipulation.

## Contours of the field

During the Muromachi period (1334–1573), Kyoto's field of elite culture – which had once been the exclusive domain of the court aristocracy – expanded. Continuing a process that had begun several centuries earlier, many members of the aristocratic class were no longer able to secure the rents from their estates in the countryside. They had little choice but to offer their services as instructors in ancient art forms and ritual in exchange for financial assistance. Military leaders also supported such arts as Noh drama, which developed outside the court tradition, and carried them into the field of culture in the capital. These men hosted lavish gatherings, where participants collaborated in such social arts as linked verse (*renga*) poetry and games of object matching (*monoawase*), while enjoying food and libation amid elaborate displays of Chinese art objects. At times the drinking of bowls of tea was also included. These cultural affairs were held in specially constructed buildings, called banquet-room complexes (*kaisho*), where such architectural features as alcoves (*tokonoma*), divided shelves (*chigaidana*), and built-in writing desks (*shoin*) first appeared. Tea practitioners would later incorporate these elements in their tea room designs.

The aesthetic which dominated the decoration of these gatherings was "love for Chinese things" (*karamono-suki*). Objects such as Chinese paintings, lacquerware, ceramics, and bronze vessels were used to decorate the banquet-room complex and functioned as symbols of wealth and power. Not only the military and nobility coveted these objects. Some wealthy merchants also collected and became experts in connoisseurship. The Ashikaga shogunate gathered perhaps the most impressive collection; artifacts once part of this collection have remained some of the most highly valued pieces in Japan to the present day.

The owners of great collections of Chinese art generally entrusted the objects to the curatorship of a group of men who came to be known as the "companions" (*dōbōshū*). The term was used in the war-torn fourteenth century to refer to men who served on the battlefield by caring for the dying and dead. These individuals were characteristically members of the Ji sect of Buddhism, were of low social status, and adopted the Buddhist suffix -*ami* to their names. At the residences of the military elite the companions served in a variety of positions, from servants and clerks to curators and connoisseurs of Chinese art. The most famous of these curators are Nōami (1397–1471), Geiami (1431–1485) and Sōami (d. 1525), who are known to have been greatly respected for their knowledge of Chinese art.[3]

Curators such as the companions of the Ashikaga collection seem to have played a role in the early formation of tea ritual, in which tea was performatively prepared and served in front of the assembled guests. Among the compiled letters attributed to the priest Gen'e (1279–1350), we find one such example of an early form of serving tea at the residence of a military lord. The assembled guests were first served sake, noodles and foods of the mountain and sea, and other delicacies before making their way to the second story of a lavishly decorated tea pavilion from which the moon could be viewed. The room had been decorated with Chinese paintings by Muqi and Zhang Sigong. Bronze vases, incense burners, tea jars, tea kettles and many other treasures were displayed on tables covered with golden brocades. The guests sat in chairs luxuriously draped with leopard skins. The host's son served sweets to the guests and then Chinese Jian ware (Japanese: *temmoku*) bowls were distributed. Next a "young man" with a kettle of hot water in his left hand and a tea whisk in his right moved from guest to guest in order of rank preparing tea. After this the guests enjoyed additional sake and later a tea judging contest (*tōcha*) was held.[4] Several other similar gatherings are recorded, such as when a Chinese embassy visited Ashikaga Yoshimitsu's (1358–1408) Kitayama residence in 1407 and when another Chinese embassy was entertained at the Muromachi compound of Ashikaga Yoshinori (1394–1441) in 1434.[5]

The servant who made the tea, quite possibly a specialist in the handling of tea wares, was thus granted a degree of interaction with the assembled elite guests. In the examples above many utensils were displayed, a minimum were used, and the actual procedures of preparing the tea itself were rather simple. By the middle of the fifteenth century, however, complex ritual tea-preparation procedures had developed centering around the use of a Chinese-made utensil stand (*daisu*).[6] These procedures were probably created by "companions" in conjunction with tea utensil merchants, influenced by rules for the handling of tea in temples as well as concepts of Chinese geomancy. Over time the tea specialist's duties came to include instructing others in the proper procedures to drink tea and handle the utensils, although it was not until late in the fifteenth century that warriors would study the ritual procedures to make tea. In this manner, tea specialists gained prestige by becoming ritualists and potentially teachers.

Shops specializing in tea utensils could be found in Kyoto by at least the late fourteenth and early fifteenth centuries.[7] By the mid-fifteenth century some merchants had gained sufficient wealth to collect the Chinese utensils needed to practice the new ritual art of tea. Merchants who concentrated on the sale of Chinese utensils seem likely to have been the first to practice the ritual, inspiring a trend among their peers. Unlike warrior leaders who enjoyed collecting tea utensils and drinking tea at banquets, these merchants prepared tea themselves in front of their guests. This important development is surely closely related to belief in the value of demonstrating ritual skill. In order to be acknowledged, the specialized knowledge that the complex ritual of tea constituted had to be demonstrated. Elite merchants did not duplicate the architectural structures or style of entertaining which were practiced by the military lords, but instead developed their own mode of tea practice, known as the grass-hut (*sōan*) style of tea, in which they invited guests to partake of tea while manipulating the valuable objects they had collected.

## The struggle for autonomy

Yamanoue Sōji (1544–1590) in his *Record of Yamanoue Sōji* [*Yamanoue Sōji ki*] (*c.*1589) credits Murata Shukō (also read Jukō, 1421?–1502) as the founder of grass-hut tea culture, the man who most influenced the beginning of a transformation away from the warrior style of tea.[8] Modern historians have repeated this claim, although a lack of documentary evidence makes it impossible to clearly determine Shukō's activities. Nevertheless, his place in the history of tea culture is assured by his *Letter of the Heart*, which provides important evidence of the introduction of new aesthetic ideals.[9]

Shukō is said to have been born in Nara, perhaps the son of a blind biwa-player priest, and at an early age entered the Buddhist temple of Shōmyōji.[10] The very humbleness of this account suggests to many scholars its validity, yet an equally strong argument can be made that he was said to have come from a poor yet culturally talented family to make his supposed influence on tea appear more disinterested and thus authentic. Before the age of thirty Shukō left the temple and moved to Kyoto where he somehow learned tea and became a collector and connoisseur of tea utensils.[11] He may also have been a dealer in utensils, which would help to explain how he was able to obtain the costly pieces in his collection.

In *Record of Yamanoue Sōji*, it is stressed that in Kyoto Shukō studied with the famous Daitokuji priest Ikkyū (1394–1481), from whom he received a calligraphic work by the Song dynasty Chan master Yuan-wu (J. Engo) in certification of his enlightenment. Sōji also claims that Shukō was employed by Ashikaga Yoshimasa (1435–1490), the eighth Ashikaga Shogun, as a specialist in ritual tea at his Higashiyama villa (presently the Ginkakuji or Silver Pavilion) through the introduction of the "companion" Nōami, who Shukō taught his new style of tea practice. Yamanoue Sōji further states that, under the influence of Ikkyū, Shukō realized the potential for tea to become a discipline of spiritual attainment and perhaps ultimately Buddhist enlightenment and was thereby inspired to develop his new style.[12]

No other extant documents substantiate these claims. It is known that Nōami died before Yoshimasa retired to his Higashiyama villa, so it is unlikely that he introduced Shukō to Ashikaga Yoshimasa. Furthermore, the name Shukō does not appear in any of the documents related to either Yoshimasa or Ikkyū. Shukō does appear in later records of Daitokuji, however, which indicates that he probably did have dealings with the temple after Ikkyū's death, if not before. In addition, references to Shukō appear in the writings of the Noh master Konparu Zenpō (1454–1520) and also in a letter from the *renga* poetry master Sōgi (1421–1502) to the incense expert Shino Sōshin (d. 1480).[13] It is therefore fairly certain that Shukō was active in artistic circles in Kyoto at this time, although his links to powerful figures such as Yoshimasa, Ikkyū, and Nōami are suspect.

Shukō wrote *Letter of the Heart* for Furuichi Harima (1452?–1508), commonly known by his Buddhist name of Chōin. The latter entered the temple of Kōfukuji when he was 13 and succeeded his father as the leader of a group of warrior monks (*shuto*) at the age of 23. From this position he later became a minor domainal lord in the town of Furuichi outside of Nara, and is known to have been a patron of Kōfukuji temple and various artists, possibly including Shukō. During the late fifteenth century the Furuichi family was also known to have held elaborate bathing parties which included the composition of *renga* and *waka* poetry, food, sake, and the drinking of powdered green tea. It is said that Chōin requested the letter from Shukō to assist in his practice of tea; it is very similar in form to a work on poetry in Chōin's possession. In 1646 the Nara lacquer merchant who then owned the letter, Matsuya Hisashige (1566–1652), brought it to the influential tea practitioner Kobori Enshū (1574–1647) for authentication. Enshū, himself a member of the samurai class, served as tea master to the Tokugawa government and played an important role in defining tea practice in the early seventeenth century. Enshū arranged for authentication of the letter from the head priest of Daitokuji. He then had this authentication mounted together with Shukō's letter as a hanging scroll.[14]

*Letter of the Heart* begins by proclaiming that in following the path of tea, the greatest errors are insolence, attachment to self, and the scorning of beginners. Next, it states the need to dissolve the line between Chinese and Japanese wares. Shukō is quick to condemn those "mere beginners," however, who use such native wares as Bizen and Shigaraki, claiming to be "advanced and deep." The ideal that was promoted was the "withered (*kare*), [which] means owning splendid pieces, knowing their savor fully, and from the heart's ground advancing and deepening so that all after becomes chill (*hie*) and lean (*yase*)." The letter concludes with another admonition to avoid insolence and the need for a "painful self-awareness."[15]

Although framed in statements expressing the sincerity and spiritual purity needed to practice the "way" (common injunctions in such writings), the force of the letter is an appeal to a new aesthetic that is expressed by combining Chinese and Japanese wares: the "withered," "chill" and "lean." Although this was new to tea culture, contemporaneous records show that such ideals were commonly expressed in the literary arts. "Chill" and "lean" were originally drawn from Chinese literature, and all three terms appear in works on *waka*, *renga*, and Noh. The mixture of Japanese and Chinese was also similar to the popular *wakan* form of poetry that alternated verses in Japanese and Chinese. Reference to tea as a "way" (*michi*) was adopted from the literary world as well. The concept of "the way" had developed in poetry from the thirteenth century and had gradually broadened to include diverse activities ranging from singing popular ditties to tree climbing.[16]

*Letter of the Heart* represents the interests of a new group of tea practitioners, mostly wealthy merchants, struggling to define a new mode of tea practice. The merchants' wealth and corresponding power made it possible for them to practice tea; now they were attempting to change the contour of the field to express their social position and interests. The nature of the field, however, was such that only a limited number of changes could be made. The merchants had to choose a position within the field that would appear reasonable in the eyes of their contemporaries while imposing change on all practitioners.[17] Mixing a few pieces of native pottery into the ritual under the respected aesthetic ideal of the "chill" and "withered" satisfied both requirements. By relating tea practice to other established art forms through the use of this ideal, tea – as well as those merchants who practiced it – gained in prestige. Other records verify that it was indeed at this time that domestically produced ceramics began to be used in tea culture.[18] *Letter of the Heart* can thus be read as a statement of the merchants' strategy to establish themselves within the field.

This strategy had other advantages as well. In contrast to the aesthetic of banquet-room tea, in which exclusively Chinese wares were used, *Letter of the Heart* both promotes a new aesthetic and attempts to limit who can claim to understand it. The letter is quick to condemn "mere beginners" who try to use native pieces, before it has even elaborated on what mixing Chinese and Japanese wares was meant to express. The implication is that before one can use Japanese objects they must first own splendid pieces (*yoki dogu*) and savor them fully. The struggle to impose the legitimate definition of tea practice was also a struggle to define who could practice tea and what utensils they could use. The rarefaction of entry requirements served to increase the prestige of the art as well as the stakes involved. In promoting this new ideal, elite merchant tea practitioners were also trying to monopolize the power to consecrate objects for themselves.

Chinese utensils, characterized by brilliant glazes, elegant forms, and technical perfection, were easily distinguished from Japanese wares in this period. The appreciation of Chinese utensils in general took no great training, although considerable skill was needed to distinguish between superior and inferior pieces. The relationship of these rare objects to wealth and power was transparent. In contrast to this, unglazed Shigaraki and Bizen ceramics were made in Japan and available for only a fraction of the cost of Chinese pieces. Merchant tea practitioners claimed that what was required to use and appreciate these native wares was an ability to evaluate them according to acknowledged canons, so-called "good taste," not wealth or power.

For native wares to be appreciated, a belief in both their symbolic and economic value was needed; tea as a ritual provided an ideal atmosphere. The connoisseurship of utensils had always been central to tea practice, and the admiration and examination of art objects continued to play a central role in tea gatherings. Japanese utensils were used together with acknowledged Chinese treasures, thus gaining validation through the association of juxtaposition. The merchants now claimed authority to choose which objects could be used; the ritual itself insured the appreciation of Japanese utensils. This created enormous potential for merchant tea practitioners to "discover" native wares, create a belief in their value, and resell them at a vast profit.

In the latter half of the fifteenth century the new grass-hut mode of tea culture was practiced primarily by rich merchants, and these men formed a group which functioned in many ways like an elite club. Entrance into the practice of grass-hut tea was limited to those few who could obtain the necessary ritual objects, while more importantly, unlike banquet-room tea, full participation required that the movements of the ritual itself be learned so that the rite could be performed before others. Tea practice was not a body of writings to be discussed, but a set of movements of the body to be practiced. All of the seemingly small and insignificant actions of the practice combine to erase their artificial production and produce a misrecognition that allows a naïve, pre-reflexive compliance to be imposed. The imposition of a definition of the legitimate mode of tea practice requiring proficiency in the procedures granted experts control over the bodies and thus the beliefs of all who practiced the art. The appeal to a higher aesthetic ideal was in fact a struggle by elite merchant tea practitioners to employ a potent means of social control.[19]

The tea practice of the dominant military elite, in which Chinese utensils were displayed, reinforced a hierarchical definition of society in which the warrior leaders were distinguished by their wealth and power. In response, the merchants created grass-hut tea culture by positing the ideal of the "chill" and "withered." To gain a position of dominance within the field of grass-hut tea culture, proficiency in expressing this ideal using a limited number of Chinese utensils together with Japanese wares had to be demonstrated. The merchants, by presenting what they claimed was a purer and more profound form of tea culture, negated the style of using exclusively Chinese utensils and placed their "grass-hut" mode above that of the military lords. At the same time, the merchants arrogated to themselves the power to assign value, both real and symbolic, to simple native objects and tried to limit the manipulation of these objects as symbols of power. The practice of grass-hut tea was removed from the exclusive control of elite warriors, so that relationships of domination within grass-hut tea culture no longer strictly paralleled those outside the field but instead followed a relatively autonomous principle of hierarchization; the practice as such constituted a counter-ideology.[20]

## Practice redefined

What were the actual changes that merchant tea practitioners made? In the late fifteenth and early sixteenth centuries, rather than the banquet-room style of architecture popular with military lords, merchant tea practitioners built six or four-and-one-half *tatami* mat sized rooms (approximately 9 by 12 and 9 by 9 feet respectively) of simple construction, often set alone in a garden at the back of the house.[21] This style of architecture was borrowed from practices popular in the larger cultural field of the period.

One example is the structure that Sanjōnishi Sanetaka (1455–1537), an influential court poet, constructed in 1502. Sanjōnishi purchased an existing six-mat building, had it moved to his estate, and rebuilt it as a four-and-a-half mat structure. His interest in the project is made clear by the ten entries in his diary beginning 6/2/1502, when he sent someone to inspect the building, through 8/16 when he celebrated the completion of the project by drinking sake in the new hut, called the "Corner Hut."[22] The building had such architectural features as a raised display area with a wooden floor (*oshi ita*), shelves, walls covered in paper or plaster, and a *tatami* mat-covered floor.[23] His diary suggests that the cottage was used for gatherings to compose poetry, and at least once for the display of a ceramic object he had recently acquired, an event which was attended by important members of the court.[24]

Evidence of a similar structure can be found in the diary of the *renga* poetry master Sōchō (1448–1532), where it is recorded on 8/15/1526 that Sōju (also read Sōshu) had recently built a four-and-a-half mat room and a six-mat room near some tall pine and cryptomeria trees at his home in the southern part of Kyoto.[25] Sōju was the adopted son of Shukō, and his rooms are also described in a work by the Middle Counselor Washinoo Takayasu (1485–1533) where he wrote, "Sōju's tea room is splendid. The atmosphere of a mountain dwelling it creates is most impressive. Truly, it is a hermitage within the city."[26]

It is noteworthy that not only merchants but also warlords and noblemen sponsored the construction of small, intimate gathering spaces. Peter Stallybrass and Allon White, in their study of high–low oppositions in Britain from the seventeenth through the twentieth centuries, point out:

> Each "site of assembly" constitutes a nucleus of material and cultural conditions which regulate what may and may not be said, who may speak, how people may communicate and what importance must be given to what is said. An utterance is legitimated or disregarded according to its place of production and so, in large part, the history of political struggle has been the history of the attempts made to control significant sites of assembly and spaces of discourse.[27]

In these small cottages within the city, noblemen, warriors, priests, and merchants met together to share in various cultural activities. As tea practitioners appropriated these structures, they were indeed taking "control of significant sites" where, through the ritualized procedures of tea culture, they could influence the discourse, bodies, and beliefs of elite participants.[28]

Many military lords and wealthy merchants sought in tea culture the marks of civility and culture. These Japanese counterparts to the "Booby Squires" of Britain were in part drawn to tea by the relative ease of entry into the field. Compared to the vast knowledge of canonical writings required for proficiency in the highly regarded art of poetry, wealth was all that was needed to purchase utensils and practice tea. As competence in the actual procedures of tea came to be required in grass-hut tea culture, however, practitioners were forced to make a considerable investment of time. In the small rooms for tea there were undoubtedly concepts introduced which could not be expressed in a larger more public forum. Practitioners selected and arranged less utensils in the new, small tea rooms, for example, one or two scrolls, an incense container, a flower vase, and perhaps a writing set. Practitioners still used Chinese utensils, but they preferred objects of less refined beauty, such as ash-glaze Jian ware bowls and celadon pieces with a cloudy glaze. Domestically produced flower containers and waste water jars were increasingly used in place of Chinese ones, though a substantial collection of Chinese utensils was still required.[29] Overall a quality of restraint came to be seen as elements not strictly related to the drinking of tea were removed.

## Shifting boundaries

Throughout the first half of the sixteenth century, the field of tea culture continued to turn toward greater simplicity. Tea practitioners further reduced the number of objects displayed and increasingly replaced Chinese utensils with Japanese as well as rare Korean and South Asian ones.[30] At the same time the popularity of tea continued to spread throughout Japan, apparent in the *Record of Tennojiya*, a diary of tea gatherings hosted and attended by four consecutive generations of the Tsuda merchant family of Sakai. In the first part of the work, written by Tsuda Sōtatsu (1504–1566) between 11/1548 and his death in 1566, the popularity of the tea culture is apparent. Appearing in the diary are merchants from the cities of Sakai, Kyoto, Osaka, and Hakata, as well as from the prefectures of Yamato (present day Nara prefecture), Harima (Hyōgo), Ōmi (Shiga), Ise (Mie), Echizen (Fukui), Mino (Gifu), Awa (Tokushima), Suruga, Hizen (Nagasaki), Bungo (Oita), and Satsuma. Sōtatsu also shared tea with such domainal lords as Hatakeyama Takamasa (d. 1576) from Kawachi, Ikeda Nobuteru (1536–1584) from Settsu, Saitō Toshimasa (1494–1556) from Mino, Matsunaga Hisahide (1510–1577) from Yamato, and the powerful lord Miyoshi Chōkei (1523–1564) who controlled parts of Awa, Settsu, Kawachi, and Izumi (modern Osaka prefecture). In 1559 even such high ranking courtiers as the former Chief Minister of State (*Kanpaku*) Kujō Tamemichi and former Major Counselor (*Dainagon*) Kuga Haru-michi visited Sōtatsu's home for tea.[31] Merchants, warriors, and even noblemen built teahouse complexes and met regularly to perform tea. Although the earlier style continued to be practiced, by the mid-sixteenth century grass-hut tea had become firmly established as the predomin-ant mode.

Modern scholars of tea have frequently pointed to the mixing of mer-chants and warriors at tea gatherings as evidence of the ideal of equality in the new cultural matrix of grass-hut tea. It should be noted, however, that a large number of the merchants of port cities like Sakai had once been lower-level samurai who were assigned by their lords to handle shipments for the fief. Over time these men developed private trading businesses and became independent merchants. Many domainal lords had also been lower-ranking members of the samurai class who, when their commanders had moved to Kyoto, had stayed behind in the country and developed local ties that allowed them to grasp the reins of power.[32] Although the two groups were quite different in regard to military strength, the similar-ity of backgrounds contributed to an ease of social intercourse. It was not, in other words, as dramatic a mixing as is sometimes conveyed.

Sitting in the same small room and sharing tea culture would have nat-urally led to a certain degree of camaraderie, although it is not possible to know exactly how "equally" individuals were treated. It can be argued that for elite merchants, sharing the practice of grass-hut tea culture with military lords and noblemen provided the opportunity to try to appear to be their social equals. We must not, however, confuse equality in the elite field of tea with the modern ideal of egalitarianism. Above all, ritual has the power of "instituting a lasting difference between those to whom the rite pertains and those to whom it does not pertain."[33]

## Collecting power and ritualizing legitimacy

In the latter half of the sixteenth century, many domainal lords were suc-cessful in consolidating their territory into larger holdings. This was particularly true in the case of Oda Nobunaga (1534–1582), who brought relative political stability to the area around Kyoto and Sakai. This had a profound effect on many aspects of Japanese culture, including tea. After gaining military control, Nobunaga continued to strengthen his position by other means. One of his techniques was to arrogate the semblance of legitimacy through association with the emperor and Shogun, two tradi-tional sources of authority.[34] His collection of famous tea objects, particu-larly those that had once been in the Ashikaga collection, provided one source for this association.

When Nobunaga occupied Kyoto in 9/1568, Matsunaga Hisahide sub-mitted to Nobunaga and presented him with a famed eggplant-shaped tea caddy. This Chinese object was purported to have been owned by Ashik-aga Yoshimitsu (1358–1408), and subsequently purchased from the Shogun's collection by Shukō for the price of ninety-nine *kan*.[35] The name of this piece, "Tsukumo" was written with the characters for ninety-nine (*kyūjūkyū*), while the reading was taken from a poem in the famous *Tales of Ise*.[36] The Asakura warrior family later purchased the caddy for 500 *kan*. Next the Kosode merchant family bought it for 1,000 *kan*. It then entered Matsunaga's collection and finally Nobunaga's.[37] In a similar example, the Sakai merchant and tea practitioner Imai Sōkyū (1520–1593) visited Nobunaga in the capital and presented him with two famous tea utensils: a tea leaf storage jar named *Matsushima*, which had once been in the Ashikaga collection; and an eggplant tea caddy ostensibly once owned by Takeno Jōō.[38] This pattern of presenting famous objects to Nobunaga would be repeated many times in the following years, as Nobunaga applied his considerable skill in the manipulation of symbols of power to the field of tea culture.

Although Nobunaga seems to have had little interest in tea before enter-ing Kyoto, he quickly realized the potential uses of the art. In 1569 he declared that he would begin collecting Chinese utensils and famous objects, as he had no lack of precious metals or rice. This is known as his "famous-utensil hunt" (*meibutsu-gari*).[39] In Kyoto he confiscated several famous objects from merchants, warriors, and temples, including a tea caddy named "Hatsuhana" (literally "first flowers," which refers to plum blossoms), formerly in the Ashikaga collection.[40] In 1570 he extended the hunt to Sakai, where he obtained four other famed pieces.[41] In addition, Nobunaga continued to add to his collection by confiscating utensils from defeated enemies as well as obtaining unsolicited gifts from individuals who sought his favor.[42]

After being "presented" with the requested utensil, Nobunaga custom-arily paid the owner what was considered to be a fair price for the piece. Records indicate how one such exchange, in which confiscation was dis-guised as a gift through the use of middlemen, took place. At midday on 12/20/1574, Tsuda Sōgyū (d. 1591) invited Imai Sōkyū to tea. His real purpose was to show Sōkyū a letter bearing Nobunaga's vermilion seal requesting a tea bowl named "Matsumoto," named after its former owner, the mid-Muromachi period merchant Matsumoto Shuhō. It was in the col-lection of Sumiyoshiya Sōmu (1538–1603). The two men discussed how to obtain the "gift" and decided on a price of five thousand *kan*, a consider-able sum. Sōgyū borrowed the money from two other merchant families, received the bowl from Sōmu and then presented it to Nobunaga.[43] Mer-chants such as Sōgyū who were involved in Nobunaga's tea practice and utensil collecting also played major roles in outfitting his troops with sup-plies. Serving Nobunaga undoubtedly provided merchant tea practitioners with ample opportunities for profit, both symbolic and economic.

Nobunaga not only gathered famous utensils but also gave them away, upon occasion even returning them to their original owners. This movement of valued tea utensils through sometimes circular consecration cycles of gift giving provided another means, at times more expedient than military force, for Nobunaga to exercise control through a form of "generosity" that cultivated both dependency and indebtedness.[44] The eggplant-shaped tea caddy once owned by Jōō is a good example. As mentioned above, Imai Sōkyū initially presented Nobunaga with the caddy. Nobunaga later returned the caddy to Sōkyū, who then, after Nobunaga's death, presented it to Toyotomi Hideyoshi (1536–1598). Hideyoshi later returned it to Sōkyū, and his descendants eventually presented the tea caddy to Tokugawa Iemitsu (1603–1651). Likewise, a round tea caddy once owned by Shukō was presented to Nobunaga, who later returned it to its earlier owner, Tsuda Sōgyū.[45]

Nobunaga also used tea utensils to control members of his own status group. He is known, for example, to have rewarded victorious generals with gifts of famous objects. He is also thought to have decided who among his warrior forces was allowed to host formal tea gatherings, as stated in a letter in which Toyotomi Hideyoshi (1536–1598) expresses the appreciation he felt for receiving this honor from Nobunaga in 1582.[46]

## Changing ideals and preserving autonomy

Nobunaga's vast collection of tea utensils and his political manipulation of practitioners threatened the influential position of merchant followers of grass-hut tea. He and other powerful domainal lords created the largest collections of their day, in the process limiting the use of collected objects by others. Although Nobunaga did not own all of the famed pieces, he had made it clear that he could obtain virtually any piece he wanted. Famed utensils still functioned as symbols of power, yet the extensive collections that Nobunaga and his like amassed greatly reduced their value as symbolic capital. Tea practitioners thus had to reformulate the relative value of specific forms of capital, which they did through the creation of the *wabi*, or rustic, mode of tea practice. In tea culture the *wabi* ideal was expressed through the use of only a few Chinese utensils contrasted with primarily Japanese wares: an aesthetic that again had been borrowed from the literary field.[47] Practitioners of the *wabi* mode emphasized the simple and the quotidian, using rustic tea rooms as small as only two *tatami* mats (approximately 6 by 6 feet) and placing tea utensils directly on the mats rather than on stands. A new mode of practice was created in which the quantity and importance of famed utensils were further decreased, effectively devaluing the capital that the military lords were able to control. Using this ideal, merchant tea practitioners could restore their share of symbolic capital, stressing that "less is more" and thereby making a virtue of necessity.

Taian, an extant two-mat room in Yamazaki said to have been designed by Rikyū and built around 1582, is the most famous example of a tea room in the *wabi* style. In addition to its size, other significant features include a smaller alcove, fewer windows so that the interior is darker than earlier tea rooms, and a special crouching entrance (*nijiriguchi*) that forces guests to bow down to enter the room.[48] Hideyoshi is believed to have had five tea rooms at his Osaka Castle, which he occupied in 1583. One of these was two mats in size. Rikyū reportedly had a room of only one-and-one-half mats, the smallest known example.[49]

The institution of the use of smaller tea rooms was a major development in tea culture. Participants in these new rooms were in such close physical proximity that feudal hierarchies could not have been strictly upheld. The host would invite one, two, or possibly three guests to his small rustic tea room, where in the dim light of the paper lattice windows he would serve a meal and ritually prepare tea. Within these spaces relationships of relative equality between the participants were objectified, thus divisions and hierarchies broke down, and the result demonstrated an alternative to the dominant hierarchy of the military rulers.

## The structuring power of the field

In 1576, Oda Nobunaga rewarded his vassal Toyotomi Hideyoshi for his military accomplishments with a scroll painted by the admired Chinese artist Muqi. In 1577, Nobunaga presented Hideyoshi with a well-known kettle from his own collection. In this same period, Hideyoshi began to have dealings with tea practitioners, the beginning of his studies in tea culture. When Nobunaga was assassinated in 1582, Hideyoshi emerged as the new leader of Nobunaga's vassals. He thereby gained control of Nobunaga's territorial holdings, as well as his collection of tea utensils. In his tea practice we find evidence of the multi-layered structures of the field of tea culture.

Hideyoshi's first known tea gathering occurred on 10/15/1578, while he laid siege to the castle of Bessho Nagaharu (1558–1580) in Harima (modern Hyōgo prefecture). The Sakai tea practitioner Tsuda Sōgyū assisted him, and they used utensils such as the Muqi scroll and kettle he had received from Nobunaga, a handled bucket for a water jar, the "Forty Koku" tea leaf jar,[50] a Jian ware tea bowl for thick tea, and a style of Korean tea bowl said to be in Shukō's taste for thin tea.[51] Pieces were added to Hideyoshi's collection on 12/22/1581 at Azuchi Castle when he was granted twelve famous utensils from Nobunaga's collection, and again on the twenty-seventh when he received eight additional pieces.[52]

In 1583, the year after Nobunaga's assassination, Hideyoshi held an exhibition of utensils at his castle in Osaka. Rather than showing exclusively his own treasures in the style of Nobunaga, he invited five merchant tea practitioners, including Sen Rikyū and Tsuda Sōgyū, to display pieces from their own collections. Of the approximately forty utensils used, the majority were Hideyoshi's.[53]

On 3/8/1585 Hideyoshi held a tea on an unprecedented scale and put his collection on display at Daitokuji temple in Kyoto. In typical fashion, he mixed the old warrior tea mode of displaying large quantities of objects with the grass-hut style of more intimate, participatory tea. Rikyū and Sōgyū used Hideyoshi's utensils to make tea in rooms nearby. They served tea first to priests of Daitokuji, then to warriors in attendance, next to Sakai tea practitioners, and finally to all others.[54] Hideyoshi also personally prepared and served tea to guests, presumably as many as one-third of the 150 who attended. This act indicates the degree to which Hideyoshi accepted the grass-hut value of demonstrating skill in ritually manipulating the utensils of tea culture as necessary to his own tea practice.

On 10/7/1585 Hideyoshi was promoted to the office of Chief Minister of State (*Kanpaku*). In the same year he took the unprecedented step of holding a tea gathering in the imperial palace for the emperor and courtiers. While his motive may have amounted to nothing more than self-promotion, the gesture both brought attention to tea and increased its legitimacy. Following traditional custom, he used all new utensils to serve the emperor. Next, Rikyū made tea for the courtiers in a neighboring room using a stand and Hideyoshi's famous utensils. The number of nobles who attended that day was so great that he continued to serve tea throughout the afternoon until early in the evening. Hideyoshi performed tea for the emperor again in 1586 using his famed golden tea house. This structure was constructed in complete disregard for the *wabi* aesthetic. It consisted of a three-tatami mat room almost completely gilt in gold. He also commissioned various new utensils, also gold, to serve the emperor. Imperial precedent ruled out the use of famous objects, so Hideyoshi went to the furthest opposite extreme to procure valuable new tea wares. After using it at the palace, Hideyoshi set up his golden tea room at Osaka Castle. He frequently showed it to visitors, and on occasion brought it with him on his travels; it served as physical testimony to Hideyoshi's relationship to the emperor.[55]

In contrast to such ostentatious tea gatherings, Hideyoshi also held numerous smaller teas in the *wabi* mode in this same period. When entertaining visitors Hideyoshi often hosted *wabi* gatherings, preparing tea himself or instructing one of his assistants to do so. He used a few special famous utensils from his collection at these gatherings, along with assorted Japanese wares. Hideyoshi thus used *wabi* tea practice to impress his visitors with both his utensils and his skill in manipulating them, thereby employing the ritual setting to profit from the symbolic negation of power/riches and encouraging such needed values as intimacy and mutual trust.

Hideyoshi often held grass-hut and *wabi* tea gatherings with merchant tea practitioners. Examples include a gathering in Yamazaki in the fall of 1582, shortly after Nobunaga's death, in which the guests were Rikyū, Sōkyū, Sōgyū and Yamanoue Sōji. After moving into Osaka Castle in

1583, Hideyoshi hosted a gathering on 7/2 for Rikyū and Sōgyū, and then daily for a week beginning on 7/7. At the opening of a two-mat tea room in Osaka Castle on 1/3/1584, Hideyoshi made tea for Rikyū and Sōgyū. In the first month of 1585, Hideyoshi traveled to the hot baths at Yūshima with Rikyū, Sōgyū and Yamanoue Sōji, where they held many gatherings together.[56] In 1587 Hideyoshi spent several weeks in the company of tea practitioners in Hakozaki. During this time Sōgyū hosted Hideyoshi in a tea room in the style of a salt-making hut, while on another day Hideyoshi made tea for the merchant tea practitioners Kamiya Sōtan (1551–1635) and Shimai Sōshitsu (1539–1614) in a three-mat hut. Later Sōtan hosted Hideyoshi in a two-and-one-half-mat hut thatched with miscanthus.[57]

Later in the same year, on the first day of the tenth month, following a victorious campaign in Kyūshū, Hideyoshi held what was perhaps the largest tea gathering of all time, the Grand Kitano Tea Gathering.[58] Here, perhaps more than at any other time, the combination of the seemingly contradictory elements of grand display and *wabi* tea culture in Hideyoshi's tea practice are apparent. For this event Hideyoshi had sign boards posted at all the major crossroads in Kyoto as well as throughout the Kansai area and along the seven major roadways which issued an open invitation for all tea practitioners to come. This announcement provides important evidence as to the state of the field of tea culture at the time as well as Hideyoshi's position within the field. The most significant points are:

Item: It is ordered that, weather permitting, a tea gathering will be held in the forest at Kitano for a period of ten days beginning on the first day of the tenth month. All of the Kampaku's famous objects, without exception, will be placed on display. This event is being held so that devotees of tea culture can view the collection.

Item: Devotees, whether they are military attendants, townspeople, farmers, or others, should come, and each should bring a kettle, a well bucket for use as a water jar, a drinking bowl, and either tea or roasted and powdered rice tea-substitute.

Item: Since the seating will be in a pine field, two mats should suffice for each person. *Wabi* persons, however, may use either mat covers or coarse straw bags.

Item: In regard to what has just been said, the Kampaku has made these arrangements for the benefit of *wabi* persons. Accordingly, those who do not attend will henceforth be prohibited from preparing even tea-substitute. This prohibition will extend also to persons who visit those who do not attend.

In addition: Lord Kampaku has declared that he will personally prepare tea for all persons who attend, not only those from distant places.[59]

Hideyoshi's unquestioned political dominance and his massive collection of utensils allowed him to exert tremendous influence in the field of tea culture. At the Grand Kitano Tea Gathering, all practitioners of any social status were not only invited to come, but threatened with prohibition from practice if they failed to appear. The recommendations for those participating (a kettle, tea bowl, well bucket to use as a water jar, and a two-mat enclosure) served to limit everyone except Hideyoshi himself to an austere display of utensils.

The display of Hideyoshi's utensils did not strictly follow the *wabi* ideal, although a number of austere utensils did appear. Hideyoshi's golden tea room was assembled in the shrine hall and two additional three-mat rooms were constructed to each side. In each of these rooms a formal stand and utensils from Hideyoshi's collection were displayed. The display included extremely famous utensils such as a gourd-shaped tea caddy and the painting *Temple Bell in Evening* by Yu Qian (previously in the Ashikaga collection), and some austere objects such as a Bizen waste-water receptacle once owned by Jōō. Outside, an additional four rooms of four-and-one-half-mat size were arranged, in which Hideyoshi, Rikyū, Sōgyū, and Sōkyū prepared tea during the event. Again, Hideyoshi's utensils were exclusively used in these four rooms. Along with famed pieces such as the *Hatsuhana* tea caddy that Hideyoshi had received from Tokugawa Ieyasu (1542–1616), a Bizen cylindrical vase made an appearance. In the other rooms, treasured Chinese pieces, a Japanese Bizen water container, bamboo lid-rests, and bent-wood waste-water receptacles were used.[60] There were as many as 1,500 tea houses constructed on the grounds of Kitano Shrine for this event, although some were of such simple construction that they seem to defy the appellation of "house."

On the morning of the first day, the golden tea room and flanking rooms with their various displays of famed utensils were open to be admired. Groups of guests were chosen by lottery to be served tea in the four rooms outside. Hideyoshi and his assistants served 803 bowls of tea that morning. In the afternoon, Hideyoshi toured the grounds and observed the utensils and tea rooms that had been assembled by the various participants.[61] He is reported to have stopped at just two sites. The first was at the enclosure of Ikka, who had come from Mino (modern Gifu prefecture) to attend. He had made his "tea room" by hanging straw mats from a cluster of small pines and spreading sand on the ground as well as arranging roof tiles around a fire pit. Hideyoshi drank his only bowl of tea, actually tea substitute, here. Later he paused where Hechikan, a descendant of the prosperous Sakamotoya merchant family of Kyoto, had erected a large parasol to shade where he sat ready to serve tea.[62]

Hechikan had a tea hut in Yamashina, to the east of Kyoto, and was praised by later tea practitioners as an exemplary tea practitioner.[63] Late in the afternoon Hideyoshi reached the huts of the noblemen that were grouped together to the east of the shrine. Hideyoshi seems to have left the event that day in high spirits, yet during that night the word spread that the event would not continue the remaining nine days as planned. The official reason for the sudden cancellation was an uprising in Kyūshū.[64]

Many historians have been greatly troubled by the apparent contradiction between Hideyoshi's involvement in grandiose displays of his famed utensils such as the Grand Kitano Tea Gathering, and his interest in *wabi* tea culture. Perhaps the simplest resolution is to cast Hideyoshi as an ignorant interloper who merely exploited tea culture for self-aggrandizement; who loved the ostentatious gold tea room and never understood the "profound beauty" of *wabi*. Those historians who place Hideyoshi in this role often credit the involvement of Rikyū to explain the time Hideyoshi spent in his small tea room practicing *wabi* tea culture.[65] To occupy a dominant position within the field of tea culture, however, one had to struggle to gain this position by using the rules of the game as they had been established. All tea practitioners, including Hideyoshi, were restricted to a limited number of possible position-takings by the structures of the field. Moreover, within the field, the strategies which could be employed were closely related to the relative value of specific capital as defined by the legitimate mode of practice, namely the *wabi* style of tea culture.[66]

The *Record of Yamanoue Sōji*, a document contemporaneous with the Grand Kitano Tea Gathering, offers evidence as to what types of capital were required to hold a dominant position in tea at this time. The following definitions of tea practitioners, listed from lowest to highest position, are given.

> One who gathers a collection of old and new Chinese utensils and devotes himself to the artistic display of famous objects is known as [a practitioner of] "elite warrior tea culture" [*daimyō cha*]. One who is skilled in both judging the value of utensils and tea culture, and makes his way in the world by instructing tea practice is known as a tea person [*chanoyu sha*]. One who does not own even one [famed] utensil, but incorporates the three qualities of resolution, creativity and skill, is known as an admirer of *wabi* [*wabi suki sha*]. One who owns Chinese utensils, can judge the value of utensils, is skilled in tea culture, has the three above qualities [of resolution, creativity and skill] and aspires to a deep understanding of the way [*michi*] is a master [*meijin*].[67]

These categories of tea practitioners indicate that to reach the dominant position of "master" within the field one had to exhibit various qualities, or types of capital, which included the possession of Chinese utensils, taste, skill in the ritual procedures of tea culture, and "a deep understanding of the way." It should be noted that the possession of Chinese utensils was the only one of these qualities that could be simply purchased by those with sufficient wealth. All of the others qualities, which defy precise definition, constituted forms of capital that could be gained only by consensus of the members of the field, and viewed from outside the field of tea culture, can be seen as almost completely arbitrary.[68] It is in fact the seemingly arbitrary nature of assignment of this capital, which did not follow the dominant hierarchy of the field of power, that maintained the relative autonomy of the field.

If Hideyoshi sought a dominant position in the field of tea culture, as he seems to have done in other fields, he could not rely simply on grand displays of famous objects, but also had to exhibit his taste, skill in the ritual procedures, and a deep understanding of the art. At Kitano, when he displayed his collection and made tea in the morning, and then in the afternoon stopped and admired some of the more extreme examples of *wabi* tea culture present, he was performing his accomplishments, and thus his dominant position, for the entire assembled community.

Hideyoshi had entered the field of tea culture during the 1570s. During his rise to power he collected Chinese as well as native wares and gained proficiency in the rituals of tea, and he continued to demonstrate his interest until his death. Hideyoshi, like other tea practitioners, acquired a disposition through the *habitus* of tea culture to follow the logic of the field. This included a belief in the relative value of the various forms of specific capital.[69] Hideyoshi was forced to play by the rules of the game, and ultimately it was a game he could never win, because *wabi* tea culture as a relatively autonomous mode of practice was structured in a manner which was fundamentally opposed to the dominant principle of hierarchization on which Hideyoshi's political power was based. Indeed, it was through this requirement of engagement in the *wabi* mode that the art of tea culture was able to resist the dominant principle of hierarchization that powerful warlords such as Hideyoshi sought to impose, allowing both the field of tea culture and tea practitioners to preserve some measure of autonomy.

## Conclusion

As the tea ritual was modified by practitioners of various social groups, the earlier warrior style of tea gave way to the grass-hut and finally *wabi* styles, as well as mixtures of these three modes of practice. Within these new styles, the requirement of specific forms of capital, including skill in judging utensils and their ritual manipulation, together with the wealth certain merchant tea practitioners were able to amass, served to break down the earlier relationship between owning tea utensils and the superior power of dominant military lords. The leading figures within grass-hut and *wabi* tea culture were not those who dominated society. It was not merely those removed from the center of power, however, who practiced grass-hut and later *wabi* tea culture, for by the early sixteenth century the neat division between warrior tea/political rulers/hierarchization and grass-hut tea/elite merchants/counter-ideology had shifted, as engagement in the grass-hut mode was imposed on all tea practitioners who sought recognition within the field.

To understand the contradictions seen in tea gatherings held by certain warlords, it must be realized that practice of the grass-hut mode of tea culture was required for dominance *within the field* of tea culture, while at the same time this mode opposed the dominant hierarchy of the military lords *outside the field* of tea culture. When military lords such as Hideyoshi sought recognition within the tea world, tension between these elements of the grass-hut mode were certain to appear, as we have seen above. This conflict between grass-hut tea and the dominant hierarchy could only be resolved by creating new and different modes of practice, which is what occurred at the beginning of the seventeenth century as tea culture fractured into different social groups and styles.

## Notes

1 In considering these issues, the concept of the "field of cultural production" as developed by Pierre Bourdieu, has been a particularly useful model. Pierre Bourdieu, *The Logic of Practice* (Stanford University Press, 1990); *The Field of Cultural Production* (Columbia University Press, 1993); *Distinction: A Social Critique of the Judgment of Taste* (Harvard University Press, 1984).

2 Beatrice M. Boddart, "Tea and Counsel: the Political Role of Sen Rikyū," *Monumenta Nipponica*, 32.1 (1977): 50–74; Theodore M. Ludwig, "*Chanoyu* and Momoyama: Conflict and Transformation in Rikyū's Art," in Paul Varley and Kumakura Isao (eds), *Tea in Japan: Essays on the History of Chanoyu* (University of Hawai'i Press, 1989), pp. 71–100.

3 For a discussion of the *dōbōshu* see Richard Stanley-Baker, "Mid-Muromachi Paintings of the Eight Views of Hsiao and Hsiang" (Ph.D. diss., Princeton University, 1979), pp. 139–151 and 154–163; see also H. Paul Varley, "Ashikaga Yoshimitsu and the World of Kitayama: Social Change and Shogunal Patronage in Early Modern Japan," in John Whitney Hall and Toyoda Takeshi (eds), *Japan in the Muromachi Age* (University of California Press, 1977), pp. 188–191.

4 Gen'i, "Kissa ōrai," transcribed in Hayashiya Tatsusaburō, Yokoi Kiyoshi, and Narabayashi Tadeo (eds), *Nihon no chasho*, vol. 1 (Heibonsha, 1971), pp. 122–125; also vol. 2 of Sen Sōshitsu *et al.* (eds), *Chadō koten zenshū* [hereafter cited as *CKZ*], 12 vols (Tankō Shinsha, 1956–1962), pp. 176–179.

5 Respectively "Nokitoki-kyō ki," in Tokyo Teikoku Daigaku (ed.), *Dai Nihon shiryō* 7–9 (Shiryō Hensanjo, 1943), p. 125; and "Manzai Jugō nikki," as cited in Nakamura Toshinori, "Early History of the Teahouse II," *Chanoyu Quarterly* 70 (1992): 36.

6 Although no records of how the *daisu* was used are available, the highest level procedures of tea culture today, extremely complex movements which are transmitted orally, use a *daisu* and are said to have been preserved from this time. The *daisu* is a large stand with a base board and one shelf on which all

the other utensils rest. The other utensils include a kettle and brazier; a *kaigu*, a set of matching bronze utensils which include a *mizusashi* (water jar), *kensui* (waste water receptacle), *futaoki* (lid rest) and *shakutate* (ladle stand), a Chinese tea caddy (tea container), and a Chinese tea bowl.

7  Moriya Takeshi, "The Mountain Dwelling Within the City," *Chanoyu Quarterly* 56 (1988): 18.
8  "Yamanoue Sōji ki," in *CKZ*, vol. 3, p. 11. There are several extant versions of the text dating from 1588 to 1590. For a discussion of this document in English, see Tanihata Akio, "Men of Tea: An Evaluation by Yamanoue Sōji, Part 1," *Chanoyu Quarterly* 28 (1981): 50–51.
9  The authenticity of the letter is not certain. However, the majority of tea historians today make frequent reference to the letter as a reliable source. For the complete text and commentary, see "Kokoro no fumi," in *CKZ*, vol. 3, pp. 1–24. For a traditional account of the letter with a complete English translation see Dennis Hirota, "Heart's Mastery: *Kokoro no fumi*, The Letter of Murata Shukō to His Disciple Choin," *Chanoyu Quarterly* 22 (1979): 7–24.
10  "Kokoro no fumi," in *CKZ*, vol. 3, p. 11.
11  Ibid.
12  Yamanoue Sōji, "Yamanoue Sōji ki," in Hayashiya, *Nihon no chasho*, vol. 1, pp. 140–143.
13  "Kokoro no fumi," in *CKZ*, vol. 3, pp. 12–17; and Hirota, "Heart's Mastery," p. 11.
14  "Kokoro no fumi," in *CKZ*, vol. 3, pp. 4, 8; Hirota, "Heart's Mastery," p. 7; Murai Yasuhiko, "The Development of *Chanoyu*: Before Rikyū," in Varley and Kumakura, pp. 19–20.
15  Hirota, "Heart's Mastery," pp. 9–10; "Kokoro no fumi," in *CKZ*, vol. 3, pp. 3–6.
16  For a concise discussion of *michi*, see Kon'ishi Jinichi, "Michi and Medieval Writing," in Earl Miner (ed.), *Principles of Classical Japanese Literature* (Princeton University Press, 1985), pp. 181–208.
17  See Bourdieu, "The Field of Cultural Production," *Logic of Practice*, pp. 66–67; "The Production of Belief: Contribution to an Economy of Symbolic Goods," *Media, Culture and Society*, 2 (1980): 262; *Distinction*, pp. 30–32.
18  Akanuma Taka, "Wabi no chaki – shikisai no hensen," *Tankō* 8 (1993): 26–27.
19  For a discussion of the relationship between belief and the body, see Bourdieu, *Logic of Practice*, pp. 67–69.
20  This concept of "relative autonomy" within Bourdieu's field theory should not be confused with concepts of art as an "autonomous realm" removed from relations of power, but rather considered an attribute of values or ideals which oppose the dominant principle of hierarchization. See Bourdieu, *The Field of Cultural Production*, pp. 319–320.
21  "Kadoya," also read "Sumiya." Moriya, "The Mountain Dwelling Within the City," pp. 7–21.
22  Takahashi Ryūzō (ed.), *Sanetaka-kō ki* (Zokugun Shoruishō Kanseikai, 1980), vol. 4, part 1, pp. 22–52; vol. 6, part 2, pp. 210, 226–227.
23  Nakamura Toshinori, "Early History of the Teahouse," part 1, *Chanoyu Quarterly* 69 (1992): 9–10.
24  The entry merely states, "*chawan-biraki* [first display of *chawan*]." At this time the term *chawan* was sometimes used for pottery in general so it is not clear if this was, in fact, a tea bowl. "Sanetaka-kō ki," Daiei 6/2/19 and Daiei 3/12/6 respectively: Takahashi, vol. 6, part 2, p. 156; vol. 6, part 1, p. 103.
25  Nakamura, "Teahouse," part 1, pp. 11–12. Also Moriya, "The Mountain Dwelling Within the City," p. 10.

26 *Nisui ki*, entry for Kyōroku 3 (1530)/9/6 as cited in Nakamura, "Teahouse," part 1, p. 12.
27 Peter Stallybrass and Allon White, *The Politics and Poetics of Transgression* (Cornell University Press, 1986), p. 80.
28 For further discussion of the relationship between the body and belief see pages 25–26 above as well as Bourdieu, *Logic of Practice*, pp. 66–79.
29 Akanuma, "Wabi no chaki," p. 27.
30 Ibid., p. 28.
31 Tanihata Akio, "Wabicha no hatten to Sakai no chajintachi," *Tankō* 8 (1993): 107–108.
32 For information of the development of these merchant and warrior groups in the city of Sakai see V. Dixon Morris, "Sakai: The History of a City in Medieval Japan," (Ph.D. diss., University of Washington, 1970), pp. 38 and 45.
33 Bourdieu, *Language and Symbolic Power* (Harvard University Press, 1990), p. 117.
34 Herman Ooms, *Tokugawa Ideology: Early Constructs, 1570–1680* (Princeton University Press, 1985), pp. 26–27.
35 Roughly equivalent to 1,000 copper coins.
36 For the complete poem see Iwanami Shoten, *Nihon koten bungaku taikei*, vol. 9 (Iwanami Shoten, 1957), p. 146.
37 Tsutsui Hiroichi, *Yamanoue Sōji ki o yomu* (Tankōsha, 1987), pp. 259–260. This tea caddy was lost with Nobunaga in the Honnōji fire.
38 Morris, "Sakai," pp. 190–193.
39 Kuwata Tadachika (ed.), *Shinchō kōki* (Jinbutsu Ōraisha, 1965), p. 95.
40 Ibid., pp. 95–96. A total of six pieces were "received" by Nobunaga. In addition to the *Hatsuhana* tea jar that had been owned by the Kyoto Daimonjiya family, these are: a *kabura nashi*-shaped vase from Ikegami Jyokei; the *Fuji nasu* tea caddy from Yūjyōbō; a bamboo tea scoop; a painting of geese; and the *Momosoko* vase from the Emura family.
41 Kuwata, *Shinchō kōki*, p. 101. The four pieces are: a painting of sweets from Tsuda Sōkyū; the *Komatsushima* tea jar from the Rakushiin; a ladle stand from Aburaya Jōyū; and a painting of a bell from Matsunaga.
42 One way to prevent Nobunaga from taking a *meibutsu* was to destroy it. While under siege by Nobunaga in 1577, Matsunaga Hisahide, before taking his own life, destroyed a famed kettle to prevent Nobunaga from obtaining it. Paul Varley and George Elison, "The Culture of Tea: From Its Origins to Sen no Rikyū," in George Elison and Bardwell L. Smith (eds), *Warlords, Artists, and Commoners* (University of Hawai'i Press, 1981), pp. 327–328, n. 59.
43 Yonehara Masayoshi, "*Chanoyu*," in Okamoto Ryōichi (ed.), *Oda Nobunaga jiten* (Shin Jinbutsu Oraisha, 1989), p. 328.
44 For a discussion of such cycles see Bourdieu, *Logic of Practice*, pp. 125–126.
45 Ikeda Iwao *et al.* (eds), *Chadō bijutsu kanshō jiten* (Tankōsha, 1980), pp. 146 and 182 respectively.
46 There is some debate among scholars as to whether Nobunaga did actually control the practice of tea by his generals. It should be noted that Hideyoshi's letter, the major piece of evidence to support this claim, was written after Nobunaga had died and may have been simply another of Hideyoshi's many strategies for legitimization. See the letter from Hideyoshi to Okamoto Jirozaemon no Jō and Saitō Benba no Suke, Tenshō 10/10/18 as cited in Tanihata Akio, "Nobunaga no meibutsugari to ochanoyu goseidō," *Tankō* 9 (1993): 96.
47 For a discussion of the development of *wabi* see Haga Kōshirō, "The *Wabi* Aesthetic through the Ages," in Varley and Kumakura, pp. 195–230.
48 Nakamura Masao, *Chashitsu to roji*, Book of Books, *Nihon no bijutsu* 19

(Shōgakukan, 1972), p. 174; Itō Teiji, "Sen Rikyū and Taian," *Chanoyu Quarterly* 15 (1976): 9.

49  Ludwig, "*Chanoyu* and Momoyama," pp. 86–87; *Nihon no chasho* 1, p. 174.

50  *Shijū-koku* or "forty *koku*," so named because it was once exchanged for a piece of land which produced this quantity of rice annually.

51  Tanihata Akio, "Tenkajin Toyotomi Hideyoshi to chanoyu no kakudai," *Tankō* 10 (1993): 93–94.

52  Kuwata, *Shinchō kōki*, Tenshō 9.12.22 (1581) as cited in Tanihata, "Tenkajin Hideyoshi," p. 94.

53  Tanihata, "Tenkajin Hideyoshi," p. 96.

54  Tanihata, "Tenkajin Hideyoshi," pp. 96–97. Ludwig, p. 83.

55  Ludwig, "*Chanoyu* and Momoyama," pp. 85–86.

56  Ibid., pp. 84–85.

57  Ibid., pp. 88–89.

58  For the following discussion I have borrowed extensively from Louise Allison Cort, "The Grand Kitano Tea Gathering," *Chanoyu Quarterly* 31 (1982): 15–44.

59  Translation by Paul Varley, slightly modified, in Kumakura Isao, "Sen no Rikyū: Inquiries into his Life and Death," in Varley and Kumakura, pp. 39–40. For the original text, see *CKZ*, vol. 6, pp. 3, 36.

60  *Matsuya kaiki*, in *CKZ*, vol. 9, pp. 132–134; *Genryū chawa*, in *CKZ*, vol. 3, pp. 474–477; *Kitano ōchanoyu nikki*, *CKZ*, vol. 6, pp. 4–7.

61  Cort, "Kitano Tea Gathering," p. 35; Tanihata, "Tenkajin Hideyoshi," pp. 98–99.

62  *CKZ*, vol. 3, p. 360.

63  *CKZ*, vol. 3, p. 467.

64  *Tamonin nikki*, entry for Tenshō 15.10.4 as cited in Cort, "Kitano Tea Gathering," pp. 36–38.

65  For a brief overview of some of the views by major tea historians on Rikyū and Hideyoshi see Ludwig, "*Chanoyu* and Momoyama," pp. 91–93.

66  Bourdieu, *The Field of Cultural Production*, pp. 312–313.

67  The original text with commentary appears in Tsutsui, *Yamanoue Sōji ki*, pp. 22–23. I have also borrowed from the translation given in Elison, "The Culture of Tea," pp. 204–205.

68  For a discussion of the manner in which this consensus was derived, see Christy Allison Bartlett, "The *Tennōjiya kai-ki*: The Formative Years of *Chanoyu*" (MA thesis, University of California at Berkeley, 1993), pp. 28–36.

69  For a discussion of *habitus* see Bourdieu, *The Logic of Practice*, p. 53.

# 3 Shopping for pots in Momoyama Japan

*Louise Allison Cort*

## Introduction

Imagine that it is autumn, 1606; you are a successful merchant from an established textile shop in Kyoto, and you have a problem. You have invited five close friends to a tea gathering for the occasion of opening your jar of new tea, which was picked in the spring at the best plantation in Uji. The new-tea season is especially festive in Kyoto, and you're eager to plan a stylish event. The centerpiece of your display, naturally, will be the fine antique Chinese tea-leaf storage jar you inherited from your grandfather. Your friends know that jar already, since it's famous in tea circles, and you want to surprise them with at least one utensil they've never seen before, something that will make them fiercely jealous. Perhaps a tea bowl. You had thought of using your Shino tea bowl but, although it's a treasure, you bought it a good ten years ago and styles have certainly changed. That's it – you need a new tea bowl.

That very afternoon, you leave your store on Teramachi Street and stroll west along Sanjō to the neighborhood where all the antique dealers have their shops. The narrow shops fronting the busy thoroughfare offer a dazzling variety of ceramics – Chinese and Korean heirlooms, new imports from China and Southeast Asia, and brand new ceramics from kilns in Kyoto and the provinces. One dealer you know specializes in pots from the Mino kilns, where your Shino bowl was made. You've heard intriguing rumors about the novel styles of Mino tea wares coming out of the new kiln built just last year.

You're in luck. The dealer has just received a shipment of tea bowls from Mino, and you can see why everyone's talking – these bowls are amazing! All of them bear shiny black glaze, with big white patches painted boldly in black in an array of patterns that resemble the latest textile designs you feature in your own shop (Figure 3.1). Finally you settle on the perfect one and order a padded silk storage bag and wooden box. The bowl will be delivered next week. You stroll home, relieved and full of anticipation about your forthcoming tea. It's going to cause a sensation!

*Figure 3.1*  Tea bowl, Black Oribe ware, Mino kilns, Japan, excavated from Kyoto
site. Momoyama period (1573–1615), *c.* 1605–1615. Stoneware with
black glaze and iron pigment under clear glaze, h. 6.3–7.0 cm.;
d. 12.1–13.4 cm. Kyoto-shi Maizō Bunkazai Kenkyūjo.

Although this scenario might seem like pure fantasy, it is based on
recent archaeological excavations of Momoyama period (1573–1615) and
early Edo period (1615–1868) sites in Japan. Since 1988, three excavations
conducted on plots along Sanjō Street in Kyoto have uncovered the sites of
dealers' shops together with the troves of ceramics that once lined their
shelves. The Sanjō finds mingle antiques and brand new pots, from China
and Korea as well as Japan; South-east Asian pots appear in other sites.
These astonishing finds of raw data, combined with the rich information
supplied by heirloom ceramics and by tea diaries, and other primary documents of the Momoyama period, provide an extraordinarily detailed
picture of the presence of ceramics in Momoyama Japan.

This chapter discusses the ceramics of the Momoyama period through
the focal point of the market: what kinds of ceramics were available,
where they came from and where they were sold, who sold them, who
bought them and for how much, and how the buyers used their purchases.
This approach draws upon current archaeological investigation of urban
consumer sites – kitchens, storerooms, and rubbish heaps of tea masters,
merchants, and warriors – and on related research that brings to light the
personalities of the merchants who made the vital connections between

provincial kilns or international ports and eager consumers. This new evidence challenges an earlier tendency to consider Momoyama period Japanese ceramics exclusively as objects of aesthetic appreciation, created purely for the pleasure of their users and divorced from any connection to commerce, and to view them in isolation as "uniquely" Japanese manifestations, without reference to contemporaneous ceramics made elsewhere in Asia.

That approach reflected the way Japanese ceramics are often viewed in relationship to the development of tea culture (*chanoyu*), which reached its mature form in the Momoyama period and was the primary cultural framework for ceramic use and appreciation. The standard view of *chanoyu*'s development in the course of the sixteenth century holds that it began as a form of displaying collections of Chinese ceramics, gradually incorporated Korean bowls and "found objects" culled from Japanese utilitarian pottery, and culminated in new forms of Japanese ceramics made explicitly for tea use. In this standard view, both *chanoyu* and Japanese ceramics of the Momoyama period are discussed in an essentially national framework.

This chapter proposes that both *chanoyu* and Japanese ceramics of the Momoyama period could only have developed as they did because of the intensely *international* nature of the age. In the sixteenth century, Japan constituted one node in a vigorous trade network that linked it to the Ryūkyūs, Ming China, Choson Korea, ports in northern and central Vietnam, Indonesia, the Philippines, and the Ayutthaya kingdom in Siam, and even indirectly to India, the Near East, and Europe. Japan was a key source of the silver and gold that were exchanged in these transactions.[1] In exchange for silver, an unprecedented diversity of international goods flowed into Japanese markets. Wealth from this trade fueled *chanoyu* activities and ceramic production. The availability of tempting foreign goods helped to create the mature form of *chanoyu* and exerted a powerful influence on the emergence of Momoyama ceramic styles. The transformation of *chanoyu* from a codified display of standard Chinese vessel types to an exuberantly experimental, mix-and-match combining of utensils celebrated the new range of choice in the market – the enormous diversity of ceramics as well as metalware, lacquerware, basketry, and textiles. Mature *chanoyu* is an art of eclecticism; it flourished in response to the flood of varied objects into the market and the Japanese desire to find a meaningful and coherent way of incorporating these exotic goods into their lives.

Likewise, the distinctive new Japanese tea ceramics – Bizen, Shigaraki, Iga, Raku, Mino, and Karatsu in the late sixteenth century; Takatori, Agano, Satsuma, and Hagi in the early seventeenth – were not invented wholly within a framework of native taste, although that also played an important part.[2] They are better understood as imaginative, often brilliant, reinterpretations of foreign wares, not simply Korean (as long assumed) but also contemporary Chinese and South-east Asian as well. The dynamic international marketplace of the Momoyama period assembled most, if not all, of the foreign ceramic models that served as immediate inspiration for new Japanese ceramic forms. Reinterpretation of these hybrid Momoyama forms, in turn, created the subject matter of much Japanese ceramic production throughout the Edo period.

## Where ceramics were sold

The consumerism dignified by *chanoyu* was an urban phenomenon. The major urban centers that arose in the fifteenth and sixteenth centuries were the nodes for gathering, dispersing, and displaying the wealth of ceramics available in Momoyama Japan. The merchants in those cities – owners and users of ceramics through their roles as participants in *chanoyu* – were also inventors, commissioners, and vendors who played an active role in bringing new native wares into being.

In the late sixteenth century, the aspiring national rulers Oda Nobunaga (1534–1582) and Toyotomi Hideyoshi (1536–1598) created policies for expanding wealth by stimulating commerce and craft manufacture, rebuilding towns and cities, and organizing markets and financial systems. Throughout the country, but especially in western Japan, towns with periodic markets became full-fledged cities with standing markets, sending specialty products to the capital of Kyoto and dispersing Kyoto's manufactured products and luxury goods. Kyoto was the cultural, political, and commercial heart. Hideyoshi's building policy for Kyoto included orderly reinvention of the city structure. He concentrated mercantile activity in a new center along Teramachi Street west of the Kamo River, connected by Sanjō Bridge to the land route eastward. A water route linked central Kyoto to Sakai and Osaka to the west.

The major international ports were Hakata (modern Fukuoka) and Nagasaki in western Japan and Sakai (part of modern Osaka) in the center. Hakata's key location on the north coast of Kyūshū made it an important entrepôt in international trade. Hakata sent copper, lead, and sulfur to Korea and received, in turn, cotton cloth, various luxury goods, and Buddhist scriptures. From South-east Asia, Hakata merchants imported dyestuffs, pharmaceuticals, and spices.[3] After Hideyoshi took control of Kyūshū in 1587, he rebuilt Hakata and promoted commercial growth by establishing nearby Nagoya Castle as headquarters for his invasions of Korea. Nagasaki was the chief port in Japan for Portuguese merchants based in Macao, who served as intermediaries in a triangular private trade linking Japan, China, and other Asian countries. They exchanged Japanese silver for Chinese raw silk (used in the Kyoto textile industry).[4] Located at the head of Osaka harbor, Sakai owed its prosperity to its position in the Kyoto-centered marketing structure, serving as Kyoto's window to the international market. The free port was governed by its leading merchants (who were also the country's most influential practitioners of *chanoyu*) until Nobunaga seized control of Sakai in 1569. By the early seventeenth century, Sakai was eclipsed by the commercial rise of Osaka.

New answers to the questions of where ceramics were sold and used emerge from recent urban archaeology. A necessary precedent was the archaeological work that identified and characterized the places of ceramic manufacture. From the 1950s onward, excavations followed the opportunities created by reconstruction of the nation's infrastructure. Highways, water systems, and railroads cut through undisturbed rural areas, including former centers of ceramic production, and brought to light hundreds of kiln sites in both known and newly discovered centers. Specialists in the new field of historical ceramic archaeology established basic sequences of production for the individual centers. A synthetic view of Momoyama period ceramics became possible once archaeology pursued the shift in construction, during the real-estate boom of the 1980s, to redevelopment of existing urban spaces and changed its focus from production to exchange and use. In Kyoto, demolition of old townhouses to make way for modern shop buildings with deeper foundations cut into the underground storerooms of Momoyama period merchants. In Sakai, construction of a ring road turned up pots in merchant establishments; in Hakata, construction of a new subway line had the same result.

## How ceramics were sold

Transactions during the Momoyama period took place in the triple coinage system of gold, silver, and copper coins, with native coinage replacing imported Chinese coins.[5] Coin equivalencies were measured out by weight, using scales. Policies established by Nobunaga and Hideyoshi dictated that imported items such as raw silk, medicines, damask, and tea bowls had to be paid for with gold and silver.[6] Since rice harvested from land holdings was the principal measure of wealth, the value of a ceramic expressed in metal coinage can be understood from the amount of rice that could be obtained by exchange (the exchange rate fluctuated from year to year, depending upon the harvest). Rice was measured in *koku*, equivalent to 180 liters. To give an example, a letter written in 1588 by the tea master Sen no Rikyū (1522–1591) records a price of fifty pieces of gold for an antique Chinese tea-leaf storage jar called Hannya. Around that time, one gold piece would buy at least 10,620 liters of rice, so the Chinese tea jar Hannya was worth upwards of 540,000 liters.[7] This represented the peak of the market; new imports cost less, and local Japanese ceramics far less.

## Who sold them

Traders involved in the market for ceramics and other tea utensils were known as *karamonoya*, or merchants of Chinese goods (*karamono*). In its earliest usage, *karamono* referred narrowly to Chinese imports, but as the varieties of imports from other countries multiplied, the term became an umbrella for all imported goods. At the same time, as *chanoyu* participants avidly sought imported utensils from the mid-sixteenth century onward, *karamonoya* became closely associated with tea utensils. The Kyoto excavations show that, as new varieties of Japanese tea ceramics came to be produced, *karamonoya* became involved in their marketing as well. By the early seventeenth century, some documents referred to *imayaki-mono* (new ceramics people) in place of the older term.[8]

Research by the Kyoto scholar Oka Yoshiko has brought the role of *karamonoya* into sharper focus. Her investigation is based on the *Kakumeiki*, the diary of Hōrin Shōshō, an abbot of the Kinkakuji in northwestern Kyoto.[9] Spanning thirty-four years from 1635 to 1669, the diary postdates the Momoyama period but offers unparalleled richness of anecdotal information. Hōrin, who was active in tea circles, dealt regularly with two Kyoto *karamonoya*. His diary shows that the two men had differing specialties: Ōhira Gohei handled chiefly domestic ceramics, including Seto, Kyoto, and Bizen wares, while Fujita Jirōzaemon dealt with Chinese and Vietnamese ceramics as well as Imari porcelain from Arita. Fujita also supplied cotton and other "Nagasaki goods" (by then, Nagasaki was the only Japanese port open to official international trade). His connections were mainly with western Japan, whereas Ōhira's were with the center and the east.

As the abbot of a prominent Kyoto temple, Hōrin did not have to go out shopping: Ōhira and Fujita usually brought their wares to him for inspection. They supplied the full range of tea utensils and accessories, had storage bags and boxes made, and arranged for repairs. (Ōhira also sold paintings by Shūbun [Tenshō Shūbun, active 1414–before 1463] and Sesshū Tōyō [1420–1506] to Hōrin.) The two dealers regularly brought gifts to their esteemed customer, and they introduced other merchants who had rarities to sell. Hōrin socialized with them, joining Ōhira, for instance, to watch the Gion Festival procession.

The *Kakumeiki* shows that Ōhira Gohei lived near the intersection of Sanjō and Yanaginobanba streets. Other records refer frequently to "Karamonoya so-and-so of Sanjō," indicating that many *karamonoya* had their combined shops and homes there. Screens depicting activities in Kyoto show merchants' shops lining both sides of the busy thoroughfare. In recent years this evidence from texts and paintings has been brought to life through the spectacular archeological discoveries in the vicinity of Sanjō.

Masses of Momoyama period tea ceramics and imported wares have been discovered at the three sites situated within two hundred meters of one another along Sanjō. The Benkeiishi-chō site, located just west of the Kawaramachi–Sanjō intersection, excavated in 1987–1988, yielded over 120 crates of ceramics (Figure 3.2).[10] The 1989 find at the Nakano-chō site, further west near the corner of Yanaginobanba, produced 300 crates

*Figure 3.2* Ceramic finds excavated from Benkeiishi-chō site, Sanjō district, Kyoto. Japanese Shigaraki, Bizen, Mino, and Karatsu wares and Chinese Zhangzhou ware. Momoyama period (1573–1615), *c.* 1590s. Kyoto-shi Maizō Bunkazai Kenkyūjo.

(Figure 3.3), while the 1995 find at Shimo Hakusan-chō, located between the previous two sites, was on a similar scale (Figure 3.4).[11] The finds were distinguished by dozens of nearly identical wares – twenty-eight Shigaraki ware freshwater jars, for example (Figure 3.5) – far more than any one person would have needed for his personal *chanoyu* activities. Meanwhile, tea ceramics of the same sorts that crowd the Sanjō shops have been discovered individually at dozens of other sites throughout Kyoto, probably

*Figure 3.3* Ceramic finds excavated from Nakano-chō site, Sanjō district, Kyoto. Japanese wares, including Shigaraki, Bizen, Mino, Karatsu, and Takatori. Momoyama period (1573–1615) or early Edo period (1615–1868), *c.* 1610–1620. Kyoto-shi Maizō Bunkazai Kenkyūjo.

*Figure 3.4* Ceramic finds excavated from Shimo Hakusan-chō, Sanjō district, Kyoto. Japanese Shigaraki, Bizen, Iga, Mino, and Takatori wares and Chinese Zhangzhou ware. Early Edo period (1615–1868), mid-1620s. Kyoto-shi Maizō Bunkazai Kenkyūjo.

*Figure 3.5* Freshwater jar, Shigaraki ware, Japan, excavated from Benkeiishi-chō, Sanjō district, Kyoto. Momoyama period (1573–1615), *c.*1590s. Unglazed stoneware, h. 15.7 cm. Kyoto-shi Maizō Bunkazai Kenkyūjo.

the homes of *chanoyu* participants who shopped on Sanjō. The range of probable dates for the three sites, from the 1590s (Benkeiishi-chō) through about 1610–1620 (Nakano-chō) to the mid-1620s (Shimo Hakusan-chō), shows the enduring vitality of this commercial sector.

## What kinds of ceramics were available

Highly valued antique Chinese ceramics changed hands in the Momoyama period as old warrior families fell from power. These included Southern Song (1127–1279) and Yuan (1279–1368) dynasty celadon ware from the Longquan kilns, black-glazed bowls from the Jian kilns, and iron-glazed tea caddies and tea-leaf storage jars from kilns near Foshan, in Guangdong Province. These rarely found their way to the open market, however; more often they were given as "gifts" to facilitate important private negotiations. For example, a Sakai merchant secured the favor of Oda Nobunaga through the presentation of an antique Chinese tea caddy, as discussed by Watsky in Chapter 1.

Many varieties of newly made Chinese ceramics became available in the sixteenth century, however, such as the "Luzon" tea-leaf storage jars acquired by Japanese merchants from the Spanish trading base in the Philippines (Figure 3.6).[12] Excavations of warrior residences and urban

*Figure 3.6* Tea-leaf storage jar, Guangdong Province, China. Ming dynasty (1368–1644), sixteenth century. Stoneware with amber glaze, h. 37 cm, d. 30 cm. Freer Gallery of Art, Smithsonian Institution, Washington, DC. Gift of Charles Lang Freer, F1900.22.

sites show that surprising quantities of Chinese blue-and-white dishes were also in use.[13] Recent excavations within the newly identified Zhangzhou kiln complex in southern Fujian Province have clarified that it was the source of these and most other thin, rather brittle blue-and-white porcelain commonly found in Japan (Figure 3.7).[14] (Fine porcelain from Jingdezhen, the great center of Chinese blue-and-white porcelain manufacture, is rare

*Figure 3.7* Bottle, Zhangzhou kilns, Fujian Province, China, excavated from Benkeiishi-chō site, Sanjō district, Kyoto. Ming dynasty (1368–1644), sixteenth century. Porcelain with underglaze cobalt blue decoration, h. 17.1 cm, d. 11.0 cm. Kyoto-shi Maizō Bunkazai Kenkyūjo.

in Japanese sites and collections.) The Zhangzhou kilns also produced much of the enamel-decorated porcelain found in Japan. Especially popular were bowls or dishes of a size appropriate for use as serving dishes for *chanoyu* meals (Figure 3.8). Small molded boxes bearing lead glazes in green, yellow, and purple were known in Japan as Kōchi (Cochin, i.e. Northern Vietnam) ware, although their true origin was a mystery until the 1997 excavation of the Tiankeng kiln site, part of the Zhangzhou complex.[15] Zhangzhou kilns also produced large and small dishes with two-color or three-color lead glazes that appear in Kyoto sites (Figure 3.9). The abundance of various Zhangzhou wares in Japan (including the coarse porcelains long known as "Swatow") is readily explained by the kilns' proximity to the port city of Xiamen.

The importance of Korean *punch'ong*-style stoneware bowls (called *mishima* in Japan), decorated with white slip over a dark body, as tea bowls from the mid-sixteenth century onward has long been recognized.

*Figure 3.8* Bowl, Zhangzhou kilns, Fujian Province, China, excavated from Benkeiishi-chō site, Sanjō district, Kyoto. Ming dynasty (1368–1644), sixteenth century. Porcelain with overglaze enamel decoration, d. 19.7 cm. Kyoto-shi Maizō Bunkazai Kenkyūjo.

*Figure 3.9* Bowl, Zhangzhou kilns, Fujian Province, China, excavated from Kyoto
site. Ming dynasty (1368–1644), sixteenth century. Pottery with green
and yellow lead glazes, d.29.0 cm. Kyoto-shi Maizō Bunkazai
Kenkyūjo.

Urban excavations show that quantities of plain white Korean porcelain
were also imported, probably for use as tableware (Figure 3.10).

Knowledge of ceramics exported to Hakata and Sakai from South-east
Asia has been greatly expanded by excavations there. The well-known
iron-decorated bowls, bottles, and boxes from the Si Satchanalai and
Sukhothai kilns in Thailand are just one example of South-east Asian
imports. Numerous coarsely glazed utilitarian jars also arrived as containers for various tropical products, although they were almost never converted to use for tea-leaf storage: despite their exotic origin, they retained
their utilitarian nature in Japan.[16] Surprisingly, unglazed South-east Asian
ceramics seem to have found a place more readily as tea utensils. The occasional earthenware cooking pot that survived the trip became a freshwater
jar. Varieties of utilitarian stonewares known collectively as *namban*

*Figure 3.10* Bowl, Korea, excavated from Benkeiishi-chō site, Sanjō district, Kyoto. Choson period (1392–1910), sixteenth century. Porcelain with clear glaze, h. 5.3 cm, d. 19.6–19.7 cm. Kyoto-shi Maizō Bunkazai Kenkyūjo.

precise origins, began to be used as *chanoyu* freshwater jars and vases by the late fifteenth century and reached a peak of importance in the Momoyama period.[17] It seems increasingly clear that arrival in the Japanese market of these unglazed (hence utilitarian) but imported (hence important) South-east Asian wares stimulated the appreciation in the *chanoyu* aesthetic context for unmatched groupings of found objects, including unglazed Japanese utilitarian ceramics, with important consequences for the status of native wares such as Shigaraki and Bizen.

In Japan, the Seto kilns produced iron-glazed bowls and tea caddies (Figure 3.11) that served as inexpensive native substitutes for Chinese brown-glazed ceramics. Conservative Seto production was eclipsed from the mid-sixteenth century onward by that of adjacent Mino, whose potters created a rainbow of new glazes – including Yellow Seto splashed with copper-green (Figure 3.12), Black Seto (Figure 3.13), and the white feldspathic glaze called Shino (Figure 3.14) – on imaginative new shapes. The iron decoration on much Shino ware is the first pictorial decoration on a Japanese ceramic. The popularity of these fresh, dynamic wares is clear from their abundance in the Kyoto shop sites, and the role of the *kara-monoya* in creating a market for the new products is now clear.

Around 1600 another new Mino ware called Oribe (Figure 3.15), made in a range of styles combining copper-green glaze or black glaze and iron painting on asymmetrical, molded forms, debuted at Motoyashiki, the first of a new type of multi-chambered climbing kiln built in Mino. Excavations in Kyoto and elsewhere have profoundly changed the image of Oribe ware, which used to be interpreted as a limited-production luxury ware because of the rarity of heirloom pieces. Now it is seen to have been plentiful and affordable – even thrown away with other Mino wares in a rubbish heap

*Figure 3.11* Tea caddy, Seto kilns, Japan. Muromachi (1392–1573) or
Momoyama period (1573–1615), *c.*1550–1600. Stoneware with iron
glaze; ivory lid, h. 6.5 cm, d. 3.8 cm. Freer Gallery of Art, Smithsonian
Institution, Washington, DC. Gift of Charles Lang Freer, F1905.38.

in the Osaka fish market.[18] The *karamonoya* of the Nakano-chō site
(Figure 3.3) seems to have specialized in Black Oribe tea bowls (Figure
3.1). While one such bowl is strikingly bold, hundreds of them – as heaped
in excavation crates – are overwhelming, almost nauseating. Not surprisingly, the aggressive Oribe ceramic style was short-lived, ending by
around 1630.

Unglazed stoneware jars – utilitarian products – sent to Kyoto markets
from provincial kilns in Shigaraki and Bizen had been picked out for use as
*chanoyu* vases and water jars by adventuresome connoisseurs by the late
fifteenth century. Tea wares made as such appeared much later, in the

*Figure 3.12* Individual serving dish, Yellow Seto ware, Mino kilns, Japan. Momoyama period (1573–1615), late sixteenth century. Stoneware with yellow glaze and copper-green and iron-brown pigments, d. 15.9 cm, h. 5.1 cm. Freer Gallery of Art, Smithsonian Institution, Washington, DC. Gift of Charles Lang Freer, F1905.219.

*Figure 3.13* Tea bowl, Black Seto ware, Mino kilns, Japan. Momoyama period (1573–1615), *c.* 1580–1605. Stoneware with black glaze, h. 7.5 cm, diam. 12.5 cm. Freer Gallery of Art, Smithsonian Institution, Washington, DC. Gift of Peggy and Richard M. Danziger, F1998.15.

*Figure 3.14* Tea bowl with design of gate and seedling pines, Shino ware, Mino kilns, Japan. Momoyama period (1573–1615), late sixteenth century. Stoneware with iron-brown decoration under white Shino glaze, h. 8.9 cm., d. 14.3 cm. Freer Gallery of Art, Smithsonian Institution, Washington, DC. Gift of Charles Lang Freer, F1902.234.

1580s (Figure 3.16). The Benkeiishi-chō site in Kyoto shows that the same dealer handled tea utensils in similar styles from both Bizen and Shigaraki (Figure 3.2), suggesting that he commissioned the shapes. His inventory of Bizen and Shigaraki also included numerous table wares, including sake bottles and serving dishes, indicating an expansion of the roles for wares from provincial kilns.

The rise of ceramic production in Kyūshū is associated with the relocation of Korean potters to the domains of warriors in western Japan who participated in Hideyoshi's two invasions of Korea, in 1592 and 1597, although certain kilns producing Karatsu ware appear to have been active for some time prior to the invasions. Karatsu pieces appear earliest in the Sanjō sites (Figure 3.2, center right). A letter of *c.* 1602 written by Nabeshima Naoshige (1538–1618), lord of the domain within which most Karatsu kilns lay, mentions hearing at a tea gathering in Kyoto that some Sanjō dealers in "new ceramics" (*imayaki*), who had already placed orders at the Karatsu kilns before, intended to do so again. Naoshige's letter requests that the ordered wares be well executed, for the sake of Karatsu ware's reputation in Kyoto.[19]

A few tea utensils appear among the utilitarian repertory of the earliest Takatori ware, made by immigrant Korean potters in the Chikuzen domain of Kuroda Josui (1546–1604). The tea wares that were made in far greater quantities at the Uchigaso kiln (operated 1614–1624), however, exhibit

*Figure 3.15* Ewer, Oribe ware, Mino kilns, Japan. Momoyama (1573–1615) or early Edo period (1615–1868), early seventeenth century. Stoneware with copper-green glaze and iron-brown decoration under clear glaze, h. 19.7 cm. Freer Gallery of Art, Smithsonian Institution, Washington, DC. Purchase F1969.21.

dramatically distorted, large-scale shapes of a distinctly non-Korean style. Takatori tea and table wares from this kiln made a splash in Kyoto: they constituted 8 percent of the ceramics excavated from the Nakano-chō site (Figure 3.3). Takatori wares from the Shimo Hakusan-chō site are strikingly oversized (Figure 3.17), but so are the wares from the same site made in Bizen, Shigaraki, Iga, and Tamba (Figure 3.4). Wares of this type are sometimes categorized as "Oribe" style, referring to the warrior and influential tea practitioner, Furuta Oribe (1544–1615), rather than the Mino ware named after him. It is probably more appropriate to think of a homogenous "late Momoyama" style executed at various provincial kilns. In recognition of the role of the Sanjō dealers in creating this unified period style, this ware might even be called "Sanjō *imayaki*" style. The common

*Figure 3.16* Freshwater jar, Bizen kilns, Japan. A similar vessel was excavated
from a Kyoto site. Momoyama period (1573–1615), *c.*1590–1605.
Unglazed stoneware; black-lacquered wooden lid, h. 11.0 cm., diam. of
rim 21.0–23.5 cm. Freer Gallery of Art, Smithsonian Institution,
Washington, DC. Gift of Peggy and Richard M. Danziger, F1998.17.

traits of this style are the large size and the distorted form – features for
which the regular, wheel-thrown foreign models cannot account.

The Sanjō excavations and other sites are spurring new analysis of the
development of ceramic production within Kyoto itself. The oldest glazed
ceramic tradition in Kyoto had been thought to be Raku ware, associated
with a tile-maker named Chōjirō, who used the cylindrical, updraft tile
kiln to fire lead-glazed ceramics. The majority of Chōjirō's works are
black- or red-glazed tea bowls, but a famous large dish with green and
yellow lead glazes can now be understood as a copy of Zhangzhou ware.
Recent excavations have introduced, moreover, a contemporaneous type
of lead-glazed tea bowl previously unknown among heirlooms and quite
distinct from Raku, using white slip over red clay and splashes of copper-
green on the outside, often with black glaze on the inside (Figure 3.18).
Viewed together, early Raku ware and the newly discovered bowls from
the 1580s and 1590s seem to show a powerful design influence of southern
Chinese lead-glazed ceramics.

The earliest workshops in Kyoto for glazed stoneware (*kyōyaki*) are
thought to have been set up soon after 1600 by potters brought from Seto

*Figure 3.17* Freshwater jar, Takatori kilns, Japan, excavated from Shimo Hakusan-chō site, Sanjō district, Kyoto. Early Edo period (1615–1868), mid-1620s. Stoneware with applied and natural ash glazes, h. 20.5 cm. Kyoto-shi Maizō Bunkazai Kenkyūjo.

and Mino. Tea caddies – standard Seto–Mino wares – are the first *kyōyaki* shapes to appear in tea records, and they may correspond to a class of Seto–Mino tea caddies known as *nochigama* or "latter kilns," associated with potters working in Kyoto in the early seventeenth century.[20] Early *kyōyaki* kilns were built along the slopes of the mountains to the east of Kyoto. As Oka Yoshiko points out, they were located directly across the Sanjō Bridge from the shops of the *karamonoya*, who probably played a role in underwriting production.[21] Hōrin's *Kakumeiki* describes a visit from Ōhira Gohei escorting a potter from the Awataguchi kiln, whose presentation of new pottery work elicited an order from the abbot. This procedure indicates that some "shopping" took the form of orders rather than off-the-shelf purchases. The rise of the Kyoto kilns, more

*Figure 3.18* Temmoku-shaped tea bowl, Kyoto kilns, Japan, excavated from a Kyoto site. Momoyama period (1573–1615), late sixteenth century. Earthenware with white lead glaze and copper-green and iron-manganese pigments, h. 5.8 cm., d. 9.8 cm. Kyoto-shi Maizō Bunkazai Kenkyūjo.

conveniently located than Mino or Karatsu, increased the frequency of such ordering activity, as brokered by *karamonoya*.

## Who bought them and how they used them

Nobles, warriors, and abbots were customers of *karamonoya* for ceramics during the Momoyama period, but many clients were fellow merchants. Their names appear in tea diaries, and now excavations are turning up the remains of their collections. Intense competition to show off new discoveries is also recorded in *chanoyu* diaries. The Sakai merchant Tsuda Sōgyū (?–1591), for example, carefully documented his purchase of a Shigaraki water jar from a Kyoto merchant and, just eight days later, its surprise debut in his tea room.[22] "My guests could not have known that I bought it," he gloated.

## Momoyama eclecticism

The aesthetics of Momoyama *chanoyu* developed in tandem with available utensils, expanding the rules of display to make room for an international mixture of antique and new, coarse and refined, local and imported ceramics. Similarly, native Japanese ceramic wares responded magnificently to the wealth of new models available in the markets from the mid-sixteenth century onward. The efflorescence of new Japanese ceramic styles seems to coincide with the introduction of new ceramic technology, suggesting that more remains to be learned about the sources and processes of encouragement for such late sixteenth-century innovations as Yellow Seto, Black Seto, and Shino glazes in Mino or Raku and the hitherto unknown lead-glazed tea bowls in Kyoto. A few decades later, the new form of climbing kiln first introduced to Kyūshū spread like a forest fire to Mino and Kyoto, as though its introduction met a pent-up anticipation.

It may well be that this eagerness for access to improved facilities for making glazed ceramics grew through contact with the varieties of imported wares. Such technology enabled *chanoyu* enthusiasts, working through the agency of the Sanjō *karamonoya*, to reshape the foreign models to their own taste. In a surprising departure from the description of Momoyama ceramics as "uniquely Japanese," some Japanese scholars have recently discussed the most "purely Japanese" wares in terms of their relationships to foreign models – of Yellow Seto ware to the green-and-yellow lead-glazed dishes from Zhangzhou; of iron-decorated Shino ware to the cobalt-painted porcelain from Zhangzhou, of Oribe ware as a sort of hybrid of these two influences.[23]

The relationships of model to interpretation are not simple, for they involve translations into new materials (with an unprecedented emphasis on the visual and tactile qualities of the regional clays) and a distinctive new scale, one that probably relates to issues of scale in other media, notably architecture. The phase of assimilating new palettes and decorations was quickly succeeded, moreover, by dynamic interactions among domestic wares as, for example, Mino potters imitated Iga and Karatsu formats, Takatori imitated Mino, or Kyoto potters imitated Seto, creating a new type of hybrid. In both the adoptive and the cross-fertilizing phases, the role of Kyoto *karamonoya* cannot be underestimated. The international marketplace of Momoyama Japan created eager shoppers, who in turn helped to create a new panoply of Japanese ceramics.

## Notes

1   In sixteenth-century Japan, the production of gold and particularly silver grew so significantly that it left a mark on world economic history. Indeed, Japan may have accounted for as much as one-third of the world's silver output at the end of the sixteenth and beginning of the seventeenth century. This expanded production began in the 1530s and had an important impact on the form and content of trade in East Asia.
(Asao Naohiro, "The sixteenth-century unification," in John Whitney Hall (ed.), *The Cambridge History of Japan*, vol. 4 Cambridge University Press, pp. 60–61)

2 Archaeologist Narasaki Shōichi discusses the role of Japanese literature in providing subject matter for the new type of iron-painted decoration on Shino tea bowls from the Mino kilns (Figure 3.14). Narasaki Shōichi, "Mino Momoyama-tō no seiritsu," *Seto-shi Maizō Bunkazai Sentaa kenkyū kiyō* 7 (1999): 176–178.

3 Jurgis Elisonas, "The Inseparable Treaty: Japan's Relations with China and Korea," in John Whitney Hall (ed.), *The Cambridge History of Japan* (1991), vol. 4, p. 246.

4 Jurgis Elisonas, "Christianity and the Daimyo," in John Whitney Hall (ed.), *The Cambridge History of Japan* (1991), vol. 4, p. 326.

5 Asao Naohiro, "The sixteenth-century unification," p. 61.

6 Ibid.

7 Tokugawa Bijutsukan and Nezu Bijutsukan (eds), *Chatsubo* (Tokugawa Art Museum and Nezu Institute of Fine Arts, 1981), p. 137.

8 Kawahara Masahiko, "Kyōyaki ni tsuite no oboegaki," *Bunkazaihō* (1983): 3–4.

9 Oka Yoshiko, "*Kakumeiki* ni miru karamonoyatachi – kinsei shotō no tōjiki ryūtsū," *Shisō* 48 (1991): 245–262; "Karamonoya oboegaki – Ōhira Gohei to Katsuyama Chōji" in *Kan'ei bunka no nettowaaku: "Kakumeiki" no sekai* (Shibunkaku Shuppan, 1998), pp. 199–208.

10 *Kyoto-shi maizō bunkazai hakkutsu chōsa gaiyō* (Kyoto-shi Maizō Bunkazai Kenkyūjo, 1987). Ceramics excavated from this site became the centerpiece of an exhibition on Momoyama tea-ceremony ceramics; see Nezu Bijutsukan (ed.), *Momoyama no chatō* (Nezu Institute of Fine Arts, 1989).

11 The finds from the three Sanjō sites are summarized in Andrew Maske, "New Advances in Tea Ceramic History: Recent Excavations of Tea Wares from Consumer Sites," *Chanoyu Quarterly* 70 (1992): 8–21. Objects from the sites appeared in a two-part exhibition, *Rakuchū Momoyama tōki no sekai – Sanjō kaiwai shutsudo* (Kyoto-shi Kōko Shiryōkan, 1998–1999). The question of why such quantities of ceramics were found in the sites of dealers' shops remains to be fully explained. Many of the pieces were recovered from burial pits, suggesting that they had been discarded, perhaps when the property changed hands or after the dealer had abandoned hope of selling goods that had gone out of fashion. Unless some sort of disaster is proposed, the excavated pieces can be assumed to represent leftovers after the best pieces had been sold. Although several fires occurred in the Sanjō area during the early seventeenth century, the three sites show no signs of fire damage.

12 After Hideyoshi took control of trade in Nagasaki in the late 1580s, he exchanged a huge quantity of rice for silver, which he used to buy up raw silk, lead, gold, mercury, and "Luzon" jars reaching Nagasaki on Portuguese ships; he then resold the goods at a profit to domestic merchants. Asao Naohiro, "The sixteenth-century unification," p. 63. A.L. Sadler retells the tale of a Sakai merchant who became rich by selling fifty Luzon tea jars to Hideyoshi's retainers. A.L. Sadler, *Cha-no-yu: The Japanese Tea Ceremony* (Charles E. Tuttle Company, 1962), p. 133.

13 An underground storehouse on the grounds of a merchant residence, uncovered during construction of the Hakata subway, contained a Bizen-ware vat full of Chinese blue-and-white dishes and turquoise-enameled dishes. Fukuoka-shi Hakubutsukan (ed.), *Sakai to Hakata ten – yomigaeru ōgon no hibi* (Fukuoka-shi Hakubutsukan, 1992), p. 52.

14 Fujiansheng Bowuguan, *Zhangzhou yao* (Fujian Renmin Chubanshe, 1997).

15 Chadō Shiryōkan (ed.), *Kōchi kōgō – Fukenshō shutsudo ibutsu to Nihon denseihin* (Chadō Shiryōkan and MOA Bijutsukan, 1998).

16 As the result of recent archaeology in Thailand, such jars are known to come

from the Maenam Noi kilns in Singburi Province, north of the port city of Ayutthaya. Two such jars excavated from a warehouse in the old merchant section of Sakai were found to be full of sulfur, an ingredient of gunpowder and thus essential to the military engagements of the second half of the sixteenth century, which were fought with weapons first introduced by the Portuguese in 1543. Sakai-shi Hakubutsukan, *Sakaishū – chanoyu o tsukutta hitobito* (Sakai-shi Hakubutsukan, 1989), p. 124. Sulfur may not have been the original contents of the jars when they were imported. Documents show that Tokugawa Ieyasu (1542–1616), founder of the Tokugawa government, repeatedly sought gifts of saltpeter, another ingredient of gunpowder, from the king of Ayutthaya, finally receiving it in 1621. Morimura Ken'ichi, "Jūroku-jūnana seiki shotō no Sakai Kangō Toshi iseki shutsudo no Tai shijikō," *Bōeki tōji kenkyū* 9 (1989): 149.

17 Louise Allison Cort, "Vietnamese Ceramics in Japanese Contexts," in John Stevenson and John Guy (eds), *Vietnamese Ceramics: A Separate Tradition* (Art Media Resources with Avery Press, 1997), pp. 67–69. Recent Japanese-Vietnamese joint excavations and surveys have identified production sites for some such ceramics in northern Vietnam, others in central Vietnam. Morimoto Asako, "On the Vietnamese Trade Ceramics Excavated in Japan and Their Production Places," *Tōyō tōji* 23–24 (1993–1995): 49.

18 Imai Shizuo, sup. ed., Toki-shi Mino Tōji Rekishikan (ed.), *Momoyama no hana – Osaka shutsudo no Momoyama tōji* (Oribe no hi jikkō iinkai, 1993), pp. 35–36.

19 Kawahara Masahiko, "Kyōyaki ni tsuite no oboegaki," pp. 3–4.

20 Louise Allison Cort, *Seto and Mino Ceramics* (Freer Gallery of Art, 1992), pp. 136–139.

21 Oka Yoshiko, "Kyōyaki no hatten," in Yabe Yoshiaki (ed.), *Nihon yakimono-shi* (Bijutsu Shuppansha, 1998), p. 112.

22 Louise Allison Cort, "Gen'ya's Devil Bucket," *Chanoyu Quarterly* 30 (1982): 31–40.

23 Nezu Bijutsukan Gakugeibu, *Kanan no yakimono: Kiseto, Oribe, Aode Kokutani no genryū o motomete*, Kanshō seriizu I (Nezu Institute of Fine Arts, 1998); Narasaki Shōichi, "Mino Momoyama-tō no seiritsu," pp. 161–179.

# 4 Sen Kōshin Sōsa (1613–1672)
## Writing tea history

*Morgan Pitelka*

## Introduction

The Sen house of professional tea practitioners experienced a dramatic transformation in its fortunes over the course of the seventeenth century. When the warlord Tokugawa Ieyasu (1542–1616) came to national power in 1598, the members of the Sen house were still recovering from the forced suicide of their founder, Sen no Rikyū (1522–1591), and the accompanying temporary confiscation of their holdings. Though the Sen had many friends in the capital city of Kyoto and in their ancestral home, the port city of Sakai near Osaka, it seemed unlikely that they would regain the prominence and influence known under Rikyū. By the end of the seventeenth century, however, they had established three separate but mutually supportive Sen tea schools that would come to dominate the tea world. The standing of the Sen tea masters was sustained, on the one hand, by the growing reputation of Rikyū as one of the great cultural luminaries of the previous age, and on the other by strong occupational relationships forged with members of the ruling warrior elite.

This chapter will examine one of the key figures in this seventeenth-century re-emergence of the Sen house, Sen Kōshin Sōsa (1613–1672). In addition to being the great-grandson of Rikyū, tea master to the Kii branch of the Tokugawa house, and the founder of the Omotesenke school of tea, Kōshin was the first conscious chronicler of his house's history. His life and writings provide a singular glimpse into the early systematization and institutionalization of tea culture in the second half of the century, a process that was shaped by the social stability and economic growth of the new Tokugawa state. Kōshin's attempt to record his own tea activities is particularly notable because it set a precedent in the Sen tea tradition from which writing could be understood as a form of tea practice.

## Kōshin Sōsa: fourth generation of the Sen house

Until recently, scholars of tea history have devoted little attention to Kōshin, seeing him as a significant historical personage only in his close relationship with his famous tea practitioner father, Sen Sōtan. This was true in spite of the fact that Kōshin founded the Omotesenke tea school, which has survived to the present day as one of the most powerful cultural institutions in Japan. In part Kōshin has been ignored because Omotesenke has traditionally claimed Rikyū as its founder, relegating Kōshin to the rather unglamorous position of "fourth generation" in the lineage of school leaders.[1]

For most of the twentieth century, little was known about Kōshin but the following. He was born in 1613, Sōtan's third son but his first by his second and final wife. His oldest brother was Sōsetsu (who died young, estranged from the family), followed by Ichiō, who would later found the Mushanokoji Senke tea lineage. He also had a younger sister, Kure,[2] and a younger brother, Sensō, who would found the Urasenke tea lineage. After several aborted attempts to gain employment as a tea master, Kōshin was hired by Tokugawa Yorinobu, domainal lord of Kii, in the early 1640s. His father Sōtan retired in 1646 and passed the headship of the house to Kōshin. In 1670 Kōshin passed the headship of the house to his adopted son Zuiryūsai and died two years later at the age of 60.[3]

While factually accurate to the best of our knowledge, this narrative reduces Kōshin to nothing but one of the fourteen generations between Rikyū the founder and the present head of Omotesenke. He becomes a mere transmitter of tradition rather than a producer of it. Recently published texts authored by Kōshin, however, transform the picture of his place in the complex development of early modern tea culture. These texts provide great detail about the myriad activities of a professional tea master, a position that brought intimate contact with various social groups and geographical regions in the Tokugawa system. Kōshin's writings also reveal two formative relationships that lay the groundwork for his cultural accomplishments, connections that demonstrate the mediating role tea played in the socio-political matrix of the period. The first relationship was between Kōshin and his father, Sen Sōtan, the grandson of Rikyū. The second was between Kōshin and his eventual patron, Tokugawa Yorinobu. It was Kōshin's ability to positively negotiate both associations that allowed him to firmly establish his branch of tea in the increasingly competitive cultural market of seventeenth-century Japan.

## Son of Sōtan

Kōshin's father was the famous tea practitioner Sen Sōtan (1578–1658), well known among students of tea today for having revived the reputation of the Sen house after the death of Rikyū. Born to Shōan (1546–1614), Rikyū's adopted son,[4] Sōtan entered the Kyoto Zen monastery Daitokuji as a youth, and thrived under the guidance of the abbot Shun'oku Sōen (1529–1611).[5] According to records left by Shun'oku, Sōtan displayed considerable talent at writing poetry as part of his Zen education, and great things were expected of him as a Zen devotee.[6] In 1591, however, while the 14-year-old Sōtan was still engaged in his studies, Rikyū committed suicide. Rikyū's Kyoto residence and holdings were confiscated. Shōan, recently made head of the Sen house, fled and was given shelter by a powerful disciple of Rikyū in the provinces. Within several years Shōan was pardoned and Rikyū's tea utensils returned to the household, but the incident was to have a major impact on Sōtan, the effects of which shaped the development of tea for generations.[7]

Sōtan emerged from his years of study and practice at Daitokuji to devote himself to the Sen house business of tea with his father Shōan. He begins to appear in records of tea gatherings in 1608,[8] and with his father's death in 1614, took control of the house and began teaching tea. He was known posthumously primarily for his continuation of Rikyū's austere, *wabi*-style tea practice, a characteristic that has been linked with his Zen training as a youth, and also earned him the sobriquet "beggar Sōtan."[9] This vision of Sōtan as rustic tea hermit was reinforced by the belief that he lived a life completely removed from the world of warrior politics, having learned to avoid the whims of the ruling political elite from the example of Rikyū's untimely end. Scholarship of the past three decades, however, has demonstrated that Sōtan was deeply concerned with aligning the Sen house with political leaders to ensure its stability and continuity. Furthermore, though he himself avoided direct affiliation with any warrior, he enjoyed frequent contact with members of the nobility, wealthy commoners, and other social and economic powerholders of seventeenth-century society.

Sōtan was particularly adept at navigating the elite circles of early seventeenth-century Kyoto. The noble Konoe Nobuhiro (1599–1649), for example, an active participant in the tea, flower, incense, and literary salons of the imperial court, visited Sōtan's tea house and enjoyed Sōtan's particular style of tea preparation.[10] His son Konoe Hisatsugu and Empress Tōfukumonin (1607–1678) also interacted with Sōtan, which demonstrates Sōtan's willingness to associate with the luminaries of the seventeenth-century court, if not those in command in Edo.[11] Sōtan also had frequent interaction with Hōrin Jōshō (1593–1668), the abbot of Rokuonji temple (the complex well known today for its Golden Pavilion), and one of the period's most avid chroniclers. On 12/3/1639, for example, Sōtan visited Hōrin at Rokuonji, the two had tea, and Sōtan chanted "The Tale of Heike."[12] Hōrin's records of his interactions with Sōtan also reveal that Sōtan had financial problems. On 4/2/1640, for example, Hōrin returned a promissory note to Sōtan, effectively canceling a loan he had given to the struggling tea master.[13]

Sōtan's pecuniary troubles may help to explain the zeal with which he launched his sons onto professional paths different from his own. In 1633, Sōtan sent Kōshin to Edo in search of the very kind of employment he had avoided: a position as tea master to a major domainal lord.[14] In 1639,

Sōtan made similar efforts on behalf of his second oldest son Ichiō.[15] The following year, Sōtan began to contemplate sending his youngest son Sensō to be an apprentice with a doctor,[16] an idea he acted upon in 1641.[17]

It is apparent from Sōtan's letters that he was a concerned parent who worried constantly about his children. Fortunately, several of his closest associates from Daitokuji were in Edo at the time of Kōshin's arrival in 1633, and were able to lend the young man assistance. Arrangements were soon made for Kōshin to assume the position of tea master to Terazawa Hirotaka (1564–1633), domainal lord of the Karatsu domain. Sōtan wrote a typically paternal letter to Kōshin expressing his joy:

> I am so pleased that you have been employed by Terazawa [Shimadono]. I can't believe the energy the abbot devoted to the task. This is also the place I secretly hoped you would be employed . . . Terazawa has been interested in tea for some time, so there should be much to talk about.[18]

Unfortunately, Hirotaka died that year, and his son Katataka's harsh administration led to the Shimabara Rebellion, which resulted in embarrassment for the *bakufu* and dispossession of the Terazawa house.[19] Kōshin found himself once again unemployed.

Eventually, after a similarly disappointing miss with the Ikoma house,[20] Sōtan's hopes for his son were realized when Kōshin was appointed tea master by the Kii[21] branch of the Tokugawa house, arranged via the offices of the *fudai* domainal lord Yagyū Muneyori (1571–1646), Takuan Sōhō, and the Kii Tokugawa retainer Watanabe Ichigaku (1601–1668). Yagyū had been personally enlisted by Sōtan in the project of finding Kōshin, as well as his older brother Sōsetsu, work among the powerful elites of Edo.[22] Sōtan wrote in a letter to Kōshin of his deep satisfaction upon hearing the news, and instructed him to write the appropriate letters of thanks.[23] Kōshin thus became the first member of the Sen house to be hired by a warrior politician since Rikyū, precisely fifty years after his great-grandfather's suicide.

## The Kii Tokugawa

Kōshin's employment with the Kii Tokugawa proved to be, along with his frequent contact with his father, one of the most sustaining relationships of his career as a tea master. The patronage of this powerful Tokugawa branch house became the base for Kōshin's tea activities, bringing economic support, political connections, and access to cultural capital in the form of the extensive Kii collection of tea utensils. Though the Sen name and lineage were powerful symbols that brought Kōshin additional work, and his teaching and connoisseurship skills presumably kept his clientele satisfied, it was the funding, experience, and prestige gained from his association with the Kii Tokugawa that ensured the success of his branch of tea in the seventeenth century. His work as domainal tea master exposed him to a wide range of warrior leaders and took him both to Edo, where the Kii Tokugawa had a sizeable mansion, and the castle town of Wakayama, capital of Kii, on a regular basis as part of the larger flow of culture and technology in the system of alternate attendance. Tokugawa Yorinobu, in turn, enjoyed the prestige of employing a tea master descended from Rikyū.

The enthusiasm for tea culture shown by members of the warrior status group was nothing new in the mid-seventeenth century. The precedent for Yorinobu's employment of Kōshin can be found in the late sixteenth century, when warrior leaders such as Oda Nobunaga and Toyotomi Hideyoshi patronized tea for pleasure, cultural legitimacy, and to strengthen their ties with the commoner and religious elites of Kyoto, Sakai, Osaka, and Hakata.[24] Rikyū had been particularly active in warrior circles, indicated by several later sources that list seven Rikyū disciples, each of whom was a prominent military personage.[25] By the early seventeenth century, many of the most active tea practitioners came from warrior families, the most well known being Furuta Oribe (1543–1615), Oda Uraku (1547–1621), Kobori Enshū (1579–1647), and Katagiri Sekishū (1605–1673). By the second and third decade of the seventeenth century, tea was becoming more than just the odd cultural pursuit for interested warriors, but a common element in the education of the ruling military elite.[26]

Tokugawa Yorinobu (1602–1671) was born the tenth son of Tokugawa Ieyasu two years after the Battle of Sekigahara, at the height of his father's machinations to replace the deceased warlord Hideyoshi as sole ruler of the archipelago. In the second month of 1603, Ieyasu was granted the rank of Shogun, though his position was still insecure with the presence of Hideyoshi's son and heir, Hideyori, at Osaka Castle, and a variety of hostile domainal lords in the provinces. In the eleventh month of the same year, Ieyasu made the 2-year-old Yorinobu domainal lord of the Mito domain with a revenue of 200,000 *koku*,[27] raised the following year to 250,000. Ieyasu in fact brought Yorinobu with him to Sumpu Castle, leaving retainers to administer the domain in the boy's stead. In the twelfth month of 1609, Ieyasu made the now 8-year-old Yorinobu domainal lord of Suruga, Tōtōmi, and Higashi Mikawa, with a combined revenue of 500,000 *koku*.[28] He replaced Yorinobu in Mito with his eleventh son, Yorifusa, who became the founder of the Mito branch of the Tokugawa house. This brought Ieyasu's well-known strategy of placing family members in important domains to near conclusion, with his ninth son Yoshinao in Nagoya (Owari), his second son Matsudaira Hideyasu in Kitanoshō (Echizen), and his sixth son Tadateru in Takata (Echigo). Ieyasu died in 1616, having defeated the Toyotomi at Osaka and laid the base for the Tokugawa political structure that would be further developed by his descendants.[29]

The final move for Yorinobu came in the seventh month of 1619 when the second Tokugawa Shogun, his older brother Hidetada, placed him at the head of the Kii domain, which included the problem-ridden Wakayama and Ise domains, and had a combined revenue of 555,000 *koku*.[30] The previous domainal lord, Asano Nagaakira (1586–1632), who had distinguished himself at the battles at Osaka Castle despite rebellions at home and a family connection to the Toyotomi, was transferred to Aki (Hiroshima).[31] Placing a son of Ieyasu in Wakayama allowed the Shogun Hidetada to maintain a Tokugawa influence in central Japan, where the Kyoto court still enjoyed considerable influence. Eighteen-year-old Yorinobu quickly installed vassals in the castles at Tanabe, Shingū, and Ise, and began a major reconstruction of Wakayama Castle. Over the next several decades, Yorinobu launched a series of new policies for the domain in line with the range of Tokugawa programs.[32] As one of the three Tokugawa branch families from which the position of Shogun could be drawn,[33] Wakayama became one of the most important domains in the Tokugawa political structure, sending Yoshimune (1684–1751) to Edo as Shogun in 1716.[34]

Another facet of Yorinobu's activities as domainal lord of Kii was his patronage of the arts. Like his father Ieyasu, Yorinobu was a fan of Noh, bringing sixteen Noh actors with him when he arrived in Kii and employing several more soon after. Yorinobu was also a patron of the painter Kano Kōi (d. 1636), who is well known for his involvement in the training of Kano Tan'yū (1602–1674). In 1627 Yorinobu hired Kōi's son Kōho (d. 1671) as official painter to the domain of Kii, following the example of the employment of Tan'yū as official painter of the Tokugawa government in 1617. Kōho's two brothers each went to work for one of the other Tokugawa branch house domains, and Kōho established an atelier in Wakayama that became known as the Kii School of Kano Painting.[35] Kōho passed the headship of the lineage and the position of official Kii painter on to his heir Kōeki in 1660.[36]

In 1641, Yorinobu added a tea master to his staff with the hiring of Kōshin at an annual stipend of 200 *koku*. Kōshin was expected to spend considerable time in Edo and in Wakayama, overseeing not only actual tea gatherings, but the entire complex of operations related to the maintenance and use of a tea collection:

The responsibilities of the tea master (*sadō*) are to manage the tea utensils, scrolls, and calligraphy of the lord; also, to organize and care for utensils, to hold regular ceremonies, to decorate the inner chambers and outer rooms of the lord's residence, to hang scrolls, and to arrange flowers.[37]

## Tea master Kōshin

The recently published writings of Kōshin Sōsa provide us with a fuller picture of the various responsibilities and activities of a professional tea master than was heretofore ascertainable. These records are unique in their detail and depth, which leads to the question, why did Kōshin feel inclined to leave written records in addition to oral teachings? There was some precedent in the writings of a handful of tea practitioners from sixteenth-century Sakai and Kyoto. These men left precise tea diaries, records of tea gatherings attended and/or held, and the occasional entry provides details about personages active in the tea community, relations among them, and contemporary news and gossip. But nearly all of these men (and extant tea records from this period are universally written by men) pursued tea in addition to or as a part of their activities as merchants; their records are whimsical and inconsistent without any clear purpose. Kōshin, on the other hand, was a professional tea practitioner, and seems to have put his brush to paper with an eye to the future of his house. As a result of this difference of perspective, Kōshin's writings are technical and practical, professional notes for himself and his descendants.

Kōshin's writings reveal that his primary duty as tea master to the Kii Tokugawa was to prepare tea for Yorinobu and his associates, though it is not clear how many times this occurred between his hiring in 1641 and Yorinobu's retirement in 1667. The best extant source for such gatherings is *Record of His Lordship's Tea Gatherings Beginning in the Second Month of 1642* [*Uma no nigatsu ochanoyu no oboe*].[38] This document covers the years 1642 to 1656, a record of fifty-one gatherings, nearly all of which were held at the Kii Tokugawa residence in Edo. The honorific "*o*" prefix before the standard term for tea, "*chanoyu*," implies that Yorinobu was present at these gatherings,[39] though this is difficult to verify because Kōshin only recorded guests, omitting his and his employer's names.

The specific function of these tea gatherings also was not put to paper, perhaps because such events were quite popular in elite warrior society by the mid-seventeenth century, and it was not surprising for a powerful warrior leader, particularly a son of Ieyasu, to engage in this form of cultural practice. The gatherings were held with some regularity, recorded as follows: 1642, 14 gatherings; 1643, 8 gatherings; 1647, 2 gatherings; 1648, 12 gatherings; 1649, 2 gatherings; 1650, 5 gatherings; 1652, 1 gathering; 1654, 5 gatherings; and 1656, 2 gatherings.[40] Most of the major gaps in tea activity correspond to periods when Kōshin was allowed to return to Kyoto, or when Yorinobu, sometimes followed by Kōshin, returned to Kii.[41] Though it seems likely that Kōshin attended tea gatherings hosted by Yorinobu when they were both in Kii, he did not clearly record any such events.

The names of guests that appear in *Record of His Lordship's Tea Gath-*

*erings* show that Yorinobu invited a range of warrior politicians to tea, and occasionally other Edo residents who may have had a connection with Kōshin. Yorinobu's guests included the *fudai* domainal lord Ogasawara Tadasane of the Ogura domain, Toda Shitetsu of the Ōgaki domain, Sakai Tadakatsu of the Obama domain, Sakai Tadakiyo of the Omayabashi domain (also head of Gagaku for the central Tokugawa government), Itakura Shigemune of the Sekiyado domain (also Kyoto governor), Yagyū Munenori of the Yagyū domain, Matsura Shigenobu of the Hirado domain, and Matsudaira Tadaakira of Osaka among others. He also invited the *tozama* domainal lord Sanada Nobuyuki of Izu, Mōri Hidemoto of Nagato province, Hosokawa Tadaoki (Sansai) of the Kumamoto domain, and Ikeda Mitsunaka of the Tottori domain. Direct shogunal retainers (*hatamoto*) and Tokugawa house retainers also attended gatherings.[42]

The program, objects used, and size of each gathering varied considerably, though the manner in which decisions about such changes were made is not clear. It seems likely that it was Kōshin's responsibility to choose the objects to be used for each gathering, though he may have consulted with Yorinobu for special requests. In the evening of 3/28/1642, for example, a gathering was held with five *fudai* domainal lords in attendance, including the aforementioned Ogasawara Tadasane, Matsudaira Mitsushige, and Honda Toshitsugu. The entry is sparsely written, typical of Kōshin's notation style in *Record of His Lordship's Tea Gatherings*, recording the date, and a simple list of objects used or displayed. The scroll displayed in the alcove was attributed to the renowned Chinese Chan (Zen) monk Muqi (active thirteenth century).[43] Kōshin also notes the presence of a flower container named "Ototsure," though the displayed flower is not named. The tea caddy, which holds the powdered green tea before it is scooped into the tea bowl, was named "Ōsaka," and was accompanied by a treasured silk bag. He drew water from a ceramic water container produced at the Bizen kilns. Kōshin served tea in a white glazed, high-fired tea bowl imported from Korea. All of these objects seem to have been favorites of Yorinobu or Kōshin, as they appear frequently throughout the document. The Muqi scroll, for example, was paired with the Ototsure flower container in a gathering held ten days before this one, and again in 7/9/1643. The tea caddy Ōsaka was also used repeatedly, appearing eight times in 1642 and 1643 alone. Korean tea bowls are most common, appearing ten times, though this would seem to be Kōshin's preference rather than Yorinobu's as such bowls are frequently recorded throughout Kōshin's various writings.[44]

Without more documentary evidence, it is impossible to know the exact proceedings of this tea gathering, or the circumstances preceding and following it, but it is reasonable to conjecture that the assorted warrior leaders met with Yorinobu before or after tea to discuss political matters. Another possibility is that they arrived at the Kii Tokugawa residence in Edo specifically for the purpose of attending this tea gathering, to see

Yorinobu's new tea master and chat briefly with associates. Such gatherings may have functioned to strengthen social alliances and political ties, not only between Yorinobu and other domainal lords, but between the central power structure of the Edo government and the regional rulers who controlled the domains. The fact that numerous *tozama* domainal lords appear in the diary implies that the Kii Tokugawa played a conciliatory role between the government in Edo and those regional lords distant from the Shogun in personal relations and political power.[45]

In addition, Kōshin was responsible for the care and maintenance of the Kii Tokugawa collection of tea utensils, an impressive group of treasured and famous objects (*meibutsu*). One example is the celadon flower container mentioned in the first entry in the document, for 2/13/1642. It seems to be an example of Guan ware, the prized Chinese celadon produced in the twelfth and thirteenth centuries under the direction of the Southern Song court. Guan ceramics are famous for their thick green glaze covered with networks of crackles.[46] The tea caddy Ōsaka, mentioned above, was also a highly prized piece, a Chinese-manufactured container converted to the purpose of holding tea. Ōsaka was owned by the warrior-tea practitioner Furuta Oribe and then passed on to Yorinobu.[47] In the name-conscious world of early modern tea, pedigree was perhaps more important than the authenticity or artistic value of an object; the lineage of ownership was a primary determinant of value among tea aficionados.

Perhaps the most famous of the famous objects in the Kii Tokugawa collection was the tea caddy known as "Ake no Koromo," another Chinese-manufactured work. It was reportedly once owned by the tea master Takeno Jōō, and then passed through Tokugawa Ieyasu to Yorinobu.[48] The caddy was imbued with historical import in terms of both its place of production and its distinguished lineage of owners. Takeno Jōō (1502–1555) was a Sakai merchant, poet, Zen devotee, and one of the first tea practitioners to advocate *wabi* tea. Like his pupil Rikyū, any object associated with Jōō's name immediately assumed the status of masterpiece in early modern Japan. Ieyasu, of course, was the founder of Yorinobu's house as well as of the Tokugawa government, making the caddy something of a family heirloom as well. The caddy therefore symbolically combined the most prestigious lineage in tea culture with that of the most powerful military house in the nation.

Whether at the Kii compound in Edo or at Wakayama Castle, Kōshin thus had a variety of duties to fulfill as tea master for Yoribobu, combining elements of entertainment with the maintenance of a collection of objects. As a direct descendant of Rikyū, Kōshin also fulfilled the function of bringing prestige to an already wealthy and powerful domainal lord in a period when the fertile age of Azuchi-Momoyama was growing in the popular imagination. During a visit by the two other Tokugawa branch house leaders, Tokugawa Yorifusa (1603–1661) of the Mito domain and Tokugawa Mitsutomo (1625–1700) of the Owari domain, Kōshin was called on to serve tea. Yorinobu praised Kōshin prolifically as a tea master of the highest order from a house without peers, specifically noting that he was descended from the famous Sen no Rikyū of the late sixteenth century.[49]

## Kyoto tea society

Kōshin's work for Yorinobu represents only one portion of his total activities as a tea master. From 1640 to 1648, he spent most of his time in Edo or Kii, but from then until his death in 1672, Kōshin spent the majority of his time in Kyoto, and became increasingly active in the Kyoto tea community.[50] In 1646, Sōtan designated Kōshin head of the Sen house, giving him the Fushin'an tea room and the front of the Sen property (the "*omote*" of the Omotesenke branch of tea) in Kyoto. Sōtan retired to the Konnichian and Yūin tea rooms and gardens at the back of the property (the "*ura*" of the Urasenke branch of tea).[51] This move did not mean that father and son spent any less time in each other's company. Beginning in early 1649, Kōshin and Sōtan attended tea gatherings together as many as several times per week. Between 1649 and 1658, the year of Sōtan's death, Sōtan was present at well over half of the Kyoto tea gatherings in Kōshin's diaries. During certain years, when he was not busy working for the Kii Tokugawa in Wakayama or Edo, Kōshin attended nearly all gatherings in the company of his father. In 1649, for example, the two attended forty-six out of fifty-four recorded gatherings.[52]

Other members of the family also attended tea with Kōshin and Sōtan, and with Kōshin alone after Sōtan's death. Kōshin's younger brother Sensō, for example, was hired in 1652 as tea master to Maeda Toshitsune (1593–1658), domainal lord of Kaga, but appears in eight gatherings with Kōshin and Sōtan before leaving Kyoto.[53] He later attended numerous tea gatherings with Kōshin when back in Kyoto. Family loyalty, it seems, extended beyond the immediate household to include branch lines as well. Though competition between the Kōshin's and Sensō's respective lineages would become fierce in later centuries, initially cooperation was the norm.

Among Kōshin's written records, one of the most useful texts for the study of the Sen house's activities in Kyoto during this period is *Register of Disciples* [*Deshishū hikae*]. In this short document, Kōshin lists nine of Rikyū's disciples (conspicuously omitting such well-known Rikyū associates as Yamanoue Sōji), three previously unknown disciples of Rikyū's adopted son Shōan, thirty-four of Sōtan's disciples (omitting Sugiki Fusai and Fujimura Yōken, among others), and nine of his own disciples.[54] Among the forty-three listed Sōtan and Kōshin disciples, thirty-two appear in Kōshin's tea diaries. This list includes a wide range of individuals from mid-seventeenth century society, though the emphasis is on elite commoners who enjoyed frequent interaction with the Sen house. Again we see that though Sōtan was hesitant to associate directly with warrior patrons, he actively sought out powerful patrons from within his own status group. Six of Sōtan's disciples, for example, were members of the Kyoto Ginza or silver mint, established by Tokugawa Ieyasu in Fushimi in 1601 and moved to Kyoto in 1608.[55]

Another example is Gotō Shōsai (d. 1680), the son of the head of the Edo silver mint and a prominent metal worker and Kyoto silver mint official, who appears as a disciple of Sōtan, as a host of several tea gatherings, and as a frequent associate of Kōshin.[56] In *Writings of Kōshin* [*Hōgensai no sho*], for example, Kōshin records a visit by Shōsai to Kyoto, and later mentions him as the owner of the famous black Raku tea bowl Ōguro, one of the objects most associated with Rikyū and his distinctive brand of tea.[57] Shōsai used this bowl for a tea gathering with Kōshin on 11/16/1647. He displayed calligraphy by Rikyū in the alcove with a cylindrical bamboo flower vase; he served tea in Ōguro, matched with a new lacquer tea caddy, an Amida kettle, and a rough Shigaraki water jar.[58] On 11/28/1654, Shōsai again served tea in Ōguro with calligraphy by Rikyū, and used a tea scoop carved by Rikyū.[59] We find that tea gatherings attended by Sōtan and Kōshin often included objects attributed to or associated with Rikyū, as hosts drew from the aura of Rikyū's growing status as the patriarch of tea and simultaneously flattered their important guests.

Another commoner listed as a Sōtan disciple in the *Register of Disciples* is Seki Sōchō (dates unknown). Sōchō was a lacquerer from the Seki workshop in Nara who was active in Kyoto during the early to mid-seventeenth century and appeared frequently in Kōshin's diaries. Sōchō is well known as perhaps the first lacquer artisan to sign his works for tea practitioners, and a treasured lacquered tea caddy today still bears his name.[60] On 5/29/1649, for example, Kōshin, Sōtan, the tea practitioner Yamada Sōhen, and Sōchō attended a tea gathering at the house of another Sōtan disciple, Tani Sasuke. The host arranged calligraphy by Sōtan in the alcove, and served tea in a "new black" tea bowl, a common appellation that refers to Kyoto low-fired ceramics or black Seto ware. This bowl was matched with a Seto tea caddy from the time of Rikyū, and a rough water jar from Higo.[61] Sōchō appears again fourteen times in gatherings with Kōshin, the majority of these when Sōtan was in attendance.

Sōchō is outdone, however, by another artisan listed as a disciple of Sōtan, the founder of the Nakamura lineage of lacquerers, Nakamura Sōtetsu (1617–1695; also, Yahei). Sōtetsu appears in Kōshin's records of tea gatherings ten times as a host and thirty-one times as a guest, the most frequent of any of Sōtan's disciples.[62] Not surprisingly, a family connection lies at the root of this close relationship, starting with Sōtan and his son Ichiō. The story begins with Sōtetsu's father, a vassal of Nakamura Kazuuji (d. 1600), one of Toyotomi Hideyoshi's closest domainal lord retainers. After the defeat of the Toyotomi at Osaka Castle and the death of Kazuuji, Sōtetsu's father fled to Kyoto and established a home in the

Mushanokōji district of Kyoto, where he spent his remaining years dab-
bling at tea and lacquer with the Kichimonjiya house of lacquerers next
door. The Kichimonjiya around this time adopted a young boy to carry on
the lacquer business and the family line, a common occurrence in artisanal
houses in early modern Japan. This adopted son was Sen Ichiō, the second
son of Sōtan and future founder of the Mushanokōji Senke lineage of tea.
Ichiō took the name Yoshioka Kanemon, and learned the trade of lacquer
in the family's Mushanōkji home and workshop. Many years later he re-
established relations with his natural father Sōtan, underwent Zen training
at Daitokuji, and returned to the practice of tea. Before giving up lacquer
entirely, however, Ichiō married his daughter to the young man next door,
Nakamura Sōtetsu (Yahei), granting him the headship of the Kichimonjiya
lacquer tradition.[63] The fact that Sōtetsu was not only an important artisan
but related through marriage surely facilitated his friendship with Sōtan
and Kōshin, and ultimately cemented the success of the Nakamura as a
traditional craft lineage; during the eighteenth century, the Sen and Nakamura relationship was institutionalized with the founding of the "ten
workshops of the Sen house" (*senke jisshoku*) system, a roster of ten
artisan families who produced tea utensils for the Sen houses and their
growing schools of tea disciples.[64]

The *Register of Disciples* and Kōshin's tea diaries also reveal the Sen
house's close interactions with other professional tea masters. Kanetsune
Tokuan (1627–1686; also Matsudaira Daizen), for example, was
employed as tea master to the Mōri house, rulers of Chōshū. Kanetsune
was an infrequent participant in tea gatherings, apparently only coming to
Kyoto when in attendance to his lord Mōri Tsunahiro (1639–1689).

A more important example is Yamada Sōhen (1627–1708; also known
as Shūgaku or Sōen), who appears as host of six tea gatherings and as a
guest at eleven gatherings recorded by Kōshin.[65] He is best known as the
founder of the Sōhen school of tea, a lineage that developed into an *iemoto*
organization in the eighteenth century and is still in operation today. One
of this school's primary claims to legitimacy has been that it represents the
"true teachings" of Rikyū, passed to Sōhen through Sōtan.[66] It seems just
as likely, however, that Sōhen's lineage has been successful because of the
wide base established by the activities of its founder in the late seventeenth
century. Like Sōtan's sons, Sōhen obtained work as tea master to a
domainal lord, beginning work for the Ogasawara of the Yoshida domain
in 1655, reportedly on the recommendation of Sōtan.[67] Sōhen was
extremely active in tea, making numerous tea utensils, teaching the Ogasawara house of domainal lords and their retainers, and authoring several
books that were published as part of the larger publishing boom of the late
seventeenth and early eighteenth centuries.[68] In 1697, Sōhen entrusted the
teaching of tea in Yoshida to his descendants, and moved to Edo, where he
acquired numerous disciples among warrior leaders and their retainers.
This in turn led to the dissemination of Sōhen's tea to various regions of

Japan as oral transmissions and texts were transported back to the home domain via the system of alternate attendance.[69]

Kōshin also maintained ties with important figures in Kyoto's Zen Buddhist institutions, particularly Daitokuji. The link between tea and Zen was central to the spread of the new commoner tea from Sakai to Kyoto during the sixteenth century, fostered by the patronage of such culturally active warrior families as the Miyoshi, and by the *nouveau riche* merchant class of Sakai, represented by tea practitioners like Sen no Rikyū.[70] Though no extant records indicate that Kōshin patronized Daitokuji on the scale of Rikyū's regular donations to the Daitokuji subtemple Jukōin or his funding of the Sanmon gate,[71] Kōshin did continue Sōtan's frequent interactions with Daitokuji priests. On 11/12/1654, for example, Kōshin attended a tea gathering hosted by Gyokushitsu Sōhaku (1572–1641), a Daitokuji abbot.[72] Calligraphies bearing certificates or inscriptions by Gyokushitsu also appear more than a dozen times in Kōshin's writings.[73] Gyokushitsu's dharma heir Gyokushū Sōban (1600–1668) appears often as well, surfacing in Koshin's discussion of the pedigree of the famous water jar "Ōwakizashi" in *Summer Writings of Kōshin* [*Kōshin gegaki*], as the host of gatherings on 12/2/1640 and on 7/13/1653, and as the author of various inscriptions, certifications, and a calligraphy.[74] Gyokushū's contemporary as a student of Gyokushitsu, and later the abbot of Daitokuji, Tenshitsu Sōjiku (1605–1667), surfaces as a guest at a gathering held on 4/24/1659, and as the author of several calligraphies and inscriptions, including an inscription on a painting by the artist Kano Tan'yū on 11/21/1653.[75] These men represent the elite of Daitokuji, one of the most influential temple complexes in Kyoto during this period. The alliance between the leading monks of the temple and the Sen house was one of close cultural collaboration and mutual interest in tea practice, to be sure, but can also be understood as an institutional association that brought protection, patronage, and profit.

## Certifying the past

In 1658, at the age of 81, Sōtan died in his residence in Kyoto. Kōshin, who had left Edo upon hearing that Sōtan's health had taken a turn for the worse, later recorded the following: "I sped away from Edo on the nineteenth day of the twelfth month, but he passed away on the twenty-fourth and I wasn't able to see him on his deathbed."[76] Kōshin was 46 years old. With the death of his father and teacher, Kōshin seems to have gained a new awareness of the burden of succession and transmission. Approximately six months after Sōtan's passing, Kōshin began adding to his regular records of tea gatherings by composing notes and memoranda on Sen disciples, tea utensils, and family history, a practice that he continued until his death in 1672.[77] Particularly interesting are the first and last such documents that Kōshin composed, both of which record his comments on the tea utensils that tea practitioners brought to him for varied forms of certification.[78]

Kōshin's notes in *Register of Assorted Utensils* [*Shodōgu hikae*] begin in the sixth month of 1659. The text is not particularly long, consisting of one volume of notes on utensils viewed over a period of six years. As he himself comments at the end of the text, "I didn't record every single certification (*kakitsuke*), but wrote them down when I remembered. There were many more during these years."[79] The first entry records one small and one medium lacquered container (*natsume*) for powdered tea, examined for a monk from Seiganji.[80] Kōshin wrote a certification and, apparently, wrote or stamped names for the utensils in lacquer inside their lids.[81] What, we might ask, was he "certifying"? Tea masters were highly regarded as connoisseurs, and were frequently enjoined to verify that objects were made in this or that famous locale or by a well-known artist. In this case, because the maker's name is not recorded, Kōshin probably was providing a guarantee of quality (*kiwame*) rather than of the pedigree of production. In such cases, the approbation of the tea master became the stand-in pedigree of the object. If Kōshin accepted a fee or gift for this service he did not record it, but it does seem likely that this deed took place within a larger economy of exchange.

Another example from the same month presents a useful contrast. A certain Kohei brought several objects for certification, and Kōshin recorded the following notes:

> Item: [Bamboo] cylinder with one cut. Affidavit: "Made by Rikyū. [Previously] owned by Sōya."
> Item: Rikyū farewell poem. I prepared an affidavit: "[Previously] owned by Itamiya Sōfu of Sakai."
> Item: Writing by Rikyū. Endorsement (*uragaki*) by Sōtan. I prepared an affidavit: "Owned by Masuya Kohei."[82]

Kōshin certified that the first object was a bamboo flower container handmade by Rikyū; the second Rikyū's death poem (*jisei*); and the third unspecified calligraphy by Rikyū. We can read this encounter in a variety of ways. Kōshin may have been unaware of these utensils attributed to his great-grandfather's writing and collecting hands, in which case this was a significant opportunity to examine and comment on materials related to the founder of his house. Or, Kōshin may already have been familiar with these objects, which seems likely considering that the third object included an endorsement by Sōtan. In either case, this entry illustrates that these encounters were as beneficial to the tea master as they were to the client. With the death of Sōtan, Kōshin became one of the primary arbiters of value in all things Rikyū-related. This is borne out by the fact that Kōshin attributed forty-two of the objects noted in *Register of Assorted Utensils* to Rikyū. The assumption on the part of tea practitioners that the great-grandson would be able to recognize and discriminate amongst authentic Rikyū relics empowered Kōshin to shape and control his family's material legacy. Even objects that were outside of his immediate purview were affected, in the long run, by this practice. Because tea utensils that bear the certification of Sen tea masters accrued symbolic and economic value with each succeeding generation, those that remained "uncertified" became, *ipso facto*, less legitimate as a result.

Another type of transaction that appears in *Register of Assorted Utensils*, as well as in the later text, *Final Writings on Assorted Utensils* [*Shodōgu tomegaki*], is the naming request. On 4/13/1671, for example, a certain Yoshimura Gen'emon brought a tea bowl to Kōshin, who recorded the following note: "Red tea bowl. [By Hon'ami] Kōetsu. Yoshimura Gen'emon. Certified [on the box lid] as 'Otogoze.'" Kōshin was thus presented with a tea bowl by the influential tea practitioner and amateur Raku potter, Hon'ami Kōetsu (1558–1637).[83] He inscribed a name for the bowl on the lid of the protective wooden box, in this case a phrase meaning "plain-looking woman," this appellation is probably a humorous reference to the fact that Kōetsu's tea bowls are often asymmetrical and roughly shaped. Kōshin's conferral of a name on Kōetsu's unorthodox ceramic helped to legitimate it and bring it into the mainstream flow of objects surrounding the Sen tea schools. In contemporary Japan, Hon'ami Kōetsu is popularly known as one of the greatest artists in Japanese history; in seventeenth-century Japan, however, he was something of an eccentric. It is not an exaggeration to guess that the posthumous "patronage" of the Sen tea masters – as seen in Kōshin's writing of a box inscription for Otogoze – played a major role in guaranteeing that Kōetsu's name and material legacy would survive in the world of tea until discovered by "modern connoisseurs" in the late nineteenth century.[84]

Giving names to tea utensils was one of the ways in which a tea master could creatively engage in gift exchanges with disciples and clients. Another was to carve and bestow bamboo tea scoops (*chashaku*) and flower containers (*hanaire*), a hobby that Rikyū is said to have transformed into a key element of tea practice.[85] Kōshin's records of certification and naming exchanges indicate that tea practitioners brought bamboo utensils to him for naming and authentication more than any other type of object. In *Final Writings on Assorted Utensils*, for example, Kōshin attributes thirty-three bamboo flower containers to Sōtan and twenty-three to Rikyū.[86] Kōshin also seems to have carved many bamboo utensils himself, and granted names to these pieces on request. In *Register of Assorted Utensils* we find 121 objects for which no pedigree is listed in Kōshin's notes; scholars today assume that many of these references represent utensils made by Kōshin. They include eighty-one bamboo flower containers and fourteen tea scoops.[87] It is difficult to trace the extent of any tea master's activities as a maker of bamboo utensils, a practice that seems to have become ubiquitous in the seventeenth century but went almost entirely unrecorded. These references in Kōshin's notes, however, imply that in the Sen house, at least, large numbers of flower containers and tea scoops exchanged hands, probably serving to cement teacher–disciple relationships, to stand in for more formal forms of payment, and to extend the influence and name of the maker in the larger community of tea practitioners.

Kōshin was by no means unique in his practice of recording encounters with objects. As mentioned above, a number of tea practitioners from the sixteenth century recorded their participation at gatherings in diaries that were circulated within the tea community, and these would have been known to Kōshin.[88] Some of these writings included sketches of tea rooms and utensils, a practice that Kōshin replicated on occasion in his own tea diaries.[89] The writings by Kōshin on certification practices discussed above, however, are not records of gatherings attended but of private encounters with tea collectors and their utensils. A more direct precedent than the sixteenth-century tea diaries is the lengthy journal *Calligraphy Reproductions* [*Bokuseki no utsushi*] by the Daitokuji abbot and tea practitioner Kōgetsu Sōgan (1574–1643). In this text, Kōgetsu recorded instances of calligraphies brought to him for authentication and certification, his own sketched copies of the works, and a range of supplementary notes.[90] The contrast between the two documents, however, is perhaps greater than any similarities. Kōshin did not attempt to represent the objects he certified in the manner of Kōgetsu. Rather, his notes reverberate with a businesslike quality, reading more like a ledger of customers served than an exercise in connoisseurship. Still, both sets of writings point to an almost neurotic concern with documenting encounters with new and historical material culture in the tea community. Other textual and visual records of object appraisal from the same period, including the detailed diary of the abbot Hōrin Jōshō, the writings of members of the Kōhitsu house of calligraphy connoisseurs, and the reduced format painting sketches of the aforementioned Kano Tan'yū reflect, like Kōshin's writings, a trend toward textually and visually recording connoisseurship practices that were previously transmitted orally.[91]

## Writing history

On 9/3/1669, Kōshin wrote his last extant record of a tea gathering. The dry list of utensils includes, in characteristic fashion, a number of prized objects. He recorded that a calligraphy by Gyokushitsu with a postscript by Gyokushū was displayed. The round kettle was by [Tsuji] Yojiro, an artisan closely affiliated with Rikyū. An unattributed bamboo flower container was matched with a Bizen tea caddy, a medium black tea bowl ("unnamed"), and a Shigaraki water container. The gathering ended with a small meal, consisting of carp soup, tofu with miso, flounder, sea bass sashimi, hot *mochi* (pounded glutinous rice), and vegetables stewed in soy

sauce.[92] The text ends without any flourish or sense of completion, implying that the cessation was not meant to be permanent.

In the ninth month of the following year Kōshin began his last record,
*Final Writings on Assorted Utensils.* A number of passages in this document are written in a different brush, one that scholars attribute to
Kōshin's adopted son Zuiryūsai, whom Kōshin officially designated as his
heir on 9/29.[93] We can assume, therefore, that Kōshin was in ill health. He
soon traveled to Wakayama to see Tokugawa Yorinobu on his death bed;
his employer passed away not long after Kōshin's arrival, on 1/10/1671.
We know nothing of how Kōshin spent his time after he returned to
Kyoto, though the death of his mother Sōken on 8/24/1672 must have
been traumatic. Kōshin followed her to the grave a mere two months later
at the age of sixty.[94]

The use of the phrase "writing tea history" in the subtitle of this
chapter is not meant to refer literally to self-conscious authorship of
Rankean historical narratives for a mass audience, as was practiced by tea
collectors and tea practitioners in the modern period. Koshin's notes were
not intended for a public readership. Nor did his writings become *de facto*
historical texts as did many diaries and "secret writings" (*hidensho*) circulated among tea practitioners in the form of manuscript copies or published during the boom of print culture in the late seventeenth and early
eighteenth centuries. Until the modern caretakers of the Omotesenke collection of documents elected to sift through the extant writings of Kōshin
and select certain texts deemed appropriate for widespread dissemination,
these records (with the exception of *Summer Writings of Kōshin*) were
completely unknown to the outside world. These circumstances are
instructive as we struggle to navigate Kōshin's writings and situate them in
a larger context of seventeenth-century cultural production. We must
remember in particular that these traces are not complete, but have been
mediated at multiple points by assorted agents with differing priorities and
agendas. People who could have impacted the selection and character of
the "primary sources" on which this study is based might include:
Kōshin's early modern descendants, who took responsibility for the maintenance and protection of the house's collection of documents to varying
degrees; the previous and current *iemoto* of Omotesenke, who each made
decisions to publish volumes of Omotesenke documents and participated
in the selection of appropriate texts; historians such as Kumakura Isao,
who were called upon by Omotesenke to transcribe and interpret these
preselected documents; and the staff of the publishing house of Shufu no
Tomosha, who made editorial and design decisions that continue to affect
the way the texts are read.

This is not, then, the whole or originary textual corpus of Kōshin, but
one mediated by centuries of involved and implicated actors. This process
began, though, with Kōshin, who does emerge from these incomplete
sources as a remarkably active chronicler of his own everyday life. His

writings are not random jottings but focused records, attempts to capture his present professional activities and inscribe them in material form for his successors. This was a new practice in the Sen tea tradition. Kōshin's great-grandfather Rikyū left relatively few records other than correspondence written in a professional capacity.[95] Likewise, Kōshin's father Sōtan composed numerous personal missives but left no written tea instructions. What motivated Kōshin to take up his brush and begin recording tea gatherings, registers of associates and disciples, and encounters with objects? Kōshin was not, after all, merely "transmitting" the Sen tradition, but breaking with it by establishing writing as a further means of practicing tea.[96]

A number of interpretations are possible. Kōshin may have been encouraged by encounters with the writings of previous tea practitioners to try his own hand at jotting down notes on gatherings and objects. He may also have been motivated by a need for some sort of organizational and recollection aid. His records would have helped him to remember the ever increasing personal names and poetic object appellations relevant to his dual careers as tea master to the Kii Tokugawa and inheritor of the Sen house in Kyoto.[97] It seems unlikely, however, that Kōshin's impulse to record so many aspects of his tea life was motivated purely by contemporaneous business concerns such as recalling who owned what tea utensils. Rather, his actions are representative of a growing concern in the mid to late seventeenth century with preserving and protecting the household (*ie*) unit.[98] Kōshin acted to provide stability and continuity to his line of Sen tea by creating a core body of knowledge that could be passed on from one generation to the next in written form. His history writing was aimed not at a mass, public readership (a particularly modern notion of historical production) but at his successors.

## Notes

1 The Urasenke school, founded by Kōshin's younger brother Sensō, also follows this practice.
2 Kure is the matriarch of the Hisada lineage, a branch of the Omotesenke house and tea school. Her husband Hisada Sōri (1606–1685) is considered the second generation of the lineage, after Sōtan. Hisada Sōya, "Hisada ke no daidai," in Iguchi Kaisen *et al.* (eds), *Kyō no chake* (Bokusui Shobō, 1969), pp. 447–469.
3 *Kōshin gegaki*, a text attributed to Kōshin, has been the primary source in the study of his life and status in the Omotesenke tea tradition. Originally written sometime in the 1660s, this document was first published in the pre-war journal, *Wabi*, in 1940, and again in volume 10 of the influential series *Chadō koten zenshū*. As with Kōshin the historical personage, the text was considered important primarily for the information it contained on Sōtan and Rikyū. In 1971 Fushinan (Omotesenke) published the volume *Gempaku Sōtan monjo*, making a significant contribution to the available sources on the re-establishment of the Sen house in the early seventeenth century, printing photographs and transcriptions of 237 letters by Sen Sōtan. Surprisingly, these new sources apparently had little impact on the general vision of Kōshin's vital role

in the systematization of tea, as tea historians continued to note him as a minor figure in the pantheon of post-Rikyū tea masters. See Sen Sōsa *et al.* (eds), *Rekishi hen*, vol. 1 of *Chadō no genryū* (Tankōsha, 1981), pp. 71–72, for a standard treatment of Kōshin as the fourth tea master of the Omotesenke lineage.

4 There has been considerable debate over Sōtan's parentage among tea scholars, stemming from confusion over why Rikyū would pass the Sen house headship to an adopted son (Shōan) rather than to a natural son (Dōan) who was also an accomplished tea master in his own right. It is widely accepted today, despite a lack of documentary evidence, that Shōan was not only adopted by Rikyū but was also married to Rikyū's daughter Okame, making Shōan's son Sōtan Rikyū's grandson by blood as well as adoption. Kazue Kazu'ichi, "Sōtan no chichi oya," in Sen Sōsa (ed.), *Gempaku Sōtan monjo* [hereafter cited as *GSM*] (Chatobisha, 1971), p. 93; also Hisada Sōya, "Dōan to Shōan," in Kumakura Isao (ed.), *Oribe, Enshū, Sōtan*, vol. 4 of *Chadō shūkin* (Shogakkan, 1983), p. 200. It has also been proposed that Dōan inherited the Sakai branch of the Sen house, which subsequently died out. See Kumakura Isao, "Kan'ei Culture and *Chanoyu*," in Paul Varley and Kumakura Isao (eds), *Tea in Japan: Essays on the History of Chanoyu* (University of Hawai'i Press, 1989), pp. 149–150.

5 Sōen played a major role in the tea world as an active tea participant and as a powerful abbot of several Zen temples around the Kansai, though he is primarily associated with Daitokuji. Like the Daitokuji priest Kogaku Sōkō (1465–1548) before him, Sōen was particularly active as a bridge between Kyoto, with its large community of tea practitioners, and Sakai, the merchant city south of present-day Osaka that gave birth to the new breed of sixteenth-century tea masters. Tanihata Akio, "Daitokuji to cha no yu," in Murai Yasuhiko (ed.), *Sen Rikyū*, vol. 3 of *Chadō Shūkin* (Shogakkan, 1983), pp. 104–110; on Sōen's relationship to Sōtan, see Horinuouchi Sōkan, "Sōtan no Zen," *GSM*, pp. 52–55.

6 Shunoku Sōen, *Ichimokukō*, quoted in Horinouchi, "Sōtan no Zen," pp. 52–53.

7 On Shōan's pardon, see Kusumi Sōan's 1701 text, *Chawa shigetsushū*. The author was known as one of Sōtan's "Four Deva Kings" or four primary disciples. See vol. 10 of Sen Sōshitsu *et al.* (eds), *Chadō koten zenshū* [hereafter cited as *CKZ*] (Tankō Shinsha, 1956–1962), pp. 224–225.

8 Sōtan first appears in the entry of a gathering recorded by Matsuya Hisashige on 2/25/1608. See *Matsuya kaiki*, transcribed in *CKZ*, vol. 9, pp. 232–234.

9 On the Zen and *wabi* connection in Sōtan's tea, see Horinouchi Sōkan, "Sōtan no chafū," Kumakura Isao (ed.), *Oribe, Enshū, Sōtan*, vol. 4 of *Chadō shūkin* (Shogakkan, 1983), pp. 220–222; and Sen Sōin, "Sōtan no cha," *GSM*, pp. 3–16. Also see the description of "*wabi* Sōtan" in the recollection of Sugiki Fusai (1628–1706), one of Sōtan's disciples, in the 1834 version *Fukō chawa* in Kumakura Isao *et al.* (eds), *Shiryō ni yoru chanoyu no rekishi*, vol. 2 (Shufu no Tomosha, 1995), pp. 238–239.

10 The story of Konoe Nobuhirō's visit to Fushin'an is recorded in *Chawa shigetsushū*, transcribed in *CKZ*, vol. 10, pp. 209–210, though the rubric may be apocryphal. See also Kumakura, *Shiryō ni yoru*, vol. 2, pp. 259–261.

11 See Sōtan's letter to his sons Kōshin and Genshitsu (later Sensō) describing his exchange of gifts with Tōfukumonin: *GSM*, Figure 175, p. 234; also, Sokabe Yōko and Kiyose Fusa, *Sōtan no tegami* (Kawara Shoten, 1997), pp. 176–184. In English, Elizabeth Lillehoj describes several of Tōfukumonin's gift exchanges with Sōtan in "Flowers of the Capital: Imperial Sponsorship of Art in Seventeenth Century Kyoto," *Orientations* 27:8 (September, 1996): 65. An example of a gift from Tōfukumonin to Sōtan, a painting by the empress, is in the

Omotesenke collection at Fushinan: Figure 5, in Sen Sōsa *et al.* (eds), *Rekishi hen*, vol. 1 of *Chadō no genryū* (Tankōsha, 1983), p. 55.

12 Oka Yoshiko, "Kan'ei bunka no chanoyu," in Oka Yoshiko *et al.*, *Kan'ei bunka no nettowaaku: "Kakumeiki" no sekai* (Shibunkaku Shuppan, 1998), p. 169.

13 Cited in Sokabe and Kiyose, "Gempaku Sōtan nempyō," *GSM*, 97.

14 See Sōtan's letter to Kōshin (Jūsaburō), *GSM*, Figure 1, p. 47.

15 See Sōtan's letter to Ichiō, *GSM*, Figure 5, p. 51.

16 See Sōtan's letter to Kōshin, *GSM*, Figure 63, p. 116.

17 See Sōtan's letter to Kōshin, *GSM*, Figure 71, p. 126.

18 See Sōtan's letter to Kōshin (Jūsaburō), *GSM*, Figure 2, p. 48.

19 Sen Sōin, "Kōshin Sōsa den," in Sen Sōsa (ed.), *Kōshin Sōsa chasho* (Shufu no Tomosha, 1998) p. 402.

20 The Ikoma were domainal lords of Takamatsu, but in 1640 were demoted to Dewa, which caused the family to rescind its offer to Kōshin. Takagi Shōsaku, "Ikoma shi," *Kokushi daijiten*, vol. 1 (Yoshikawa Kōbunkan, 1979), p. 488; Sen Sōin, "Kōshin Sōsa den," ibid.

21 As was true with many provinces and domains in early modern Japan, the province of Kii also had a sinicized name, Kishū, which is widely used in the Japanese literature to refer to the branch of the Tokugawa house that administered it. In early modern sources, the family is also associated with Wakayama, their castle town headquarters and the largest domain within Kii. To maintain consistency, I will use Kii rather than Kishū or Wakayama when referring to this house.

22 See Sōtan's letter to Nodono Mokunosuke, retainer of the Yagyū house, *GSM*, Figure 74, p. 130.

23 *GSM*, Figure 81, p. 137.

24 For a brief introduction to early warrior tea patronage, see Harada Tomohiko, *Sadō bunkashi*, vol. 3 of *Harada Tomohiko chosakushū* (Shibunkaku, 1981), particularly "Daimyo cha no hassei – Hisahide to Nobunaga," pp. 64–75, and "Hideyoshi to Rikyū," pp. 88–99; also, Tanihata Akio, "Daimyo sadō no keifu," in Murai Yasuhiko (ed.), *Chanoyu no tenkai*, vol. 5 of *Chadō shūkin* (Shogakkan, 1985), pp. 137–147. In English, see Mary Elizabeth Berry, *Hideyoshi* (Harvard University Press, 1982), particularly Chapter 7.

25 According to the 1663 document *Kōshin gegaki*, Rikyū's seven disciples were Gamō Ujisatō (1556–1595), Seta Kamon Masatada (d. 1595), Hosokawa Sansai Tadaoki (1564–1645), Takayama Ukon (1553–1615), Makimura Hyōbu (1545–1593), Furuta Oribe (1544–1615), and Shibayama Kenmotsu (unknown). Later documents include other warrior tea practitioners, including Maeda Toshinaga (1562–1614), Oda Uraku (1547–1621), Araki Murashige (1535–1586), Arima Gemban (1569–1642), and Sakuma Fukansai (1556–1631). Sen Sōsa (ed.), *Kōshin Sōsa chasho* [hereafter cited as *KSC*], (Shufu no Tomosha, 1998), p. 58. See also the *Hōgensai sho*, a second version of the *Kōshin gegaki* also by Kōshin Sōsa, ibid., p. 24.

26 Perhaps the most popular brand of tea practice among warriors during this period was that propagated by Kobori Enshū, tea master to the Shogun and a disciple of Furuta Oribe. See Nomura Zuiten, *Enshū ryū: rekishi to keifu* (Mitsumura Suiko Shoin, 1987), particularly the section "Enshū to daimyo tachi," pp. 43–50.

27 Warrior stipends were paid in rice. One *koku* was roughly equivalent to 180 liters. The value of rice in relation to other commodities fluctuated depending on time and place in early modern Japan.

28 Keichō 14, *Dainihon shiryō*, vol. 12.6 (Tōkyō Daigaku Shiryō Hensanjo, 1901–).

29  See Saiki Kazuma and Iwasawa Yoshihiko (eds), *Tokugawa shoke keifu*, vol. 2 (Zoku Gunsho Ruijū Kanseikai, 1970–1984), p. 237, for a description of Yorinobu and his place in the Tokugawa lineage.

30  Genna 5, 7/19, *Dainihon shiryō*, vol. 12.31.

31  Because the Asano stipend at Kii had been 376,500 *koku*, and the revenue at Hiroshima was 426,000 *koku*, this was in fact a promotion. Gotō Yōichi, "Asano Nagaakira," *Kokushi daijiten*, vol. 1 (Yoshikawa Kōbunkan, 1979), p. 140.

32  The original construction of Wakayama Castle, enactment of land surveys, and the establishment of village headmen had already been carried out by the Asano, which left Yorinobu free to focus on the increase and reinforcement of vassal groups and domain military forces by recruiting *rōnin*; the organization of domain administration; the construction and maintenance of domain residences in Edo; and the promulgation of regulations to the various status groups of Kii. Koyama Yoshiki and Mitsuo Isao, "Tokugawa Yorinobu no Kishū nyūkoku," in Wakayama Shishi Hensan Iinkai (eds), *Kinsei*, vol. 2 of *Wakayama shishi* (Wakayama shi, 1989), pp. 103–142; Fukimoto Seijirō, Kasahara Masao, and Hiromoto Mitsuru, "Nōgyōson shihai no kakuritsu," in Wakayama Shishi Hensan Iinkai (eds), *Kinsei*, pp. 143–211; and Andō Seiichi, "Tokugawa Yorinobu no nyūkoku to han taisei no kakuritsu," in Wakayama Kenshi Hensan Iinkai (eds), *Kinsei*, a volume in the separate series, *Wakayama kenshi* (1990), pp. 58–85.

33  The official foundation of the Tokugawa branch house (*sanke*) system did not take place at the time of Yorinobu's appointment to Kii, but in 1632, when Shogun Iemitsu demoted his younger brother Tadanaga (1606–1633) from being domainal lord of Sumpu (Suruga), and ruled that the Kii, Owari, and Mito Tokugawa families, all direct descendants of Ieyasu, would occupy a special position in the *bakuhan* political system. Andō, "Tokugawa Yorinobu," p. 53.

34  See Conrad Totman, *Politics in the Tokugawa Bakufu, 1600–1843* (Harvard University Press, 1967), Chapter 6, "Related Daimyo and the Tokugawa House," for more on the *sanke*.

35  The Kii (Kishū) Kano lineage records that Kōho was employed as the founder of the school in Kan'ei 4 at 100 *koku*. Kazutaka Nobuji, "Bijutsu kōgei," Wakayama Shishi Hensan Iinkai, op. cit., pp. 236–237; and Kazutaka Nobuji, "Kishū han goyō eshi Kanoke no seiritsu to sono keifu," Wakayama Kenshi Hensan Iinkai, *Kinsei*, pp. 158–166.

36  On Kōi, Kōho, and Kōeki, see Doi Tsugiyoshi, "Kano Kōi to sono keifu," *Kinsei Nihon kaiga no kenkyū* (Bijutsu Shuppan, 1970), pp. 320–325.

37  *Nanki Tokugawa shi*, vol. 8, p. 631.

38  *Uma no nigatsu ochanoyu no oboe*, transcribed in *KSC*, pp. 207–215.

39  Hisada Sōya, "Kaidai," preceding *Uma no nigatsu ochanoyu no oboe*, *KSC*, p. 206.

40  Ibid.

41  *Uma no nigatsu ochanoyu no oboe*. Also, Sen Sōsa, "Kōshin Sōsa nenpu," *KSC*, pp. 499–513.

42  See chart 2, Sen Sōin, "Kōshin Sōsa den," *KSC*, p. 406.

43  Hayashiya Seizō, "Kōshin chakaiki ni miru chagu," *KSC*, p. 469.

44  More than 250 Korean (*kōrai*) tea bowls appear in the various Kōshin tea diaries.

45  Sen Sōin, pp. 406–407.

46  *Uma no nigatsu ochanoyu no oboe*, p. 207. Also, Hayashiya, p. 469.

47  Ibid.

48  Ibid.

49  *Nanki Tokugawashi*, vol. 7, p. 163. The late sixteenth century is referred to as

"tenka chūkō," or revival of the realm. A visit from the domainal lord of Mito and Owari is also recorded for 6/1/1652 in *Uma no nigatsu ochanoyu no oboe*, p. 213, though it is not known if this is the same gatherings as was recorded in the *Nanki Tokugawashi*. The program of objects displayed and used was not recorded.

50 Sen Sōsa, "Kōshin Sōsa nenpu," *KSC*, pp. 499–513.

51 See Sōtan's letters to Kōshin from 1646–1647: *GSM*, Figures 142–3, pp. 200–201. Also, see Sōtan's record of the division of the residence and tea utensils between his sons, *Gempaku ie yashiki yuzurijō* in the Omotesenke collection at Fushin'an, reproduced in Sen Sōsa *et al.* (eds), *Shiryō hen*, vol. 6 of *Chadō no genryū* (Tankōsha, 1983), pp. 19–25.

52 The following data present the ratio of gatherings attended by Sōtan and Kōshin to the total gatherings attended by Kōshin in Kyoto, as recorded in sources in *KSC*. 1650: 6/10; 1651: 7/11; 1652: no recorded entries for Kyoto; 1653: 27/36; 1654: 11/20; 1655: 16/40: 1656: no recorded entries for Kyoto; 1657: 22/47. Compiled from the various diaries and from "Kōshin Sōsa chakaiki ichiran," *KSC*, pp. 514–555.

53 Ibid. On Sōshitsu's employment for the Maeda, see Sōtan's letter to Kōshin in which he again expresses his joy at seeing another of his sons successfully employed as a tea master to a domainal lord. Sōshitsu is here called Genshitsu; his name change is announced in the next letter. *GSM*, Figures 194–5, pp. 256–257.

54 See *Deshishū hikae*, transcribed in *KSC*, pp. 149–150. Also, see the explanation of the document on p. 148; and Sen Sōin, pp. 418–419.

55 *Deshishū hikae*, pp. 149–150. On the silver mint, see Wakita Osamu and Wakita Haruko, "Tokken shōnin no taitō," Hayashiya Tatsusaburō (ed.), *Momoyama no kaika*, vol. 4 of *Kyoto no rekishi* (Kyoto-shi Hensanjo, 1969), pp. 404–405.

56 Sugiyama Sakon, "Gotō Shōsai," *Kadokawa chadō daijiten* (Kadokawa Shoten, 1991), p. 507.

57 *Hōgensai no sho*, transcribed in *KSC*, pp. 23 and 27. This document seems to be a final copy of *Kōshin gegaki*, the only available Kōshin text before the publication of *KSC* (see note 3); *Hōgensai no sho* was written on fine quality mulberry paper, whereas the *Kōshin gegaki* was written on scrap paper. Furthermore, numerous additions in the *Hōgensai no sho* indicate it is a later document. Hisada Sōya, "Kaisetsu," *KSC*, p. 18.

58 *Chanoyu mairi sōrō no oboe*, transcribed in *KSC*, p. 258. The tea kettle is listed as "Amidō," which could indicate the famous Amida Dō kettle used by Rikyū, but more likely refers to a general type of kettle modeled after Rikyū's piece. Sen Sōshitsu (ed.), *Kama*, vol. 10 of *Chadō bijutsu zenshū* (Tankōsha, 1970), Figure 40, pp. 80 and 187. Eventually, this type of kettle came to be intimately associated with Rikyū's tea, indicated by passages in the *Unshū fushi* and *Sadō sentei*, and various tea diaries of the late sixteenth and early seventeenth centuries. See, for example, vol. 9 of *CKZ*, pp. 187, 335, and 349.

59 *Mi no jun rokugatsu yori chanoyu no oboe*, p. 303.

60 The "Sōchō natsume" is in the Hatakeyama Kinenkan. See Ikeda Iwao, "Natsume," Ikeda Iwao *et al.* (eds), *Chadō bijutsu kanshō jiten* (Tankōsha, 1980), p. 279.

61 *Chanoyu mairi sōrō no oboe*, p. 270.

62 Sen Sōin, "Kōshin Sōsa den," p. 419.

63 Sen Sōshu, "Mushanokoji Senke," in Sen Sōsa *et al.* (eds), *Rekishihen*, vol. 1 of *Chadō no genryū* (Tankōsha, 1983), pp. 129–132, which seems to be based on Seseragi Toneri, "Senke jisshoku," in *Kibutsu hen*, vol. 3 of Sen Sōshitsu *et al.* (eds), *Chadō zenshū* (Sōgensha, 1936), p. 398.

64 Surprisingly little has been written on the system of *senke jisshoku*. They are the Raku house of potters, the Ōnishi house of kettle makers, the Nakamura house of lacquerers, the Komazawa house of woodworkers, the Nakagawa house of goldsmiths, the Tsuchida house of textile makers, the Okumura house of paper makers, the Hirai house of *Ikkanbari* lacquerers, the Kuroda house of ladle makers, and the Eiraku house of potters. See Seseragi, "Senke jisshoku"; and Horinouchi Sōkan, "Senke jisshoku," in Murai Yasuhiko (ed.), *Chanoyu no tenkai*, vol. 5 of *Chadō shūkin* (Shogakkan, 1985), pp. 85–90. In English, see Chapter 4 of Pitelka, "Raku Ceramics."

65 Sen Sōin, "Kōshin Sōsa den," p. 419.

66 See Nomura Zuiten, *Sōhen ryū: rekishi to keifu* (Mitsumura Suiko Shoin, 1987), pp. 19–23.

67 Nishiyama Matsunosuke, "Yamada ke," in Sen Sōsa *et al.* (eds), *Rekishihen*, vol. 1 of *Chadō no genryū* (Tankōsha, 1983), p. 228. Nomura, however, argues that Sōtan was actually offered the job first, and bowed out because of age and his unwillingness to work for a warrior, but there seems to be little direct evidence for this. Nomura, *Sōhen ryū*, pp. 59–61.

68 See Peter Kornicki, *The Book in Japan: A Cultural History from the Beginnings to the Nineteenth Century* (Brill, 1998) for more information on the culture of books in seventeenth and eighteenth century Japan.

69 For a partial list of Sōhen's disciples in Edo, see Nomura, *Sōhen ryū*, p. 72. See also Nomura's extensive research on the regional spread of Sōhen's tea in the same volume, pp. 169–356.

70 On the Miyoshi, Sen Rikyū, and the Sakai-Kyoto link via Daitokuji, see Greg Levine, "Jukōin: Art, Architecture, and Mortuary Culture at a Japanese Zen Buddhist Temple" (Ph.D. diss., Princeton University, 1997), particularly Chapter 2, "The Miyoshi, Sen no Rikyū, and Jukōin," pp. 76–132.

71 Ibid., pp. 125–131. Each *iemoto* of the three Sen house lines has a grave stone at Jukōin, and it is clear from this that Daitokuji remained the Sen house temple even after Rikyū's suicide and the fall from grace of the Sen house. See Haga Kōshirō *et al.* (eds), *Daitokuji to chadō* (Tankōsha, 1972), p. 189.

72 *Mi no jun rokugatsu yori chanoyu no oboe*, p. 294.

73 See, for example, the reference in *Tatsu no hachi gatsu yori chanoyu no oboe*, transcribed in *KSC*, p. 198; and *Saru no chanoyu ni aimōshi sōrō no oboe*, transcribed in *KSC*, p. 245. The influential Zen monk and onetime abbot of Daitokuji, Takuan Sōhō (1573–1645), also appears more than two dozen times in the diary in descriptions of calligraphies. See, for example, *Saru no chanoyu ni aimōshi sōrō no oboe*, pp. 229 and 249; and *Mi no jun rokugatsu yori chanoyu no oboe*, p. 293.

74 *Kōshin gegaki*, transcribed in *KSC*, p. 59. The gatherings are recorded in *Tatsu no hachi gatsu yori chanoyu no oboe*, p. 198, and *Chanoyu mairi sōrō no oboe*, p. 259. Gyokushū's inscriptions and calligraphy are recorded in *Mi no jun rokugatsu yori chanoyu no oboe*, pp. 306 and 317; and *Kanbun hachi nen saru no kai ni mairi sōrō*, pp. 374, 375, and 380, the latter being Kōshin's last record of a tea gathering, from 9/3/1669.

75 *Manji ninen yori chanoyu no oboe*, transcribed in *KSC*, p. 335; and *Mi no jun rokugatsu yori chanoyu no oboe*, p. 295.

76 *Gantan shihitsu tensho*, in the Omotesenke collection at Fushin'an, transcribed in Sen Sōin, "Kōshin Sōsa den," p. 420.

77 Not all of Kōshin's documents are dated. The text *Kigu shū*, for example, could have been written any time between 1648 and 1672.

78 I am grateful to Yukio Lippit and Louise Cort for suggesting the term "certification" as an alternative to "authentication" for understanding Kōshin's encounters with and judgments of tea utensils.

79  *Shodōgu hikae*, transcribed in *KSC*, p. 162.
80  Presumably the Pure Land Buddhist temple in Kyoto.
81  *Shodōgu hikae*, transcribed in *KSC*, p. 152.
82  Ibid.
83  See Felice Fischer (ed.), *The Arts of Hon'ami Kōetsu, Japanese Renaissance Master* (Philadelphia Museum of Art, 2000).
84  For more on modern connoisseurs' appropriation of Kōetsu as an "artist" in the modern, post-Enlightenment understanding of the word, see Morgan Pitelka, "Raku Ceramics: Tradition and Cultural Reproduction in Japanese Tea Practice," (Ph.D. diss., Princeton University, 2001), particularly the conclusion.
85  On the place of hand-made objects in tea culture, see Morgan Pitelka, "Sadō bunka ni okeru 'tezukuri' no imi," in Kumakura Isao (ed.), *Nihonshi ni okeru yūgei no shosō* (Yoshikawa Kobunkan, forthcoming).
86  Hisada Sōya, "Kaidai," preceding *Shodōgu tomegaki*, *KSC*, p. 164.
87  Hisada Sōya, "Kaidai," preceding *Shodōgu hikae*, *KSC*, p. 152.
88  See, for example, the earliest extant version of the record of Yamanoue Sōji (1544–1590) (*Yamanoue sōjiki*), reproduced and transcribed in Gotō Bijutsukan, *Yamanoue Sōjiki* (Gotō Bijutsukan, 1995).
89  See, for example, Kōshin's sketches of tea rooms, reproduced in *KSC*, pp. 382–396.
90  I am grateful to Greg Levine for allowing me to read the chapters on Kōgetsu and *Bokuseki no utsushi* in his work-in-progress, *Daitokuji: Visual Cultures at a Japanese Zen Buddhist Monastery*.
91  On Hōrin's diary, *Kakumeiki*, see Oka, *Kan'ei bunka no nettowaaku*; the six-volume transcription, *Kakumeiki* (Shibunkaku Shuppan, 1967, reissued, 1999); and Chapter 4 of Kumakura Isao, *Gomizuno'o tennō* (Iwanami Shoten, 1994; published by Asahi Shinbunsha in 1982 as *Gomizuno'o in*). On the Kohitsu house, see Komatsu Shigemi, *Kohitsu* (Kōdansha, 1972). On Kano Tan'yū's *shukuzu*, see Kyoto Kokuritsu Hakubutsukan, *Tanyū shukuzu* (Kyoto Kokuritsu Hakubutsukan, 1980–1981).
92  *Kanbun hachi nen saru no kai ni mairi sōrō*, p. 380.
93  Zuiryūsai was Kōshin's nephew by blood, the son of his sister Kure and Hisada Sōri.
94  Sen Sōsa, "Kōshin Sōsa nenpu," *KSC*, pp. 512–513.
95  Numerous "transmitted writings" (*densho*) are attributed to Rikyū, but these consist of second-hand compositions, written by his disciples. See Tsutsui Hiroichi, "Rikyū no densho," in Kumakura Isao *et al.* (eds), *Rikyū daijiten* (Tankōsha, 1989).
96  In the contemporary rhetoric of Japanese tea scholarship, Rikyū perfected or "made mature" (*taisei shita*) tea practice; this completed package was then inherited (*keishō*) by each succeeding generation. See Sen Sōin, "Kōshin Sōsa den," pp. 399–400, for one recent example.
97  This interpretation is supported by a note written by Kōshin, in the Omotesenke collection, cited in Sen Sōin, "Kōshin Sōsa den," p. 427.
98  For more information on the seventeenth-century growth of household consciousness (*ie ishiki*) in the community of tea practitioners, see Pitelka, "Raku Ceramics," particularly Chapter 3, "From Workshop to Household." In the case of Kōshin Sōsa, this analysis is also based on Kumakura Isao, "Kōshin Sōsa chasho no naka no Sen no Rikyū," in *KSC*, pp. 485–487.

# 5   *Karamono* for *sencha*
## Transformations in the taste for Chinese art

*Patricia J. Graham*

## Introduction

The term *karamono* (Chinese things) is the Japanese designation for the wide variety of Chinese arts and crafts that were exported to Japan in pre-modern times. Although Chinese arts had been imported since ancient times, this term is generally used to refer to arts that entered Japan between the thirteenth and mid-nineteenth centuries. Among these objects, some, such as incense burners and other vessels that decorated altars of Buddhist and Confucian temples, as well as painting and calligraphy scrolls by Chinese Zen masters or depicting eccentric Zen monks, originally served religious functions but were later appropriated for secular use. Others, including flower vases, musical instruments, household furnishings, writing implements and small decorative sculptures for the scholar's study, food and beverage serving utensils, and paintings with images of landscapes or plants and fauna in hanging scroll or fan format, were used from the time of their importation as residential furnishings. These would have been placed in specially designed niches or decorative alcoves (*tokonoma*), that had been designed to display these materials. Many of these things were also imported or later appropriated for use as accoutrements in secular rituals for the service of green tea or as decorations for environments in which the tea was served.

Ownership of *karamono* served as a signifier of elite status in pre-modern Japan. Not only did such objects proclaim their owners' wealth, they helped to distinguish elites because only they possessed specialized knowledge about China. Technical superiority and aesthetic qualities assured that these products were in high demand, but at first this was only true among a select group within Japan's overall population. The first aficionados were those whose upbringing, education, and wealth had instilled in them appreciation for Chinese civilization: Buddhist priests, especially those of the Zen sects, the imperial aristocracy, and high-ranking warriors. Not until the sixteenth century did a small group of commoners – wealthy urban merchants – began valuing and collecting *karamono*, and this took place within the realm of taste associated with the secular ritual preparation of powdered green tea (*chanoyu*). It was only much later, from the early nineteenth century, that *karamono* appreciation became more widespread. This development was closely tied to the popularity of another tea drinking ritual that featured tiny cups of steeped green leaf-tea, known as *sencha*.

*Sencha* emerged as an alternative tea ritual in the eighteenth century among Sinophile intellectuals. They practiced it in part to protest against the prescribed etiquette of *chanoyu* and the military regime of the Shoguns with which it had by then become closely associated. To participants in the *chanoyu* tea ritual, Chinese objects and scrolls conferred notions of status and inferred interest in spiritual ideals associated with Zen Buddhism. In contrast, *sencha* practitioners identified instead with ancient Chinese sages and their more humanistic, syncretic values derived from Confucianism and Daoism, as well as Zen. As this tea ritual developed in formality, *sencha* practitioners began to adorn their tea rooms with *karamono* similar to those favored by the Chinese scholars of the sixteenth through eighteenth centuries, including literati paintings and calligraphies; burnished, unglazed Yixing ware ceramics; and ancient Chinese bronzes.[1]

By the early nineteenth century, *sencha* had become popular among a broad spectrum of the urban population, which aspired to social parity with the elite members of society. They worked to achieve this parity by acquiring upper-class material trappings such as *karamono*, or as substitutes, Japanese-made products in Chinese styles. Under the influence of *sencha*, *karamono* came to be widely studied and collected in Japan. Still, as will be shown in this study, while *chanoyu* and *sencha* followers appreciated some similar types of *karamono*, the *karamono* favored in *sencha* circles more often differed from those admired by fans of *chanoyu*. *Sencha* aficionados admired a broad range of sixteenth- through nineteenth-century (late Ming through Qing dynasty) arts, unlike *chanoyu* participants, who, with the exception of certain types of newly-made Chinese crafts imported for their use in the early seventeenth century, preferred arts associated with imperial Chinese or Zen traditions of the twelfth through fifteenth centuries (Song, Yuan, and early Ming dynasties).

By the mid- to late nineteenth century, new significant collections of later Chinese arts had been accumulated by people involved with tea rituals for steeped rather than powdered tea. The aim of this study is to articulate more clearly the *sencha* taste for *karamono*, and to show how many modern collections of Chinese art emerged from within the circles of *sencha* enthusiasts.

## *Karamono* and *chanoyu* aesthetics

One of the most important and influential forms of Japan's secular tea ritual of *chanoyu* developed during the fifteenth century. It featured the use of Chinese tea accoutrements and the display of Chinese objects of art.

Tea was served in formal reception rooms that were decorated with Chinese arts and crafts such as cast bronze vases, carved red lacquer tea bowl stands and incense boxes, colorful painted scrolls of birds and flowers, austere black-ink scrolls depicting China's mountains or Zen monks, and ceramics with greenish-blue celadon or shiny brown "*temmoku*" glazes.[2] The atmosphere of these rooms was like that of a grand salon, sumptuous and colorful, with scrolls sometimes hung over screens and other objects displayed in decorative alcoves. Knowledge of the *karamono* collected and displayed in this period derives from detailed records of the collections of successive generations of Japan's Shoguns from this period.[3]

During the sixteenth century, wealthy merchants had begun to influence the way *chanoyu* was served and the types of utensils preferred. This formal style of tea practice, with its focus on Chinese objects, was gradually overshadowed by a new taste for accoutrements of Japanese manufacture (*wamono*). This new style of tea service evolved into rustic tea (*wabicha*), the style of *chanoyu* that is most characteristic of this tea tradition today. However, owing to the continued high prestige of Chinese cultural artifacts in Japanese society in general, and within the historical development of *chanoyu* in particular, *karamono* were not excluded from use in this new form of powdered green-tea ritual. In fact, tea masters sometimes featured prized old Chinese pieces, such as *temmoku*-glazed tea caddies or celadon porcelain tea bowls,[4] as they considered these Chinese wares to embody the essence of rustic tea taste despite their technical and aesthetic refinement. The fact that they were Chinese imparted a "touch of luxuriousness"[5] to the atmosphere of the tea room. Thus, with no apparent contradiction, Chinese objects of certain types could be simultaneously both splendid and appropriate for use in a rustic setting.

By the early seventeenth century, various factions had developed in *chanoyu*, each of which had its own preferences for types of utensils and settings for the service of the tea. *Karamono* again returned to prominence in some tea circles, one of which was led by Kobori Enshū (1579–1647), an influential domainal lord and retainer to the Shogun. Particularly prominent among the many types of arts he considered appropriate for display and use during tea rituals were contemporary, rather than antique, imported Chinese arts and crafts.[6] His interest was facilitated by increases in officially sanctioned trade between the two countries after a lull during the previous century (due to periods of political unrest on both sides). Enshū was also encouraged by the new military leaders, the Tokugawa Shoguns, who promoted the study of Chinese Confucian philosophy as a means of instilling allegiance to their authority in their vassals and the population at large. The Tokugawa hoped that loyal warrior officials would emulate the cadres of Confucian scholars who served as China's bureaucrats.

Confucian values were imparted through immersion in morally uplifting vocations: the practical study of various literary arts such as painting, calligraphy, poetry, collecting Chinese antiquities and accoutrements for the scholar's study, and participating in formal, secular ritual preparation of powdered green tea, which had become a form of mandated etiquette for the warrior class. Because of the pre-eminence of Chinese cultural studies in elite warrior circles in Japan, Chinese crafts came to play a more prominent role in warrior-sponsored tea gatherings. Not only were Chinese tea accoutrements used in the service of the tea, but tea rooms again became places appropriate for the display of participants' Chinese art collections. Although many of these collections were later dispersed, some, such as that owned by the Owari (Nagoya) branch of the Tokugawa clan, have remained intact up to the present, so knowledge about their contents is readily available.[7]

So important had many of these Chinese crafts become in Japan that a thriving export industry developed in China, with many pieces made to order for Japanese tea practitioners. Foremost among these commercial products were a wide variety of porcelains, some made at China's imperial kilns of Jingdezhen, others manufactured at regional kilns elsewhere.[8] Also among the Chinese crafts preferred by Kobori Enshū and other warriors of his time were elaborately plaited Chinese flower baskets, intended as receptacles for flower arrangements that would be displayed in tea rooms.[9] All these crafts were later appropriated for use by participants of the *sencha* tea ritual.

By the time Enshū died in 1647, the canon of taste for *karamono* considered appropriate for *chanoyu* tea gatherings had become so thoroughly fixed that it has influenced the perceptions about *karamono* by all subsequent *chanoyu* tea practitioners up to the present. After this time, *chanoyu* tea enthusiasts generally followed the taste of their predecessors for older Chinese "antiques." Perhaps this ossification occurred because no great leader emerged among the ranks of tea practitioners to set new directions for taste in *karamono*. It is also significant that by the mid-seventeenth century Chinese tea drinking customs had changed. Previously, contemporary Chinese tea caddies, bowls, and other tea utensils could be readily imported to Japan, but by this time utensils appropriate for serving powdered tea were no longer being made. Also, in the mid-seventeenth century, Japanese potters had perfected the manufacturing of porcelain in Japan, so patrons desiring such products could readily acquire Japanese-made materials.

The Japanese continued to import great quantities of marvelous Chinese art after the mid-seventeenth century, but these were largely accoutrements for the service of steeped green-leaf tea (*sencha*) and other Chinese arts favored by the Chinese literati, especially paintings and calligraphies of the sixteenth through eighteenth centuries, ancient Chinese bronzes, and writing implements and other decorative objects for the scholar's study.

## *Karamono* and *sencha* aesthetics

Appreciation for *karamono* among *sencha* participants developed gradually. Over the course of about 150 years, the types of *karamono* associated with *sencha* expanded and eventually became codified along with its ritual preparation, as had occurred within *chanoyu* circles. Changes in *sencha* participants' taste in *karamono* over time mirror both the changing demographics of participants and changes in the availability of Chinese products in Japan. For organizational purposes, these developments can roughly be divided into three overlapping and approximately dated phases: (a) the second half of the seventeenth through the first half of the eighteenth century; (b) 1800 to 1860; and (c) 1860 to 1900.

The Chinese Ōbaku Zen sect patriarch Ingen (1592–1673) is credited as the founder of *sencha* practice in Japan. Ingen and a cadre of Ming expatriate monks settled in Japan in 1654 to escape rule by the Manchu, who took control of China and founded the Qing dynasty in 1644. Ingen and his compatriots were both devoted to Buddhism and learned scholars who participated in Chinese literati pastimes, such as composing painting, poetry, and calligraphy. In addition, they brought many materials associated with Chinese literati culture with them to Japan. There, they found favor both with the Tokugawa (who were just then promoting Confucian scholarly virtues) and with educated commoners. Ingen founded the temple Manpukuji in Uji, south of Kyoto. It was an anomaly in Japan, an authentic recreation of seventeenth-century Chinese temple architecture, and it soon became a gathering place for those interested in Chinese literati customs. Nagasaki had a higher concentration of Chinese residents, but they could not freely travel around the country. Japanese residents were also then forbidden from traveling overseas. Manpukuji, which was situated a short distance from the imperial capital of Kyoto and within the densely populated Kyoto–Osaka region, was therefore a more convenient destination for those interested in encountering Chinese culture. Today, the temple still preserves Ingen's possessions, which include several Chinese Yixing ware teapots, a type prized by later *sencha* enthusiasts.[10]

With the exception of materials relating to Ingen, documentary evidence on the settings for *sencha* consumption and the types of utensils used by early *sencha* practitioners is sparse. Based on pictures in illustrated books, woodblock prints, and surviving Chinese books, we know that by the mid-eighteenth century the Japanese had access to many types of Chinese goods and possessed a great deal of knowledge about Chinese tea-drinking customs. However, it was not until the efforts of the Japanese-born Ōbaku monk, Baisaō Kō Yūgai (1675–1763), that the drinking of *sencha* grew more popular. He was responsible for transforming Ingen's Chinese manner of preparing cups of steeped green leaf-tea into what would later become a formal ritual. Baisaō was one of a number of eccentric intellectuals who gravitated to Kyoto, and he moved to the old capital in 1724 from his home near Nagasaki. Although he remained a formal member of the clergy until he was aged 70, Baisaō earned his living in Kyoto selling *sencha* as an itinerant peddler, promoting the beverage as a means of stimulating spiritual enlightenment. So revered did Baisaō become that soon after his death, his admirers began treasuring his meager possessions. They even produced a handscroll of these, later copied and distributed in printed book form. They also made reproductions of his favorite tea wares, which Baisaō had described as his "teachers." Baisaō distributed some of these to his admirers prior to his passing, while he was said to have burned others.[11]

Among Baisaō's few possessions were imported Chinese ceramics, such as an unglazed, side-handled teapot that he used both as a hot water kettle and for tea brewing (Figure 5.1, the tan teapot on the right, shown behind the porcelain cups). These kettles were cheap, mass-produced objects used for preparing medicines in China, but in Japan, due to the influence of Baisaō, they became highly admired and continued to be frequently imported for decades after his death. Large numbers of them that survive in Japan, like the present example (Figure 5.2), are preserved in boxes marked with the reign period (in this case, the Bunsei era, 1818–1830) when they entered the country. These kettles are generally known as *nanban* ("Southern Barbarian") wares, a reference to their point of origin in south China. Later Japanese potters who specialized in porcelain and other glazed wares for *sencha*, such as Aoki Mokubei (to be discussed below), also copied them, as their close association with Baisaō assured their centrality to the *sencha* canon of taste.

Baisaō also owned some porcelain vessels, such as tea cups and caddies, that were decorated with simple designs in underglaze blue (Figure 5.1).

*Figure 5.1* Chinese, side-handled kettle and set of porcelain cups with underglaze blue designs of tea plants that were owned by Baisaō, both seventeenth century. Kettle, h. 9.9 cm.; cups, h. 4.5 cm.; diam. 6.1 cm. Private collection, Japan, photo courtesy of the Osaka Municipal Museum of Art.

*Figure 5.2* Chinese-made side-handled kettle, early nineteenth century. Idemitsu Museum of Art.

Although these porcelains were more refined and elegant in appearance than the rough, unglazed teapot, they still represented types of ceramics widely produced in China. Baisaō must have liked them for their lack of colored or gold leaf decoration, which conveyed an austere impression that was in keeping with Chinese scholarly aesthetic taste. Baisaō was not affluent, and in fact made poverty a virtue in his tea ritual. He believed that to reap the benefits of the tea, rare and expensive utensils were unnecessary. Baisaō's preferences for Chinese utensils represents the first phase in the development of taste for *karamono* by *sencha* participants.

The second phase took place during the first half of the nineteenth century under the leadership of Sinophile scholars and artists. During this period, numbers of participants in *sencha* gatherings multiplied to encompass most of the educated population of Japan. This trend was concurrent with a boom in the popularity of Chinese culture in general. Even the elite warrior supporters of *chanoyu* participated in *sencha* tea-drinking rituals and constructed tea rooms especially for the purpose. In general, the participants in *sencha* rituals were divided between intellectuals, who associated it with the Chinese literati, and others who partook of the beverage because of the sophistication of taste associated with its Chinese accoutrements. At this time, following the preferences of its literati practitioners, *sencha* began to be served in a self-consciously Chinese atmosphere, with all the room decorations and utensils designed in Chinese taste, including some authentic Chinese utensils and others made by Japanese artists in Chinese styles.

Ceramic vessels for serving and drinking tea were the first Japanese crafts made especially for *sencha* service. They were initially manufactured in Kyoto by potters such as Aoki Mokubei (1767–1833), a connoisseur of Chinese antiquities who used his expertise to gain a profitable profession as a potter. He was responsible for adapting many types of Chinese porcelains that had first gained popularity in seventeenth-century *chanoyu* circles to *sencha* use. Among the types of Chinese ceramics his designs emulated, two favorites were *kinrande* ("gold brocade") with overglaze enamel and gold-leaf decoration, exemplified by this set of tea cups (Figure 5.3); and *kōchi*,[12] a multi-colored low-fired enameled ware represented by this side-handled teapot (Figure 5.4). The glazes on both these types of

*Figure 5.3*  Aoki Mokubei (1767–1833), set of *kinrande* tea cups, h. 4.5 cm.; diam. 6.7 cm. Yanagi Takashi collection, Kyoto.

*Figure 5.4*  Aoki Mokubei (1767–1833), *Kōchi*-style side-handled teapot. Yanagi Takashi collection, Kyoto.

ceramics became standards for *sencha* wares from this time up to the present. Mokubei and his many followers also continued to make utensils for *sencha* reminiscent of the styles popularized by Baisaō. One example of a fine underglaze blue ware in subdued literati taste is this tea caddy (Figure 5.5) by Ogata Shūhei (1783–1839), also a Kyoto potter and follower of Mokubei.

One person whose personal collection exemplified the taste for *kara-mono* among the Japanese literati of this period is the painter Yamamoto Baiitsu (1783–1856). Baiitsu, a native of Nagoya, lived and worked in Kyoto for most of his career. He was a serious devotee of Chinese literati culture, who became famous for his fondness for *sencha* and for his connoisseurship of Chinese paintings and antiquities. He also collected Chinese art. Two catalogues of Chinese painting exhibitions held in his honor (including paintings he and his friends owned) have survived. They indicate that he preferred Chinese literati paintings of the seventeenth and eighteenth centuries, in part because art by earlier Chinese literati was

*Figure 5.5* Ogata Shūhei (1783–1839), tea caddy with decoration in underglaze-blue, h. 8.5 cm. Kyoto National Museum.

practically impossible to acquire in Japan.[13] The most famous painting in his collection was by the Chinese literati painter Yang Wenzong (1597–1645).[14] This painting's fame in Japan is attested to by the existence of a number of faithful copies by Japanese literati artists. Baiitsu himself copied it in 1824 (Figure 5.6), several years prior to his having acquired it

*Figure 5.6* Yamamoto Baiitsu (1783–1856), *Copy of Yang Wenzong's "Landscape with Pavilion" dated 1643*, 1824. Hanging scroll; ink on satin. 134 × 49.5 cm. Photo courtesy of Kaikodo Gallery, New York.

for a large sum of money. We know Baiitsu had acquired it by 1831, the year the great Kyoto Confucian scholar–artist Rai San'yō (1780–1832) saw it, for San'yū wrote a poem about his viewing it for the first time, and inscribed the box indicating he saw it when it was in Baiitsu's collection. The story goes that when San'yū viewed the painting, he did so wearing formal attire in its honor.[15] The Chinese original hangs in the decorative alcove in this sketch of Baiitsu's study by a later literati painter, Tomioka Tessai (1836–1924) (Figure 5.7). Also visible in the sketch are assorted tea utensils Baiitsu owned.[16] Several of these are known today, having been preserved in their original wooden boxes, inscribed by Baiitsu. One is an unglazed ceramic brazier from the seventeenth century (Figure 5.8); another, a fine pewter-alloy tea caddy from the seventeenth to eighteenth centuries (Figure 5.9); and a third, a loop-handled Yixing ware teapot very much like one pictured in Tessai's sketch (in the tea utensil basket on the top shelf).[17] This last item requires further explanation.

Teapots made at the Yixing kilns were the most highly prized pieces among Chinese scholars, a fact that was known to Japanese *sencha* enthusiasts from their perusal of Chinese texts. However, few authentic Yixing teapots were imported to Japan before the nineteenth century, and as a result early collectors of Chinese art had few opportunities to examine or acquire examples. Even consummate connoisseurs of Chinese ceramics like Mokubei did not clearly understand Yixing forms and styles. Mokubei erroneously gave the title of "Yixing ware copy" to a reproduction he made of Baisaō's famous kettle (Figure 5.1), which was distinctly not an example of Yixing ceramics.[18] The fact that a nineteenth-century collector like Baiitsu owned an authentic Yixing tea bowl illustrates that *sencha* collectors of *karamono* were moving in a new direction.

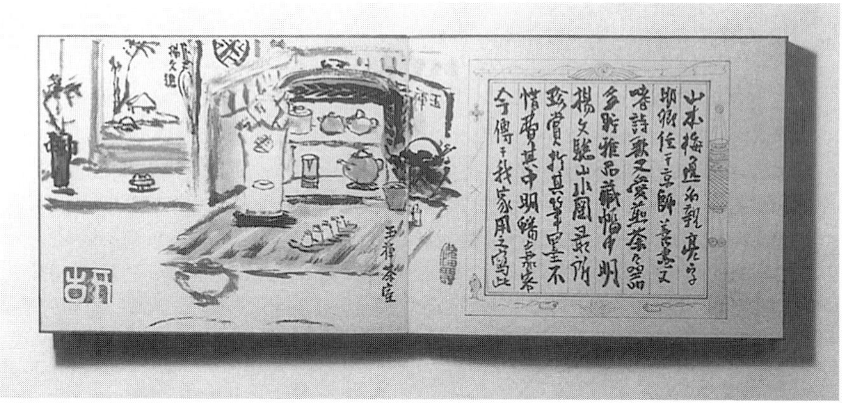

*Figure 5.7* Tomioka Tessai (1836–1924), sketch of Yamamoto Baiitsu's tea-room study, 1917, part of a larger work titled: *Leftover brushes of the way of ink [Bokuheki yohitsu].* Section of an album; ink on paper. Page size: 17.5 × 23.6 cm. Tatsuma City Archaeological Library.

*Figure 5.8* Chinese, stoneware brazier formerly owned by Yamamoto Baiitsu, seventeenth century, h. 27.6 cm. Izumi City Kuboso Art Museum, Eguchi collection.

Many of Baiitsu's paintings contain themes indicative of his interests in *sencha* and Chinese antiquities. An example is this painting of a *karamono* basket filled with flowers (Figure 5.10). Such flower arrangements played an integral role in *sencha* gatherings of the literati by conferring an air of refined elegance in Chinese taste (*fūryū*). The flowers have been arranged in a manner associated with literati taste, and the basket is obviously Chinese. By the mid-nineteenth century, when Baiitsu painted this picture, Chinese baskets had become requisite items in the tea rooms of *sencha* aficionados. As they became rarer and more difficult to acquire, expert Japanese craft makers began specializing in the production of close copies. This industry has continued to flourish up to the present day. For example, the basket in Baiitsu's painting closely resembles one by the Japanese

*Figure 5.9* Chinese, pewter-alloy tea caddy formerly owned by Yamamoto Baiitsu, seventeenth century, h. 8.6 cm. Izumi City Kuboso Art Museum, Eguchi collection.

basket-maker Tanabe Chikuhosai (1868–1945) (Figure 5.11), a member of the third generation of fine basketry crafts makers of Osaka.

Another person active as a leader in the literati *sencha* world of the first half of the nineteenth century was the literati painter, Tsubaki Chinzan (1801–1854). Unlike Mokubei and Baiitsu, he resided in Edo. A warrior by birth, his circle of acquaintances consisted largely of members of the same status group who shared his interest in Chinese literati culture. Chinzan and his friends participated in several *sencha* gatherings in the year 1838, for which they produced limited-edition, commemorative woodblock albums. One clearly shows the utensils used at these gatherings while the other illustrates the overall atmosphere.

*Figure 5.10* Yamamoto Baiitsu (1783–1856), *Flowers in a Chinese Basket*, 1849. Hanging scroll, ink and colors on silk. Former Yabumoto collection, Amagasaki; present whereabouts unknown.

The first album illustrates seven different styles of utensil arrangements. The page illustrated here (Figure 5.12) reveals how carefully these literati emulated Chinese precedents. The formal arrangement of the room with stools arranged around a table, a side table set up to hold the tea-serving utensils (enlarged on the left side of the picture), and an altar in the background flanked by curtains, is based on a drawing in a Chinese book about tea that was first published in Japan in 1829 (Figure 5.13).[19] Because some of the utensils pictured in the Chinese book differ from those in the Chinzan's print, it seems likely that his design illustrates an actual assemblage of utensils. As the picture lacks explanatory notes, it is difficult to know which of the tea implements is supposed to be Chinese, and which are Japanese-made wares inspired by Chinese models. Unquestionably, however, the two small loop-handled teapots to the left of the brazier on the top shelf of the table were Chinese Yixing wares, for Japanese potters had not yet perfected methods for reproducing them.

The second record of a *sencha* service illustrated by Chinzan is a small accordion-folded woodblock book (Figure 5.14). Guests are portrayed assembling in small groups, inspecting various tea utensils, painting pictures, and admiring completed artworks that have been spread out upon

*Figure 5.11* Tanabe Chikuhosai (1868–1945), *Flat Basket with Handle*. Bamboo and rattan. 43.2 × 50.8 cm. Photograph by Susan Einstein, collection of Lloyd E. Cotsen, USA.

the floor. This sort of gathering promoted appreciation of art in addition to tea, and served as the forerunner of many more elaborate, formal *sencha* tea gatherings that became the norm in later decades of the nineteenth century.

Like Baiitsu and other Sinophile scholars in the Kyoto–Osaka region, Chinzan and his friends collected Chinese paintings and antiquities which were displayed at exhibitions where *sencha* was served. One of the most important of these Edo collectors was the Confucian scholar and calligrapher, Ichikawa Beian (1778–1857), whose Chinese art collection was published in a catalogue in 1848. This collection included forty-three paintings now owned by the Tokyo National Museum, and several ancient Chinese bronzes, some of which scholars today consider forgeries.[20]

The third and final stage in the development of *sencha* taste for *karamono* lasted from about 1860 to 1900. Throughout this period, *sencha* gatherings continued to be forums for displays of Chinese arts, and these exhibited objects gradually replaced tea consumption as the main focus of attention. During this period greater quantities of *karamono* entered Japan, due to both increased interest on the part of Japanese collectors and

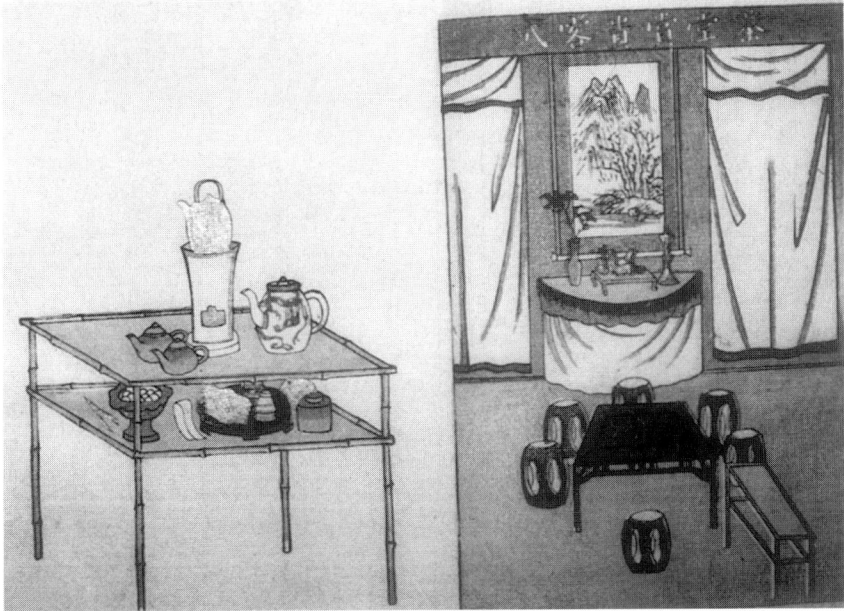

*Figure 5.12* Tsubaki Chinzan (1801–1854), page from an *Album of Sencha Utensil Arrangements*, 1838. Woodblock-printed, *surimono*-style book in ink, with colors, gold, and silver on paper, *c.* 26 × 32 cm. Private collection, Japan.

deteriorating economic and political conditions in China. Because of increased accessibility to materials, Japanese scholars and collectors were able to undertake more detailed connoisseurship studies of Chinese arts.[21] Collectors' knowledge and interest also inspired Japanese artisans to make reproductions of these Chinese crafts, especially ceramics, bronzes, and flower baskets. This period is thus marked by two contrasting trends. On the one hand, Japan's new elite – the class of wealthy merchants – began collecting *karamono* according to *sencha* taste. On the other hand, we find a popularization of *sencha* taste as Japanese reproductions of Chinese arts became more widely available.

From the beginning of this era, Sinophile scholars and Japanese literati painters continued to play leadership roles in determining the boundaries of *sencha* taste for *karamono*. Joining them as arbiters of taste and authorities on Chinese arts were the new breed of collectors mentioned above. After the demise of the Tokugawa government in 1868 and the formation of a new political and social system in the succeeding Meiji period (1868–1912), *sencha* enthusiasts came to include art dealers, businessmen, and politicians. In the active circle of *sencha* aficionados in the Kyoto–Osaka region, for example, we find examples of the former type,

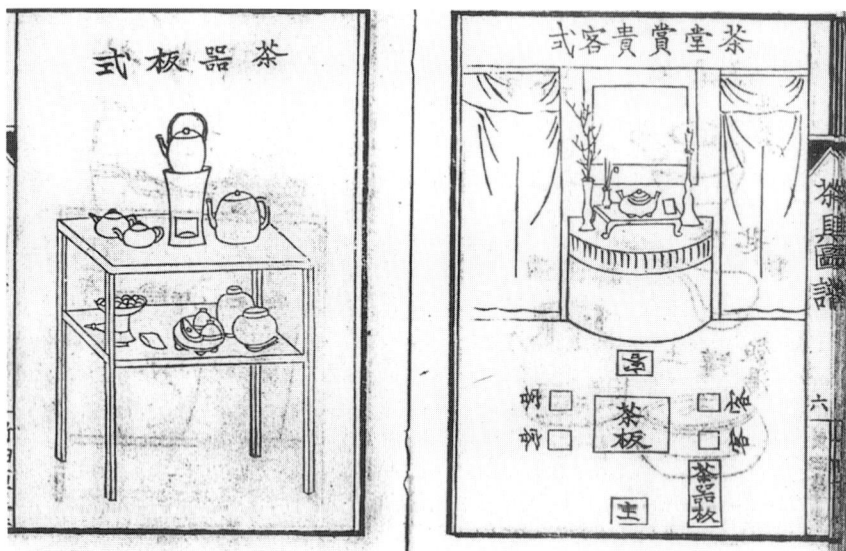

*Figure 5.13* Tanomura Chikuden (1777–1835), *Pictorial Album of Tea Utensils* (*Chagu zufu*), 1829. Woodblock book in ink on paper. 18 × 22 cm. Issa-an collection, Osaka, Japan.

*Figure 5.14* Tsubaki Chinzan (1801–1854), section of *A Small Sencha Gathering* (*Sencha shōshū*), 1838. Woodblock-printed accordion-folded book in ink and colors on paper, h. 12.4 cm. Private collection, Japan.

such as the literati painters and close friends Tanomura Chokunyū (1814–1907) and Tomioka Tessai; the proprietor of a distinguished stationery and incense shop in Kyoto, Kumagai Naotaka (1846–1875); and the Osaka art dealer Yamanaka Kichirōbei.[22] In the newly-renamed city of Tokyo, by contrast, we find examples of the latter merchant class who participated in *sencha* and collected Chinese art as a serious vocation: the wealthy businessman Oku Randen (1836–1897), and the shipping magnate Iwasaki Yanosuke (1851–1908; one of the early founders of the Mitsubishi conglomerate). All these men were actually acquaintances and participants in *sencha* services hosted by one another. They were also associates of yet another *sencha* devotee, Kido Takayoshi (1833–1877), one of the new era's most influential political leaders. Kido and other politicians of the new regime were partly responsible for turning these private *sencha* gatherings, with their obligatory displays of Chinese paintings and antiquities, into public art exhibitions. They used *sencha* gatherings as a vehicle for fostering appreciation of Chinese literati culture among the public, in whom they sought to instill values of civilization and enlightenment.

One of these public exhibitions, hosted by Chokunyū in 1874, took place in his hometown of Toyokuni in southern Japan. Over eight hundred people viewed Chinese *sencha* utensil and *karamono* displays over a three-day period. Chokunyū recorded the appearance of the galleries and made notations about each of the objects displayed in a set of three long handscrolls. The installation began with a room full of Chinese paintings and calligraphies (that also included a few Japanese literati paintings by masters of the early nineteenth century) (Figure 5.15), and then proceeded to a succession of seven other galleries, each adorned with an astonishing variety of elegant tea utensils, flower arrangements, scholars' writing accoutrements, other decorative objects, and paintings. One room (Figure 5.16) featured Chinese decorative arts arranged in a decorative alcove, reminiscent of the manner of displaying art objects at *chanoyu* gatherings. Another room was devoted exclusively to the display of scholars' writing implements and other objects found in scholars' studies (Figure 5.17). Its appearance was more exotic, with a tigerskin rug on the floor under a low Chinese table covered with a Chinese rug.

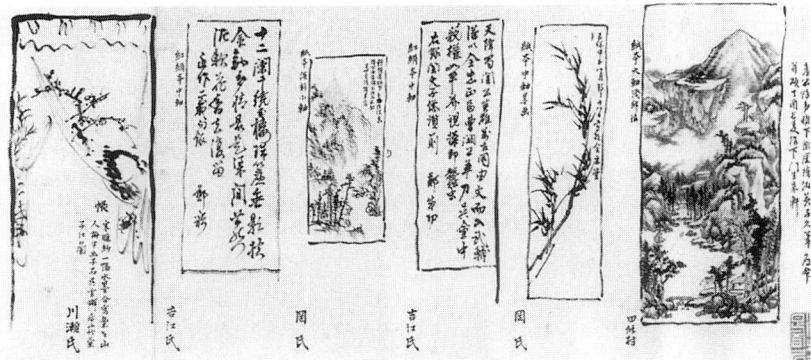

*Figure 5.15* Tanomura Chokunyū (1814–1907), *Chinese Painting Gallery*, section of: *A Record of a Sencha Tea Ceremony*, 1874. Section of one of a set of three handscrolls; ink and colors on paper, h. 26.7 cm., the Saint Louis Art Museum.

*Figure 5.16* Tanomura Chokunyū (1814–1907), *Display of Sencha Tea Utensils and Chinese Decorative Arts*, section of *A Record of a Sencha Tea Ceremony*, 1874. Section of one of a set of three handscrolls; ink and colors on paper, h. 26.7 cm., the Saint Louis Art Museum.

*Figure 5.17* Tanomura Chokunyū (1814–1907), *Display of Chinese Scholars' Accoutrements*, section of *A Record of a Sencha Tea Ceremony*, 1874. Section of one of a set of three handscrolls; ink and colors on paper, h. 26.7 cm., the Saint Louis Art Museum.

Although Kido and other politicians promoted these events, they left connoisseurship to experts such as Chokunyū and other serious collectors. One of these men was Kumagai Naotaka, who collected Chinese-style *sencha* utensils made by Aoki Mokubei,[23] as well as authentic Chinese arts and furnishings, such as this small wood and wicker cabinet (Figure 5.18). Another was the art dealer Yamanaka Kichirōbei, who authored perhaps Japan's first illustrated catalogue of an exhibition of Chinese antiquities in

*Figure 5.18* Chinese, eighteenth- or early nineteenth-century wood and wicker cabinet formerly owned by Kumagai Naotaka of the Kyūkyōdō shop. Tekisendō collection, Tokyo.

Osaka in 1874. These objects were displayed at another public *sencha* congregation that featured thirteen rooms, in which Chinese arts were displayed *in situ*. Chokunyū contributed illustrations to the book published in 1875 to commemorate this gathering, the *Pictorial Record of Famous Utensils Used at the Azure Sea Tea Gathering [Seiwan meien zushi]*. The page reproduced in Figure 5.19 contains a small cabinet similar in

*Figure 5.19* Tanomura Chokunyū (1814–1907), room one, from the *Pictorial Record of Famous Utensils Used at the Azure Sea Tea Gathering* [*Seiwan meien zushi*], 1875. Woodblock-printed book in ink on paper. Double page size: $17 \times 20$ cm. Private collection, USA.

appearance to that owned by Kumagai Naotaka (Figure 5.18). Pages of room illustrations were followed by pages of detailed drawings and descriptions of the most important objects displayed. The ancient Chinese bronze vessel filled with flowers (with its lid placed alongside it) that sits atop the cabinet, has been singled out (Figure 5.20). This type of connoisseurship study on Chinese art was a relatively recent phenomenon in Japan at the time, and seems to have been initiated under the auspices of *sencha* gatherings.

Perhaps the earliest focused study of a particular type of Chinese art was Tomioka Tessai's 1867 publication on Yixing wares, *Tessai's Tea Records* [*Tetsusō chafu*]. In the first volume of this two-volume text, Tessai illustrated various Chinese Yixing teapots (Figure 5.21), arranged by maker, followed by his translation into Japanese of an important Chinese treatise on Yixing wares.[24] The great desirability of Yixing ceramics among contemporaneous Japanese tea drinkers is evident from the increased imports of these wares, and from the efforts of Japanese potters to copy them. The unglazed, burnished surfaces of Yixing wares were thought to impart a better flavor to the tea. Japanese potters at the ceramics-production town of Tokoname, near Nagoya, began attempting to

*Figure 5.20* Tanomura Chokunyū (1814–1907), bronze vessel illustrated in room one, from the *Pictorial Record of Famous Utensils Used at the Azure Sea Tea Gathering* [*Seiwan meien zushi*], 1875. Woodblock-printed book in ink on paper. Single page size: 17 × 10 cm. Private collection, USA.

replicate Yixing ceramics from about 1854. They did not succeed until 1878, when they received assistance from Jin Shiheng (Japanese: Kin Shikō), an emigrant Chinese scholar and potter who had settled there the previous year.

Tessai's study was followed nine years later, in 1876, by another publication on Yixing ceramics. This book, the *Pictorial Record of Famous Tea Pots* [*Meiko zuroku*], was published in Tokyo, and authored by the merchant and politician Oku Randen. Large views of thirty-two teapots owned by Randen and his friends are provided (Figure 5.22),[25] arranged

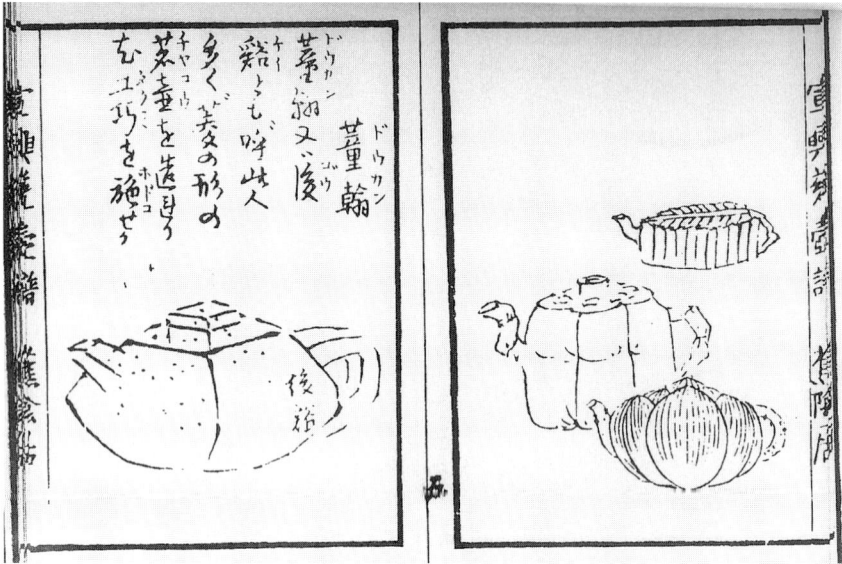

*Figure 5.21* Tomioka Tessai (1836–1924), page from *Tessai's Tea Records* [*Tetsusō chafu*], 1867. Woodblock-printed book; ink on paper. Double page size: 12.5 × 16 cm. Issa-an collection, Osaka, Japan.

here not by maker, but by color and shape, the method still used for classifying these wares in Japan today.

An exhibition completely devoted to Randen's own collection of Chinese antiquities appropriate for use and display at *sencha* tea services was held in Osaka in 1891. A catalogue, *Marvelous Treasures with Black Edges* [*Bokuen kishū*] was produced two years later, illustrated by the female literati painter Noguchi Shōhin (1847–1917).[26] Randen's preference for Chinese art in literati taste is clear from the catalogue, which includes Chinese paintings and calligraphies, as well as actual tea-serving implements and scholars' writing implements, with most works ranging in date from the fifteenth through eighteenth centuries (Ming and Qing dynasties). When he died in 1897, Randen bequeathed many of the Chinese teapots, paintings, and other antiquities illustrated in his published catalogues to the shipping magnate Iwasaki Yanosuke. They remain in his family's collection, now housed in the Seikadō Art Museum and Library (*Seikadō Bunko*) in Tokyo.[27]

By the time Iwasaki Yanosuke began to collect *sencha* paraphernalia and related Chinese literati arts, the canon of *karamono* materials considered appropriate for *sencha* had been clearly defined. Iwasaki, his son, and friends continued to participate in lavish *sencha* gatherings where these objects could be appropriately displayed. For the next two decades,

梨
皮
泥

士 居 中 藏

奥
蘭
田
蔵

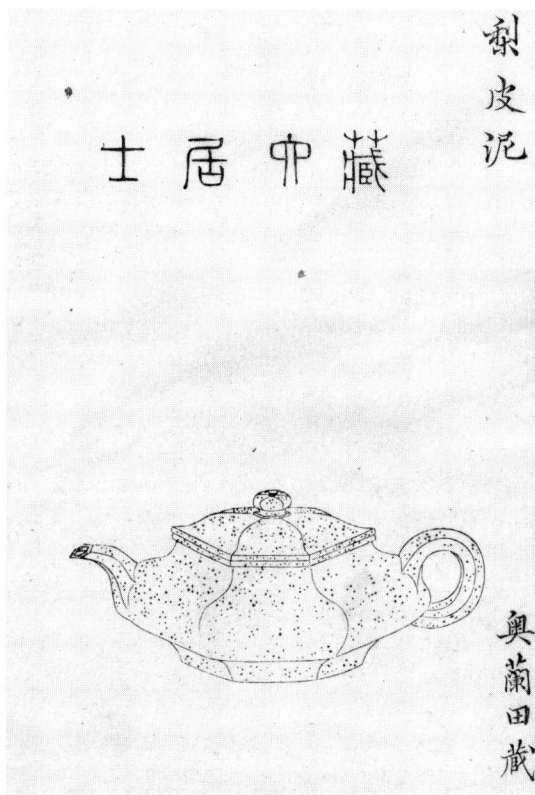

*Figure 5.22*  Line drawing of a Chinese Yixing ware teapot from the book *Pictorial Record of Famous Tea Pots* [*Meiko zuroku*], by Oku Randen. Nihonbashi (Tokyo): Isando, Meiji 9 (1876). 21 × 14 cm. From the Library of the Freer Art Gallery of Art and Arthur M. Sackler Gallery, Smithsonian Institution, Washington, DC.

they continued to hold *sencha* gatherings accompanied by formal displays of Chinese arts and paintings, either in Osaka or Tokyo. Many of these served as memorial services for deceased relatives and friends, either businessmen or prominent art dealers (such as Yamanaka Shunkōdō, father of Kichirōbei). These events rivaled similarly grand art exhibitions held in association with tea services for *chanoyu*, and hosted by another new industrialist, Masuda Takashi (1848–1938).[28] While Masuda also admired Chinese arts, he tended to favor arts of earlier periods that were more closely associated with orthodox *chanoyu* taste. These exhibitions reveal an interesting phenomenon, a legacy in Japan of associating appreciation for particular types of Chinese art with the aesthetics of tea-serving rituals.

## Conclusion

Aficionados of Japan's *sencha* tea ritual seem at first glance to have religiously attempted to follow orthodox Chinese literati taste in Chinese art. Like the Chinese they emulated, they admired literati paintings, Yixing ceramics, ancient Chinese bronzes, and other decorative objects – such as flower baskets – that were appropriate for display in scholars' studios. Nevertheless, limited access to imported Chinese materials impacted the breadth and quality of their collections. Negatively, this meant that the Japanese collections assembled by fans of *sencha* included mostly paintings of more recent vintage (the Ming and Qing dynasties), bronzes, and Yixing ceramics. By today's connoisseurship standards, we know that although some were undeniably first-rate, not all of these materials were always what they purported to be.

Although *sencha* developed in emulation of Chinese literati ideals, its practitioners were Japanese, not Chinese nationals. Thus, they inevitably incorporated aspects of their cultural heritage (in this case, the already established rituals of *chanoyu*) into their aesthetic preferences for *sencha*. They also adapted other Chinese materials to which they had access, such as humble stoneware kettles. So, on a positive note, limited access to Chinese literati objects encouraged emergence of an independent, unique aesthetic identity for *sencha* that allowed for the use of types of crafts not generally considered in orthodox literati taste in China. Furthermore, the scarcity of the material culture of the Chinese literati in Japan was a boon to producers of Japanese arts and crafts for *sencha*, as it encouraged the emergence of Japanese handicraft industries, especially those for ceramics and basketry in Chinese taste.

## Notes

1  For a detailed study of the history of the *sencha* tea ritual in English, see Patricia J. Graham, *Tea of the Sages: The Art of Sencha* (University of Hawai'i Press, 1998).

2  Information presented here on the taste for *karamono* as one component of the aesthetic of the *chanoyu* tea ritual is based on various sections in Paul Varley and Kumakura Isao (eds), *Tea in Japan: Essays on the History of Chanoyu* (University of Hawai'i Press, 1989) and Christine Guth, *Art, Tea, and Industry: Masuda Takashi and the Mitsui Circle* (Princeton University Press, 1993), pp. 46–54.

3  For general information, see Graham, *Tea of the Sages*, pp. 40 and 206 (n. 19); for a selection of imported *karamono* see Tokyo National Museum. *Tokubetsu ten: Muromachi jidai no bijutsu* (Tokyo Kokuritsu Hakubutsukan, 1989), especially sections III (*Karamono* and its influence) and IV (The development of the tea ceremony from *karamono* taste to *wabi* taste).

4  Varley and Kumakura (eds), *Tea in Japan*, p. 80. The reference is to a tea bowl once owned by Murata Shukō, and used by Sen no Rikyū.

5  From Varley and Kumakura (eds), *Tea in Japan*, essay by Sen Sōshitsu XV, "Reflections on *Chanoyu*," p. 236 (a reference to the sixteenth-century tea master Murata Shukō's predilection for the inclusion of select Chinese objects in an overtly Japanese tea room).

6  Guth, *Art, Tea, and Industry*, pp. 52–54.
7  This Owari Tokugawa collection is now housed in the Tokugawa Art Museum, Nagoya. The museum actively publishes specialized catalogues of its collections. Most are in Japanese, but several are written in English, and have accompanied touring exhibitions of the museum's treasures in the West. Of particular relevance to this study are the following: Tokugawa Art Museum (ed.), *Tokugawa Bijutsukan no meihin shirizu: Daimyo chadōgu ten* (Tokugawa Bijutsukan, 1991); and the Montreal Museum of Fine Arts (ed.), *The Tokugawa Collection: Japan of the Shoguns* (Montreal Museum of Fine Arts, 1989).
8  For illustrations of these wares, see Hayashiya Seizo *et al.*, *Chinese Ceramics from Japanese Collections: T'ang Through Ming Dynasties* (The Asia Society, 1977) and Kyoto Kokuritsu Hakubutsukan (ed.), *Nihonjin ga kononda Chūgoku tōji* (Kyoto Kokuritsu Hakubutsukan, 1991).
9  Information presented here on the history of Chinese flower baskets in Japan comes from: Patricia J. Graham, "The Appreciation of Chinese Flower Baskets in Premodern Japan," in Joseph N. Newland (ed.), *Japanese Bamboo Baskets: Masterworks of Form and Texture* (Cotsen Occasional Press, 1999), pp. 60–83. For a more detailed discussion of the importation of Chinese baskets during the sixteenth and seventeenth centuries, and illustrations of many handed down in the collections of famous *chanoyu* tea practitioners, see Ikeda Hyōa, "*Take kago no hanaire*," in Nakamura Masao *et al.* (eds), *Chadōgu I*, vol. 10 of *Chadō shūkin* (Shogakkan, 1986), pp. 94–102.
10  One is illustrated in Graham, *Tea of the Sages*, p. 57 (Figure 9).
11  For further discussion of these utensils and an illustration of the scroll, see Graham, *Tea of the Sages*, pp. 78–82.
12  The term "kōchi" is the Japanese name for Cochin (Vietnam), where tea practitioners erroneously thought this ceramic ware was manufactured.
13  The books are entitled *Shokumoku rinrō* (1852) and *Dōge yokun* (1863). On Baiitsu's knowledge of Chinese painting, including lists from these catalogues of the paintings he and his friends owned, see Patricia J. Graham, "Yamamoto Baiitsu no Chūgokuga kenkyū," *Kobijutsu* 80 (Fall 1986), pp. 62–75. For general information on Chinese painting exhibitions in Edo period Japan, see Graham, *Tea of the Sages*, pp. 115–123.
14  The painting, today owned by the Tōyama Art Museum in Saitama Prefecture, Japan, is dated 1643. It is illustrated in Harada Kinjirō (ed.), *Shina meiga hō kan* (Otsuka Kogeisha, 1936), Plate 696.
15  Kanematsu Romon, *Chikutō to Baiitsu* (Gahōsha, 1910), p. 225.
16  For two other sketches of Baiitsu's tea room brushed by Baiitsu himself, see Graham, *Tea of the Sages*, p. 109 (Figure 26).
17  This is illustrated in Shufu no Tomosha, *Gendai senchadō jiten* (Shufu no Tomosha, 1981), p. 234, middle photo.
18  Mokubei's pot is illustrated in Graham, *Tea of the Sages*, p. 131 (Figure 38).
19  The book is the *Pictorial Album of Tea Utensils* [*Chagu zu fu*], abridged and adapted for publication by Tanomura Chikuden (1777–1835). For more on this book, see Graham, *Tea of the Sages*, p. 227.
20  Beian's catalogue is titled *Catalogue of Shōsanrindō's Collection of Painting, Calligraphy, and Scholars' Accoutrements* [*Shōsanrindō shoga bunbō zuroku*]. For illustrations of the paintings, see Tokyo National Museum (ed.), *Tōkyō Kokuritsu Hakubutsukan zuhan mokuroku Chūgoku kaiga hen* (Tōkyō Kokuritsu Hakubutsukan, 1979). For assessment of the bronzes, see Thomas Lawton, "Chinese Ritual Bronzes: Collections and Catalogues Outside Japan," in Steven D. Owyoung, *Ancient Chinese Bronzes in the Saint Louis Art Museum* (Saint Louis Art Museum, 1997), pp. 17 and 29 (n. 6).

21  Not only did greater quantities of Chinese arts enter Japan at this time, so did large numbers of Chinese painters fleeing the chaos of their home country. These developments encouraged the assemblage of new collections of Chinese arts – including later literati painting, Chinese ceramics, bronzes, and Buddhist sculpture – among collectors unaffiliated with either with *chanoyu* or *sencha* circles. To say more on this here exceeds the scope of this chapter. For additional information, see Miyazaki Noriko, "Nihon kindai no naka no Chūgoku kaigashi kenkyū," in Tokyo National Research Institute of Cultural Properties (ed.), *Ima, Nihon no bijutsushi gaku o furikaeru* (Tōkyō Kokuritsu Bunkazai Kenkyūjo, 1999), pp. 140–153 (English summary on pp. 26–28).

22  For more on the legacy of the Yamanaka company as a purveyor of Chinese and Japanese art in the West, see Thomas Lawton, "Yamanaka Sadajirō: Advocate for Asian Art," *Orientations* 26:1 (January 1995): 80–93.

23  For an illustration of his set of Mokubei utensils now owned by the Tokyo National Museum, see Graham, *Tea of the Sages*, color plate 5.

24  For more information about Tessai's book, see Graham, *Tea of the Sages*, p. 228.

25  For an illustration of the actual pot in the drawing for Figure 6.19, see Seikadō Bunko Bijutsukan (ed.), *Seikadōzō senchagu meihin ten* (Seikadō Bunko, 1998), p. 50 (Figure 66-3).

26  This catalogue is reproduced in ibid., pp. 134–139.

27  For illustrations of many of these, see ibid.

28  On Masuda's art-collecting and tea-party hosting proclivities, see Guth, *Art, Tea and Industry*.

# 6 Tea of the warrior in the late Tokugawa period

*Tanimura Reiko*

## Introduction

In the many volumes of scholarship written on Japanese tea culture, little information can be found on the tea of the late Tokugawa period, particularly the activities of warrior tea practitioners. The most thoroughly researched period is the end of Sen no Rikyū's age, the epoch of "inferior overthrows superior" (*gekokujō*). In that time of social chaos, wealthy commoner merchants like Rikyū led developments in the world of *chanoyu*. Rikyū, of course, was forced to commit suicide in 1591, just one year after the unification of Japan by Toyotomi Hideyoshi. After that symbolic event, leadership in tea was transferred from elite commoners to elite warrior tea masters. After the destruction of the Toyotomi house in 1615, the Tokugawa house established a political structure in which power was balanced between the central Tokugawa government and regional domain authorities. Loyalty was transferred to the person of the hegemon, the Tokugawa Shogun. Commoner tea masters in the Tokugawa period, though still influential, depended on elite warriors for their livelihood and status.

The Tokugawa regime required a form of tea practice that was appropriate to the new social hierarchy, a form of tea for the warrior status group distinct from Rikyū's tea. The warrior tea masters Furuta Oribe (1543–1615) and Kobori Enshu (1579–1647), for example, came to dominate the leadership of the *chanoyu* world after Rikyū, but perhaps the most successful warrior tea master was Katagiri Sekishū (1605–1673). Sekishū acquired pre-eminence in 1665 under the fourth Shogun, Ietsuna, and established a new style of tea practice for the warrior class. Other famous warrior tea masters were Matsudaira Sadanobu (1758–1829) whose tea was more highly politicized, Matsudaira Fumai (1751–1818), Sakai Sōga (1755–1790), and Ii Naosuke (1815–1860).

This chapter will consider warrior tea practice in the eighteenth and nineteenth centuries, focusing on the common bonds between Fumai, Sōga and Naosuke. The case of Naosuke is particularly revealing. He was a famous tea master of the Sekishū school as well as the most powerful politician of his age, the last Great Elder (*tairo*) of the Tokugawa regime. He is well known as a headstrong political leader who signed treaties permitting international trade without the approval of the imperial court, and who instigated the Ansei purge. His tea practice, on the other hand, has been highly esteemed as "tea for meditation" and "tea for moral improvement." It would thus appear that Naosuke had two distinct personalities. Put another way, he has conventionally been evaluated either in the context of political history or in the context of cultural history, but not holistically. This chapter seeks to provide a new framework for the study of Ii Naosuke and warrior tea by connecting his cultural and political activities. This will be accomplished by placing a famous book written by Naosuke between 1856 and 1857, *Collection for a Tea Gathering* [*Chanoyu ichie shū*], in historical context. Also, analysis of forty-four tea gatherings held by Naosuke between 1851 and 1860 will help to illuminate his activities. Close consideration of Naosuke and his fellow warrior tea practitioners will clarify the social function of *chanoyu*, and allow us to locate intersections between tea and politics in the late Tokugawa period.

## The history of warrior tea

Before entering into a detailed discussion of warrior tea, we must clarify our conception of the warrior in early modern Japan. The words "*buke*" or "*bushi*" are usually translated into English as warrior. We must, however, distinguish between the two. "*Bushi*" can be understood to refer to the social status of being a warrior, passed down within a house. "*Buke*," on the other hand, refers to the ruling social class, in other words elite politicians and bureaucrats with individual consciousness of their social status.[1] These two concepts of course overlap in many instances, and therefore the generic term "warrior" will be used throughout this chapter, supplemented by modifiers such as "elite" when necessary. It is interesting to note, however, that Naosuke referred to himself using the term "*buke*" but not "*bushi*," reflecting his awareness of his position in the social hierarchy, and his concern with establishing a model warrior culture.[2]

To begin, we will examine the history of elite warrior tea masters and the development of a distinct warrior style of tea practice. Rikyū was a member of the commoner elite, a creative artist who transformed the meaning of *wabi* and wished to create a symbolic world in tea. It is well known that elite warriors and elite commoners sat together "democratically" without attention to status differences at Rikyū's tea gatherings. Numerous domainal lords, for example, sought to become Rikyū's disciples. This is borne out by the list of his leading disciples at the time of his death, known as the "seven sages" (*shichi-tetsu*), which consists entirely of warriors. Rikyū's death, however, and the conflict that it represents, can be said to symbolize the end of the epoch in which elite commoners autonomously transformed tea practice. After Rikyū, warrior tea practitioners such as Furuta Oribe (1543–1615), who was a disciple of Rikyū, came to prominence. Oribe's tea utensils, called "oddities" (*hyogemono*) and "improperly fired" (*yakisokonai*), revealed that his tea retained a *gekokujō* flavor that went against the trend of the times. He, too, was driven to suicide by the ruling hegemon of the day. After Oribe, his disciple Kobori Enshū (1579–1647) who served in a number of posts for the Tokugawa government, became well known for his pursuit of the aesthetic of "refined beauty" (*kireisabi*).

Largely as a result of the influential stature of Oribe and Enshū, members of Japan's elite warrior class were required to master tea and sophisticated manners in addition to the martial arts. This is similar to the European concept of a rounded education for young soldier aristocrats. Sir Thomas Elyot (1490–1546), for example, said in *The Boke Named the Governour* that soldiers, having become the newly self-conscious gentry, needed a proper education in order to rule. In addition to training in martial arts and literature, they had to learn dancing, music, and other cultural forms. Cultivation of this sort would allow young rulers to conduct themselves so that the governed would develop a sense of social responsibility and respect for hierarchy.[3]

Yamaga Sokō (1622–1685), like Elyot in sixteenth-century England, had a number of suggestions for "warriors," who as a status group no longer needed to fight as an occupation. Sokō proposed that warriors should devote themselves both to self-cultivation (*shushin*) and to state governance (*chikoku heitenka*). According to his doctrine, social courtesies – in other words distinctive modes of conduct – would lead to the development of the ideal character for members of the warrior status group. Sokō constructed a new identity for warriors and demanded that they be distinctive mentally and physically, and serve both as political and ethical models for the common people. Sokō's approach proved to be very popular among members of the warrior class during the Tokugawa period.

Sokō's doctrine satisfied the need of the Tokugawa government for a warrior-specific tea practice. The warrior tea master who first injected the notion of spirituality into his tea practice was Katagiri Sekishū (1605–1673), who was born in the Izumi domain and succeeded to the position of domainal lord. He learned tea from Kuwayama Sōsen, a warrior tea master who in turn had learned tea from Dōan, Rikyū's son by blood though not his officially designated successor.[4] Therefore Sekishū and his followers argued that their tradition derived from the authentic heir of Rikyū's tea practice. Sekishū was a successful tea master and received great honor from the fourth Tokugawa Shogun, Ietsuna. Sekishū's style of tea practice was particularly popular at the elite level of warrior society. He emphasized suitable forms and a high spirituality that was imbued with the spirit of Zen Buddhism. It thus gave warriors a means of cultivating their manners, spirituality, and knowledge of the material culture of tea.

## Matsudaira Sadanobu, Matsudaira Fumai, and Sakai Sōga

The Edo Senke school of tea was founded in 1750 by Kawakami Fuhaku (1719–1807), a warrior from the Kii domain who was a close disciple of the seventh head of the Omotesenke tea school, Sen Joshinsai (1705–1751). Edo Senke became so popular in Edo that large numbers of elite warriors switched their allegiance from the Sekishū school to Edo Senke. It was thus natural that some warrior tea practitioners thought that the increasing prosperity of the Sen tea schools threatened the existence of Sekishū's tea, and by extension warrior tea as a whole. Matsudaira Sadanobu (1758–1829), for example, who became the chief minister of state in 1787, wrote several essays on tea culture after his retirement. He discussed tea from a Confucian standpoint in terms of the highest level of Tokugawa society. He proclaimed that *chanoyu* tea practice was an opportunity to confirm one's social status (*bungen*) and to affirm the legitimacy of the state.[5] In part his antipathy towards Sen tea may also have derived from his dislike for the notorious previous chief minister, Tanuma Okitsugu, who had a close relationship with Edo Senke.

Two additional warrior leaders who contributed to the development of warrior tea in this period were Matsudaira Fumai (1751–1818), domainal lord of Matsue, and Sakai Sōga (1755–1790), domainal lord of Himeji. Fumai was well known as a model ruler who restructured the finances of his domain. He was also a prominent collector and researcher of tea utensils. He devoted himself to the classification of utensils in his study, *Various Collected Famous Objects from All Ages* [*Kokon meibutsu ruiju*]. Fumai's objective and reliable ranking of tea utensils was a guide for tea practitioners. His comment in this book that famous objects (*meibutsu*) should belong neither to individuals nor to single houses was implicitly a criticism of the Sen schools. In his view, famous objects were world treasures. In a critical essay titled *Remarks on Extravagance* [*Muda goto*] he further explained the tie between social and political elements in tea, remarking that proper tea practice would bring harmony to society in the manner of Confucian rituals and music imported from China.[6]

Although Fumai himself was not interested in establishing his own school of tea, some elite warriors called themselves his disciples. Sakai Sōga (1755–1790), lord of the Himeji domain, was one of these elite warrior tea masters.[7] Like Fumai, Sōga considered himself a member of the Sekishū school. Also like Fumai, Sōga felt that spirituality was paramount in tea practice. Sōga established a regular tea salon that was patronized by powerful members of Tokugawa society such as domainal lords and aristocrats from the Kyoto court, as well as educated commoners such as artists and Noh performers. Sōga did not, however, regard *chanoyu* as a leisure pastime (*yūgei*). He traced the origins of the *kaiseki* meal during the tea gathering to the ascetic diet practices at Zen monasteries (*gyo-taku shiki*), emphasizing the meal as a spiritual rather than simply a pleasurable repast.[8]

It is also interesting to note that both Fumai and Sōga placed great stock on the teachings contained in the tea text *Nampōroku*. It has long been accepted that this text is the main scripture of Rikyū's tea practice, ostensibly discovered by a warrior tea practitioner named Tachibana Jitsuzan in the late seventeenth century. Recent studies, however, suggest that it may have been constructed by Jitsuzan himself. While the text epitomizes tea's obsession with Buddhist asceticism and the aesthetics of rustic tea (*wabicha*), its great underlying theme is the spirituality of tea practice. One scholar suggests the following about *Nampōroku*: "A retainer of the Kuroda domain of Hakata, Jitsuzan saw Rikyū through the eyes of a samurai of the late seventeenth century (*Genroku-jidai*)."[9] *Nampōroku* was not a particularly common book in the Tokugawa period; some branches of the Sekishū school even regarded it as a secret text to be passed from master to disciple.[10] Fumai commented that he would not mention the contents of the *Nampōroku* to anyone, even a disciple of the same school.[11] The belief that spirituality of the sort described in *Nampōroku* was the fundamental core of warrior tea was shared by both these men, as well as by the tea master who most clearly articulated the importance of tea practice in warrior society, Ii Naosuke.

## Ii Naosuke: the Umoreginoya period (1831–1848)

Naosuke was born in 1815, the fourteenth son of Ii Naonaka, lord of the Hikone domain, which for 200 years was one of the largest domains in Japan. In the houses of domainal lords, the eldest son was expected to succeed his father as ruler. Some of the younger sons may have been fortunate enough to be adopted by other domainal lords, but most were set up in separate residences (*heyasumi*) and consigned to a life of obscurity and relative poverty on a meager stipend. Although Naosuke's father had already retired before Naosuke's birth, Naosuke lived in his father's magnificent mansion until his father died when Naosuke was 16. During these happy years with his father, Naosuke acquired a basic education in the various arts of a young member of the warrior elite. With his father's death, Naosuke was immediately obliged to move to a small, separate residence outside Hikone Castle. He named his tiny dwelling the "House of the Buried Wood" (Umoreginoya). Needless to say, it was in stark contrast to his former life in residence with his father. At the age of 20 Naosuke composed a statement, *Record of the House of the Buried Wood* [*Umoreginoya no Ki*], which expresses the essence of his outlook on life. "Even if I am a piece of buried wood, and denied all material things and a future, I shall continue to cultivate those arts required by my station."[12]

Although a deep resentment is apparent in these words, Naosuke's self-cultivation and strong identity as a member of the elite military class (*buke*) prevented him from wallowing in despair. Instead of lamenting his fate, Naosuke devoted himself to a variety of physical, mental, and spiritual pursuits during his fifteen reclusive years in the Umoreginoya: spear handling, fencing, archery, strategy, meditation, poetry, Noh, *kyogen*, national learning (*kokugaku*) and especially tea. Towards the end of his time in the Umoreginoya, Naosuke, who was critical of popular tea practice as an elegant pastime (*yūgei*) and a threat to warrior tea, proclaimed his desire to establish his own branch of the Sekishū school.[13] In this declaration, titled *Primer* [*Nyumon-ki*], Naosuke argues that tea plays a role in self-composure and in maintaining peace throughout the nation, if not the world. Like Sadanobu and Fumai before him, Naosuke argues that tea practice contributes both to self-cultivation (*shushin*) and to state governance (*chikoku hei tenka*).[14] Naosuke, who lived on a meager stipend and did not possess any social influence, was concerned about the collapse of warrior-class tea and the disintegration of the warrior spirit in general. He continued to hold these concerns as his position became more influential in the government in the latter half of his life.

## Ii Naosuke: heir apparent

One of Naosuke's brothers, the designated successor to the house of Hikone, unexpectedly died in 1846. Naosuke was called to Edo immediately and selected as heir. For the next four years the domainal lord of Hikone – Naosuke's elder brother Naoaki – isolated Naosuke from the vassals of the Ii house out of stubbornness and ill will. Naosuke lacked funds and faced considerable distress in this period,[15] but he continued various pursuits including tea practice. He began sending questions on tea to Katagiri Sōen (1775–1864), a descendant of Sekishū. Included in this correspondence were several essays on tea by Naosuke. Among a number of interesting items, Naosuke's concern with the *kaiseki* meal emerges as a particular characteristic of his tea practice.[16]

The *kaiseki* meal is one of the main components of a formal tea gathering, which can be divided into four parts: (1) entering the tea room; (2) the *kaiseki* meal and charcoal arranging; (3) intermission; and (4) service of thick tea followed by service of thin tea. Like Sōga, Naosuke viewed the *kaiseki* meal as the spiritual cornerstone of the tea gathering. In accordance with the rules of conduct in Zen monasteries (*shingi*), he demanded that his guests follow a strict code of manners. They should repeat the names of the Buddha and use special utensils when partaking of the *kaiseki* meal. For Naosuke, the meal was a religious act or exercise (*gyō* or *samskara*). In other religions fasting is commonly regarded as a form of religious practice, but Naosuke wanted to emphasize the spirit of Zen Buddhism during the stage of eating.

Although Naosuke's emphasis on the *kaiseki* meal was stronger during his years as heir apparent than later in his life, he never lost his particular concern with the role of this repast. In his writings, for example, he consistently wrote the phrase "*kaiseki*" using the Chinese characters that literally translate as "warming stone" rather than the more commonly used homophone "party meal." The former phrase literally refers to the stone put in the breast pocket for the purpose of withstanding hunger in cold weather in Zen monasteries. In his later writings Naosuke describes a tea gathering to which he invited a powerful domainal lord with whom he was in disagreement over a public works project; it is interesting to note that because the discussion at the gathering was political, Naosuke refers to the meal as "*ryōri*" (cuisine) rather than *kaiseki*.[17] This is the only occurrence of a meal not named *kaiseki* in Naosuke's records, and provides us with some clue of the degree to which he valued the subdued and spiritual nature of the meal.

The term "*kaiseki*" (written with the Chinese characters meaning "party meal") can be found as early as the 1589 document, *Record of Yamanoue Sōji* [*Yamanoue Sōjiki*],[18] composed by a disciple of Rikyū and described by Slusser in Chapter 2 in this volume. The phrase also appears in *Three Hundred Articles of Sekishū* [*Sekishū sanbyaku kajo*], collated by Sekishū's disciples after his death in 1673.[19] The phrases "cuisine" and "party meal" appear in the 1687 *Grass of Izumi* [*Izumigusa*][20] and the 1695 text *Anthology* [*Moshihogusa*].[21] We find the phrases "party meal" and "serving" (*furumai*) in the tea diaries of various warrior tea practitioners.[22] "Party meal" also appears numerous times over the course of twenty years in the diary of an aristocrat, Konoe Iehiro.[23] It is commonly assumed among tea practitioners today that the Sen schools used the characters meaning "warming stone" rather than "party meal" to describe *kaiseki*, but the latter appears in the writings of Kōshin Sōsa, discussed elsewhere in this volume.[24] Another term used by Kōshin, as well as by a disciple of Sen Sōtan, Yamada Sōhen, is "meal" (*zen*), which literally means tray. Sōhen also refers to the meal with the more common term "*meshi*."[25] Kawakami Fuhaku, founder of the Edo Senke school, also used phrases such as "party meal," "*meshi*," and "*zen*" in his book *Notes of Fuhaku* [*Fuhaku hikki*] (1757).[26] Perhaps the ultimate example of the Sen school propensity to use the phrase "party meal" rather than "warming stone" is the record of the two hundredth memorial tea gathering for Rikyū, in which we find the characters "party meal."

The first usage of the characters "warming stone" to represent *kaiseki*, on the other hand, is found in *Nampōroku*.[27] It only appears three times in that document, however, while other appellations such as *ryōri* (meal) or *chauke-ryōri* (meal for tea), or alternatively simply writing the menu without giving this segment of the gathering a name, are used for normal meals at tea gatherings. The meaning of the use of the special characters "warming stone" is not explicitly explained in the text. It has been suggested by scholars that Naosuke was influenced by *Nampōroku* in his method of writing the word *kaiseki*, but I would argue that his attitude toward the meaning represents his own philosophy. In an undated essay titled *Explanation of kaiseki* [*Kaiseki no ben*], Naosuke rejects the use of the characters "party meal" for *kaiseki*, and argues the following:

The usage of "warming stone" for *kaiseki* is found in *chanoyu* only. The origin of this phrase is the medical stone [*yakuseki*] or monk's snack [*tenshin*] at Zen monasteries. *Kaiseki* has the same meaning as warming stone or medical stone.[28]

For Naosuke, therefore, using "warming stone" to write *kaiseki* symbolized that the meal was both physically and spiritually sustaining rather than merely entertaining.

## Naosuke as domainal lord (1850–1860): the composition of *Collection for a Tea Gathering*

In 1850, Naosuke's older brother died suddenly, propelling the once-ignored fourteenth son into the position of lord of Hikone. Initially Naosuke's work kept him from authoring more tea-related tracts. Seven years after assuming political power, however, he authored his most famous work, *Collection for a Tea Gathering* [*Chanoyu ichie shū*]. This text represents Naosuke's interpretation of the sentiment of Rikyū, and clearly shows the influence of the text *Nampōroku*. *Nampōroku* emphasizes plainness, simplicity, and equality in the tea room, and Naosuke also wrote on the disguised humbleness of the so-called grass-hut style of tea. The text is particularly well known for two concepts: the notion of "one time, one meeting" (*ichigo ichie*) and the importance of sitting alone in meditation (*dokuza kannen*). Despite the fact that the book devotes only one chapter each to these two subjects (out of a total of twenty-three chapters), scholars have long considered this book to be above all a work on the philosophy of tea. It will be argued here, however, that these two key chapters need to be reinterpreted, particularly in light of the content of the remaining twenty-one chapters.

Naosuke begins the first chapter, "One time, one meeting" as follows:

This book deals with the handling of a tea gathering, giving in detail the knowledge necessary for both host and guests. For this reason I have entitled it *Collection for a Tea Gathering*. Great attention must be paid to the tea gathering, to which we can refer as "one time, one meeting" (*ichigo ichie*). Even though the host and guests may see each other often socially, one day's gathering can never be repeated exactly. Viewed this way, the meeting is indeed a once-in-a-lifetime occasion. The host, accordingly, must in true sincerity take the greatest care with every aspect of the gathering and devote himself entirely to ensuring that nothing is rough. The guests, for their part, must understand that the gathering cannot occur again, and appreciating how the host has flawlessly planned it, must also participate with true sincerity. This is what is meant by "one time, one meeting."[29]

The phrase "one time, one meeting" indicates awareness that a particular tea gathering can never be repeated, inspiring the host and guests to respect each other and establish a sort of partnership that can be perceived as an existing whole.

At the beginning of his chapter on sitting alone in meditation, by comparison, Naosuke offers the following:

> After host and guests have expressed their feelings of regret (*yojo zanshin*) and after the final farewells have been said, the guests depart through the garden. They do not call out in loud voices, but turn silently for one last look. The host, moved, watches them until they are gone from sight. It would not do for him to rush about closing the various doors, for this would make the day's entertainment meaningless. Even though it is impossible to see the guests returning to their homes, the host should not put things in order quickly. Rather, he should return quietly to the setting of the tea gathering and, crawling through the crouching entrance (*nijiriguchi*), seat himself before the hearth. Wishing to speak a while longer with his guests, he must wonder how far they have gotten on their ways home. This "one time, one meeting" has come to an end, and the host reflects upon the fact that it can never be repeated. The highest point of a tea meeting is, in fact, to have a cup of tea alone at this time. All is quiet, and the host can talk to no one but the kettle. This is a state in which nothing else exists, a state that cannot be known unless one has truly attained it oneself.[30]

The conventional explanation of this passage is that Naosuke is suggesting that the host seek Zen enlightenment through the tea gathering and its aftermath. However, the purpose of sitting alone is not only meditation. Three aspects of *dokuza kannen* are stressed in the book: (1) reflecting on the singular nature of the gathering; (2) enjoying a cup of tea alone as a release from the toils of the phenomenal world; and (3) understanding the kettle itself as a symbol of absolute reality. Naosuke thus was able to combine the spiritual and material elements of the tea room in the single concept of pure consciousness.

The remaining twenty-one chapters, which occupy the majority of the book, are a meticulous guide to correct conduct during the tea gathering. After stating his basic goal in the opening chapter on "one time, one meeting," Naosuke explains each stage of holding a tea gathering. He begins with the proper way to write an invitation letter, and ends with a guide to writing the requisite letter of thanks. Another important topic is how to deal with presents received from guests. The book is particularly detailed in its descriptions of what would normally be considered unconscious behavior: walking, bending forward, opening doors, and so on. The book as a whole is therefore a manual of practical manners for the warrior class organized around tea practice. While Naosuke describes a general philosophy of tea in the famous opening and closing chapters, his primary goal is to prescribe the manners, rituals, and forms of tea for warriors.

Furthermore, comparison of early manuscripts of the text make it clear that the two philosophical chapters were elaborately checked, compared, and added at the final stage.[31] When Naosuke began writing *Collection for a Tea Gathering*, his goal was to set out principles for grass-hut tea gatherings at which warriors would participate, as well as to describe various practical matters for warrior tea. By the final stage of his writing, however, Naosuke had progressed to a deeper understanding of the theory and purpose of warrior tea. He took the opportunity to clarify the spirit that should be at the core of warrior conduct. Describing warrior tea practice in such detail allowed Naosuke to establish a distinctive code of normative warrior behavior.

It should also be mentioned that Naosuke described proper tea gathering behavior for female members of the warrior status group, and invited women to attend his own tea gatherings. Historical records indicate that it was quite rare for warrior women to participate in tea gatherings with men during the Tokugawa period, and very few tea texts of the period address women's practice.[32] Naosuke, however, seems to have been influenced again by *Nampōroku*'s injunction that at an ideal tea gathering every guest was to be treated impartially regardless of rank. He interpreted this, however, within his own practical understanding of strict warrior hierarchy.

Forty-one passages in *Collection for a Tea Gathering* refer to the special treatment to be afforded to high-ranking warriors and nobles at tea gatherings. It is something of a contradiction to refer to the equal treatment of guests and the special treatment of elite guests in the same book, but we can interpret this as Naosuke's attempt to apply idealistic concepts to everyday realities. As a political leader, Naosuke had to be concerned in maintaining the hierarchy of the Tokugawa regime. In his tea practice, however, it is clear that Naosuke divided his gatherings into two types: those in accord with the principles of grass-hut tea, and those that were dominated by power politics.

## Naosuke's tea gatherings

After his succession to the position of domainal lord in 1850, Naosuke began to record details of tea gatherings that he hosted. Records exist covering over 170 gatherings that he hosted or attended until the last one on 19/2/1860. Of particular interest are the forty-four tea gatherings that he hosted between 2/11/1851 and 19/1/1860.[33] Despite his ability to conceptualize tea practice in his writings, he struggled to realize his ideals in the tea room. His records illustrate the conflicts between the reality of his political existence and the principles he hoped to establish in the field of warrior tea.

For the first gathering in his records, Naosuke invited older, lower ranking vassals whom he had known since his days as a youth at Umoreginoya. This seems to have been a quiet gathering among friends, a true example of "one time, one meeting." The final gathering in his records, by contrast, was held amidst the great political and social chaos of 1860, just two months before his assassination. In 1858, Naosuke had signed treaties permitting international trade without the approval of the imperial court, provoking great criticism. He responded with the Ansei Purge, arresting and in some cases executing his critics in government and the court. Relations between the Tokugawa government and the imperial court deteriorated to their lowest point in centuries. This formed the context for Naosuke's last tea gathering.

The guests at this gathering consisted of Naosuke's eldest son, Aimaro, and a number of Naosuke's disciples. Most interesting is the calligraphy that Naosuke chose to hang in the alcove, written by the Emperor Reigen (r. 1663–1687). This piece intentionally symbolized a key political negotiation of the mid-nineteenth century, the proposed marriage of the Shogun's heir apparent, Iemochi, to the imperial princess Kazunomiya. Using poetry by Emperor Reigen harkened back to the last time that an imperial princess was engaged to a Shogun or Shogun-to-be. Emperor Reigen's daughter, Yasomiya, had been engaged to Shogun Ietsugu in 1715. The engagement was not fulfilled because Ietsugu died the next year, but it illustrated the more amiable relations between the Tokugawa and the court in that era. Naosuke's use of Reigen's calligraphy demonstrates his desire to re-establish a close political relationship, information that cannot be found in government documents or contemporary accounts of the period.

The variety of guests that appear in Naosuke's records suggests the degree to which the tea room became a site of political networking. The guests at the forty-four gatherings analyzed here may be classified into four categories: Buddhist monks (6); warrior associates of Naosuke (23); women (2); domainal lords and tea specialists (*sukiyabōzu*) (8); and tea specialists alone (5). The Buddhist monk and warrior associates who attended Naosuke's gatherings were primarily friends from his youth, as we saw at his first recorded gathering, or family and vassals, as we saw at his last. The women participants were also family: one guest was his mother-in-law and the other his wife.[34] The eight domainal lords (one was actually heir apparent) who attended Naosuke's tea gatherings were all of the highest rank, those who were seated in the Tamarinoma area of Edo Castle on official occasions (*tamarinoma zume*). Tea specialists from Edo Castle also attended Naosuke's tea gatherings when domainal lords were in attendance. These specialists were active as political conspirators and informers behind the scenes in the Tokugawa government. They were important sources of information for Naosuke, providing news of other domainal lords and governmental officers,[35] and he rewarded them amply.

At one gathering held at Hikone Castle in the fifth month of 1857, for example, Naosuke put on a magnificent display of riches for a single tea specialist from Edo.[36] It goes without saying that politically motivated tea practice of this sort is not mentioned in texts such as *Collection for a Tea Gathering*, and goes against the popular vision of Naosuke the tea master as a spiritual aesthete.

## Conclusion

Warrior tea masters like Fumai and Sōga emphasized the importance of spirituality in tea, as we have seen, but Naosuke put particular emphasis on the warrior spirit. His approach to the crisis facing Japan in the 1850s can also be understood as an attempt to restore the spirit of the Japanese warrior in the arena of domestic and international politics. His masterpiece *Collection for a Tea Gathering* was perhaps his greatest articulation of the ideals of elite warrior culture. Unfortunately, however, this most eloquent attempt only affected those people close to him, and failed to impact on Tokugawa society as a whole. Naosuke has perhaps been misjudged because the arena in which he was forced to take an actively reformist role was hostile and contentious; his more heartfelt endeavors in tea were internally and externally restricted to the point that today his tea writings are understood as inspirational tracts rather than serious attempts to affect social change.

Despite his position of political pragmatism, Naosuke maintained a conservative and sentimental attachment to the traditions of the warrior class. The seeming disjunctions between Naosuke's roles as sophisticated politician, advocate of warrior culture, and flexible tea master in fact perfectly illustrate the dilemma of the elite warrior in late Tokugawa period Japan. Domainal lords such as Naosuke had to juggle real political concerns, the demands of the crumbling status system, and their own broadening personal interests on a daily basis. Naosuke's tea writings and practice, in their concern with both spiritual ideals and practical realities, can also be understood as the ultimate example of warrior tea in premodern Japan.

## Notes

1  Ishii Shirō (ed.), *Kinsei buke shisō* (Iwanami Shoten, 1974).
2  See, for example, Naosuke's letter of 6/14/1846, in Tokyo Daigaku Shiryō Hensanjo (eds), *Dai-Nihon ishin shiryō, Ii-ke shiryō* [hereafter cited as *IKS*] vol. 1 (Tokyo Daigaku Shuppan Kai, 1959), pp. 166–168.
3  Thomas Elyot, *The Boke Named the Governour* (first edition by Henry Herbert Stephen Croft, 1531; originally published in London, 1883. Reprinted in New York, Burt Franklin, 1967).
4  See Pitelka's discussion of the succession of the Sen house after Rikyū in Chapter 4.
5  Matsudaira Sadanobu, *Oi no nami* is transcribed in *Rakuō kō isho* (Hachio Shoten, 1893).

6  Matsudaira Fumai, *Mudagoto*, in Matsudairake Henshūkai (eds), *Matsudaira Fumai den* (Keibundo Shoten, 1917), pp. 101–111.

7  Sakai Sōga, "Yukō nikki," in Kurita Tensei (ed.), *Sakai Sōga Chakaiki* (Muramatsu Shokan, 1977).

8  Sakai Sōga, *Gyo-taku shiki*, Hikone Castle Museum, document no. 2876, search no. S122. See also *Himeji Bunko*, Sōga Shiryō, Konnichian Bunko microfilm, reel no. 2, flash no. 7.

9  Kumakura Isao, "Sen no Rikyū," in Paul Varley and Kumakura Isao (eds), *Tea in Japan: Essays on the History of Chanoyu* (University of Hawai'i Press, 1989), p. 65.

10  The Ise branch of the Sekishū school is a well-known example.

11  Matsudaira Fumai, *Shin-bun*, transcribed in Matsudairake, *Matudaira Fumai den*, p. 64.

12  Ii Naosuke, *Umoreginoya no ki*, Hikone Castle Museum, document no. 6998, search no. 24682.

13  Ii Naosuke, *Nyumon-ki*, transcribed in Ii Masahiro and Kurasawa Yukihiro (eds), *Ichigo ichie* (Toei Sha, 1989).

14  Ii Naosuke, *Sadō no seidō no tasuke to narubeki wo ron heru bun*, in Nakamura Katsumaro (ed.), *Ii tairo sadō dan* (Tokyo Daigaku Shuppankai, 1978 reprint, 1917 original print).

15  See, for example, *IKS*, vol. 1 (1941), pp. 136, 218–221, 248, 251–254, 196; vol. 2, pp. 27 and 70.

16  Ii Naosuke, *Tōryu chaji keiko shidai*, in *IKS*, vol. 2, pp. 494–499; Ii Naosuke, *Shinshiki kaiseki jobun shitagaki*, Hikone Castle Museum, document no. 6663, search no. 24204; Ii Naosuke, *Sōan gyotaku shiki no shidai*, Hikone Castle Museum, document no. 6690, search no. 28193; Ii Naosuke, *Jiki kaiseki an*, Hikone Castle Museum, document no. 2702, search no. 30603.

17  Tea gathering held on 12/11/1855 (Ansei 2). Tanihata Akio (ed.), "Ii Naosuke chakaiki," *Chanoyu* 16 (1979): 55.

18  The characters for "party meal" are found three times in *Yamanoue Sōji ki*, transcribed in vol. 6 of Sen Sōshitsu *et al.* (eds), *Chadō koten zenshū* [hereafter cited as *CKZ*], 12 vols (Tanko Shinsha, 1956–1962), pp. 93 and 104.

19  Katagiri Sekishū, *Sanbyaku kajo*, transcribed in *CKZ*, vol. 2.

20  Fujibayashi Sōgen, *Izumigusa*, in Honjō Sōsen (ed.), *Ishikawa Hōten Izumigusa* (Rōsokusha, 1965).

21  Fujibayashi Sōgen, *Moshihogusa*, in Noguchi Zuiten (ed.), *Teihon Sekishū ryū*, vol. 2 (Mitsumura Suiko Shoten, 1985).

22  See, for example, the records of Shimazu Yoshitaka (1702–1703, 1727) or Yanagisawa Gyozan (1777–1778): "Kinsei daimyo no chakaiki," in Murai Yasuhiko (ed.), *Chanoyu no tenkai*, vol. 5 of *Chadō shūkin* (Shogakkan, 1985), pp. 275–278 and 279–283.

23  Konoe Iehiro, *Kaiki*, transcribed in *CKZ*, vol. 5.

24  Kōshin Sōsa, *Kōshin gegaki*, transcribed in *CKZ*, vol. 5.

25  Yamada Sōhen, *Sadō yoroku*, transcribed in *Yamada Sōhen zenshū*, vol. 2 (Yamada Sōhen Zenshū Hanpukai, 1959); Yamada Sohen, *Sadō benmoshū*, transcribed in *Yamada Sōhen zenshū*, vol. 1 (Yamada Sōhen Zenshū Hanpukai, 1958).

26  Kawakami Fuhaku, transcribed in Edo Senke Chanoyu Kenkyūjo (eds), *Fuhaku hikki* (Chanoyu Kenkyūjo, 1987).

27  Nishiyama Matsunosuke (ed.), *Nampōroku* (Iwanami Shoten, 1986), pp. 208, 211, and 223.

28  Ii Naosuke, *Kaisekinoben*, Hikone Castle Museum, document no. 6668, search no. 28062.

29  Ii Naosuke, *Chanoyu ichie shū*, transcribed in *CKZ*, vol. 10, p. 331; translated

in Paul Varley, "Chanoyu from Genroku to Modern Times," in Varley and Kumakura, *Tea in Japan*, p. 187.

30  Ii Naosuke, *Chanoyu ichie shū*, pp. 414–415; translated in Varley, "Chanoyu from Genroku to Modern Times," pp. 187–188.

31  See Tanimura Reiko, *Ii Naosuke: shūyō to shite no chanoyu* (Sobunsha, 2001), pp. 127–128.

32  Ii Naosuke, *Chanoyu ichie shū*, p. 340. Naosuke refers in this text to the suitable clothes for female participants at a tea gathering. The terms used, "*kaitori*" and "*sage obi*," refer to clothes worn by women of the warrior status group.

33  Ii Naosuke, *Tō-to mizuya chō*, Hikone Castle Museum, document no. 6695, search no. 28188; *Hikone mizuya chō*, Hikone Castle Museum document no. 6696, search no. 28189; Tanihata Akio, "Ii Naosuke chakaiki."

34  We also find that after 1852, Naosuke let maids of his mother-in-law learn tea from the wife of Katagiri Soen, and sometimes gave lessons himself. Although the chief guest at these gatherings was almost always a man, women were seated between the men or at the end. See for example, the tea gatherings on 1/26/1855 and 9/23/1859 in Tanihata Akio (ed.), "Ii Naosuke no chakaiki," in *Chanoyu bunka gakkai* 3 (1996): 123 and 175.

35  See the letter of Takahashi Eitoku to a Hikone vassal, 27/7/1857, *IKS*, vol. 5, pp. 253–254. Eitoku was a tea specialist who attended Naosuke's tea gatherings ten times.

36  Ii Naosuke, *Hikone mizuya chō*, Hikone Castle Museum, document no. 6696, search no. 28189; Tanihata Akio, "Ii Naosuke chakaiki," pp. 65–66.

# 7 Rikyū has left the tea room
## National cinema interrogates the anecdotal legend

*Tim Cross*

### Reading Rikyū in the nation

Framing representations of Rikyū in changing discourses of the nation highlights the ideologies that have shaped Japanese citizenship. Disputes about the parameters of Japanese identity have been a continuing feature of post-war Japanese public life, most recently focusing on issues of historical interpretation and how the education system transmits a selective version of modern history that angers neighboring countries. The aesthetic sphere deserves closer attention because its cultural practices and artifacts have been employed by political elites as ideological tools that seductively naturalize the politically problematic relationship between the state and those governed. The inevitable fall of cherry blossoms conveniently augmented early twentieth-century militarist claims to accept the transience of youthful human life as the greatest wartime gift to the Emperor and nation. Notions such as the four seasons continue to be important elements in aestheticizing the modern Japanese identity for domestic and international consumption. These commodifications of the national identity have helped reinvent post-war Japan as the land of harmony and support a public narrative that does not address imperial atrocities inflicted on neighboring countries.

Institutionalized tea pedagogy is a major player in this discursive slip between the divine, the natural, and the national. The deification of the sixteenth-century tea master Sen no Rikyū as innocent aesthete is an example of codifying the national identity in a manner that denies the political and commercial aspects of mass culture. This chapter will examine three films representing Rikyū, works that use tea's status as a self-appointed representative of Japanese material culture to deconstruct a monolithic Japanese identity. While these three films reconfigure national identity, they imply a continuity between the values legitimating ritual suicide (*seppuku*) and tea's tenet of cherishing the instant. This common territory became historically significant when Japanese totalitarianism demanded that citizens internalize a reified version of "samurai" values.

## Three storytellers

The first director discussed in this chapter is Tanaka Kinuyo (1909–1977), who herself appeared in more than 240 films directed by Gosho, Ozu, Naruse, and Mizoguchi, and directed six films during her nine years of working as a director. In Mizoguchi's 1946 *Victory of Women* [*Josei no shōri*], Tanaka played a hard-headed lawyer defending a female client who had killed her baby, against the zealous prosecutor, her brother-in-law. Tanaka had all her teeth extracted for Kinoshita's 1958 *Ballad of Narayama* [*Narayama bushiko*] and was recognized as the Best Actress at the 1975 Berlin Festival for her role in Kumai's *Sandakan Number 8* as an elderly woman who had been sold into prostitution at an early age.[1] Her body of work addresses the plight of Japanese women through history, and her *Love Under the Crucifix* [*Oginsama*] tautly shows the tension between female agency and social restrictions.

Teshigahara Hiroshi (1927–2001) was the son of Sōfu Teshigahara, founding *iemoto* of the Sōgetsu School of Ikebana, and was internationally active in a wide range of artistic activities. In 1962 he received the NHK New Director's Award for his first dramatic film, *The Pitfall* [*Otoshi ana*], and in 1964 *The Woman in the Dunes* [*Suma no onna*] was awarded the Special Judge's Prize at the Cannes Film Festival. He established the Sōgetsu Ceramic Kiln in Miyazaki Mura, Fukui Prefecture in 1973. Teshigahara became the third-generation Sōgetsu *iemoto* in 1980 at the age of 53. His film *Rikyū*, made with the support of Omotesenke, Urasenke, and Mushanokōji Senke, won the Best Artistic Contribution Award at the Montreal International Film Festival. In 1992 he was awarded the Order of Purple Cordon for his artistic contributions; likewise, his film *Basara: Princess Gō* [*Gōhime*] addressed the tea life of Furuta Oribe. In 1993 he organized a major tea event for the Japan Cultural Festival in Paris that was designed by Tadao Ando, Jae Eun Choi, Ettore Sottass, and Charlotte Perriand. In 1994 Teshigahara directed and provided the stage settings for a new Noh play, *Susano*, at the Avignon Festival (Bourbon Quarry, France), and in 1996 he directed and provided the stage settings for the opera *Turandot* in Geneva, Switzerland. In that year he was also awarded the French National Chevalier Title, and he directed and supervised "Hana Butai" at the Itsukushima Shrine in Hiroshima Prefecture, a stage commemorating the late Takemitsu Toru, who composed the music for the Rikyū and Oribe films. In 1997 he was awarded the Japanese National Order of the Sacred Treasure. Sōgetsu Kaikan, Tokyo was the venue for Salvatore Ferragamo's Shoes Exhibit which he supervised in 1998. In 2000 Teshigahara created the "Hermitage of Moments" tea room (Shunan) at Sōgetsu Plaza.[2]

The territory of Kumai Kei (b. 1930) is the fable of the nation, the individual costs of consuming that tale, and the possibility of being consumed in the name of the nation by that myth. Themes addressed by Kumai include unsolved murder cases purportedly linked to US Army Intelligence

(*The Japanese Archipelago*, 1965) [*Nihon rettō*], the replacement of the nation by the company as the institution requiring the absolute sacrifice (*Tunnel to the Sun*, 1968) [*Kurobe no taiyō*], prejudice among and against resident Koreans, atomic bomb victims, and *burakumin* (*The Swarming Earth*, 1970) [*Chi no mure*], and the construction of the history of *karayuki* women sold into overseas prostitution (*Sandakan Number 8*, a.k.a *Brothel Number 8*, 1975) [*Sandakan hachiban shokan: Bōkyō*]. Sato Tadao characterizes these early works as "villain films" with "power structures as the enemies of democracy."[3] This classification emphasizes how Kumai's treatment of the Rikyū legend as hearsay extended the conventional range of the history drama (*jidai geki*). His 1989 film comments on how, during the early modern period, cultural practices like tea aestheticized experience and structured a desire for an authentic participation in the national community of unnatural death. The linkage in the film of cherry blossoms with a devotional death in the name of a particular ideal invites a comparison between Rikyū's death by ritual suicide and the wartime membership of the fifteenth Urasenke *iemoto* in a "divine wind" (*kamikaze*) suicide attack squad.

## Three tales of Rikyū

In her 1962 film *Love Under the Crucifix* [*Oginsama*], Tanaka locates tea in both the female realm of the domestic sphere and the world of the court and warriors, and Christianity is a major presence throughout. The complicated romantic relationship between Rikyū's daughter Ogin and the Christian warlord Takayama Ukon dominates the narrative. This storyline allows Ukon several opportunities to make orthodox pronouncements about what is appropriate for Christians in this life and what they can expect in the next life. This tension between Ukon's focus on eternal life and Ogin's insistence on the here and now connects the film's meditation on tea, Christianity, and death. After Hideyoshi becomes smitten with Ogin, he summons her to his quarters. She is blindfolded and led down candlelit steps and across his compound to the building containing the golden tea room. Because of her affection for Ukon, Ogin does not accept the advances of Hideyoshi. Hideyoshi gives her several days to consider his offer: trade her life for the life of Ukon. As Hideyoshi's anger escalates, he rephrases his demand by substituting Rikyū for Ukon. When Ogin returns home Rikyū repeats her "Rikyū's life" phrase. That evening a stranger arrives unexpectedly from Ukon's fief and requests an opportunity to drink Rikyū's tea. Rikyū welcomes and serves him, and when the guest returns the tea bowl, he hands Rikyū a letter from Ukon. Preparations are made for Ogin's departure, but Rikyū's house has been encircled by Hideyoshi's soldiers. Ogin changes into a white kimono and is armed with a dagger when the family gathers in the tea room for her final tea. They all drink from the same black Raku tea bowl. Ogin leaves that room, and enters another, warning her maid not to follow her. The maid promises to return Ukon's fan to him. The final titles refer to Rikyū's suicide.

In the film *Rikyū*, Teshigahara rejects the notion of tea as a value-neutral activity by locating sixteenth-century tea practice at the intersection of economic, military, and cultural discourses of authority. Teshigahara integrates scholarly and anecdotal versions of history to plot Rikyū's fall from favor, pitting Rikyū against Hideyoshi as one way to support the opposition of principles and art against ambition and politics, proposed by the film's opening titles. The whole film drives with teleological certainty toward the closure of Rikyū's death. It starts with Rikyū at the peak of his career, publicly acclaimed as the foremost tea practitioner and teaching Hideyoshi privately. It then flashes back to when Rikyū was a mere leading member of the tea community held in less regard than Imai Sōkyū (1520–1593),[4] and Hideyoshi was under the command of Oda Nobunaga (1534–1582). The film chronicles Rikyū's fall by foregrounding the intrigues of Ishida Mitsunari (1560–1600), a hawkish supporter of Hideyoshi's invasion of Korea. The film's final image is Rikyū walking into the storm-lashed bamboo grove where he supposedly kills himself, and the following white text scrolls onto the black screen.

> On February 28 1591
> Rikyū committed ritual suicide.
> But his way of tea
> influenced the nation forever.
> Hideyoshi died six years later
> during his invasion of Korea.[5]

By structuring the film around the personal relationship between Hideyoshi and Rikyū, Teshigahara tacitly accepts the cult of personality underlying the genealogical strategy of the Sen tea schools.[6] And yet, viewers are taken outside the neat illusion of history unfolding by a disembodied voice-over that allows Rikyū to cross four centuries of the institutionalization of tea practice. While this device attributes a youthful omniscience to Rikyū, it also allows Teshigahara to provide tea practitioners with the means of contrasting their own experience as consumers of tea orthodoxy with one representation of that highly contested construction, the real spirit of tea.

Kumai's adaptation of Inoue Yasushi's 1981 novel, *Memoirs of the Priest Honkaku* [*Honkakubō ibun*], presents an image of one "tradition" of Japanese culture, the rustic (*wabi*) aesthetic. The film portrays the point of origin of the *iemoto* system of cultural transmission. The specter of Rikyū is shown to be an elusive figure, constructed in the distance between event, second-hand accounts, and myth. In posing questions related to the role of an aestheticized cult of death in the formation of "the authentic," the film raises the issue of how ritual suicide and cherry blossoms were rhetorically deployed by early Showa political elites to advocate the patriotic suicide oaths of *kamikaze* pilots in the Imperial Air Force. The ideological application of a nationalized cultural register as a form of social control during the period of militarism also implicates cultural practices like tea, and attendant icons and personalities such as Rikyū, in the early twentieth-century creation of a fatalistic patriotic fervor.

## Film appropriates tea's anecdotes

The 1989 films of Kumai and Teshigahara make distinctive comments on the use of anecdotes to invent tea's tradition. Typically, tea anecdotes celebrate the aesthetic components of Rikyū's life while ignoring his commercial activities and military responsibilities. These two directors draw attention to how anecdotes convey the orthodox values of institutionalized tea pedagogy while constructing tea as purely aesthetic. The ideological function of anecdotes is to erase the commercial and political aspects of mass culture, and to legitimate the self-positioning of the Houses of Sen as the authentic transmitters of the Rikyū legacy.

In the context of tea pedagogy, anecdotes serve to embrace the past and repackage it to serve the needs of contemporary tea school authorities, creating a seamlessly immutable tradition.[7] These mythical stories establish a threefold distinction between those represented, those who speak, and those who listen. Those who transmit the anecdotes tacitly align themselves with those represented and assume a representative position, superior to the listeners. In merging their subjectivity with those represented, speakers position themselves as the embodiment of the values contained in the anecdote. The authority to relate the incident implies the ability to pronounce what is and is not tea, and a significant part of the responsibilities of an *iemoto* is to determine what is officially recognized as authentic tea practice and who is competent to publicly perform these practices. It is this matrix of desire, authority, and subjectivity that demands the historic past be elevated to the heroic.

The authority of the *iemoto* is naturalized by the systemic use of anecdotes. While this ideological use of anecdotes "constructs desiring subjects (those who are legitimate as well as those who are not), it simultaneously establishes them and itself as given and existing outside of time, as the way things work, the way they inevitably are."[8] Controlling these visions of tea's continuity and interpretations of tea's past by attributing authenticity to certain anecdotes is one Sen strategy for adding value to the Rikyū legacy. Given that film functions as mass culture's storyteller, it is important to note that two of the films under discussion here were made in cooperation with the Sen tea schools. In Teshigahara's film, that cooperation included close scrutiny of Mikuni Rentaro's movements during the filming of the scene where Rikyū was pressured to use tea as a means of military assassination.[9] In Kumai's film, Sen representatives sought to eliminate realistic depictions of Rikyū's ritual suicide.[10] In both films, Rikyū's death is aestheticized by removing it from the context of the Shukoin tea room in Daitokuji,[11] a relocation that effectively depoliticizes tea culture.

## Modernist film as history: contesting tea's orthodoxy

Teshigahara's film positions its audience as consumers of historical inevitability by configuring four genres: Japanese period drama; biography; Hollywood narrative; and documentary. The film is lavish in the scale of its presentation of warrior tea, typical of a period drama. It presents the clash of individual psychologies in the biographical mode. It uses a linear Hollywood narrative to structure the account of Rikyū's fall from grace, and unreflective flashbacks modulate the film's tempo by heightening the emotional tension emerging from the relentless movement toward the inescapable closure of Rikyū's death. The occasional use of expository intertitles is a necessary interruption to the willing suspension of disbelief. Teshigahara incorporates tea anecdotes and scholarly knowledge of the period to create a neatly unfolding history. Spectators are consumers of a historical authenticity that is reinforced by Teshigahara's status as an *iemoto* of the Sōgetsu School of flower arrangement, a cultural practice sustained by transmission mechanisms resembling those of most tea schools.[12] The biographical aspects of the film can almost be read autobiographically: one grand master celebrating *the* Grand Master.

Teshigahara has structured the film by seamlessly appropriating anecdotal versions of tea history into his narrative. The opening moments of the film contest a key tenet of Sen tea discourse: the power-neutral status of tea as a cultural practice. The first titles clearly present a claim that tea was centrally located in discourses of authority, and this frames the film's ongoing concern with the relationships between aesthetics and politics, and the individual and the state. The text of these first titles is premised on the scholarly evidence documenting the almost contradictory breadth of Rikyū's activities. The first sentence proposes a binary distinction between art and politics, and the second sentence points to the contrived nature of that opposition by locating tea in the political context of a specific historical period.

> This is the story of the duel
> between art and politics,
> of the beliefs of one man
> against the ambitions of another.
> In 16th century Japan
> under a new ruling class
> the arts were flourishing
> and at the center . . .
> the tea ceremony.
> A film by Hiroshi Teshigawara
> Dedicated to Sofu Teshigawara
> Isamu Noguchi[13]

The viewer then witnesses pre-dawn preparations for a tea gathering, and here the film's documentary elements present a role model for tea practitioners of how to put tea values into practice. The pedagogical content of the film's opening scene is the legendary solitary morning glory flower incident immortalized in tea anecdotes, and those tea values assume a representative function in creating a nationally distinctive aesthetic.[14] These tea ethics celebrate and reinforce the centrality of seasonal transience for tea practitioners, and by extension, the nation.

Hideyoshi's reaction to the image of the one perfect morning glory is a textbook example of the power of simplified representations of nature to penetrate the disarray of the everyday. When natural elements are first selected and then further elevated by being isolated from the disorderliness of daily life, their inherent beauty becomes a convincing argument for the existence of a deeper divinity that spans beyond the life of an individual. This elimination of visual confusion is an important strategy in the sacramentalization of the nation. Conflating the distinction between nature and the national allows the logic of physical creation to be read as proof of the self-evident glory of social entities like nations. With this slippage between nature and the national in place, aesthetic reduction operates as a "cultural sacrament offered to the Japanese people."[15] This reductive impulse is not confined to tea ceremony, and the following version of the anecdote re-enacted in the film's opening scene demonstrates that it is a common trope in the creation of an idealized Japanese vision of nature.

> At times the quantity is deliberately reduced to a minimum. As when Toyotomi Hideyoshi, the sixteenth-century warlord and national unifier, wanting to celebrate the profusion of morning glories in a tea master's garden, came to the tea ceremony only to find that the master Sen no Rikyū had cut all the flowers, leaving a single one in a vase on the ceremonial shelf ... Another well-known story is the use of a single camellia flower in the Ikenobō School of flower arrangement. In 1816 the fortieth master of the school instructed that only six and a half leaves should be left, the others removed to reveal the pure essence of the flower. His successor went further: only three and a half leaves should be left.[16]

This movement from a single camellia flower to six and a half leaves to only three and a half leaves is an example of how creative expressions become codified and reduced to formula inside *iemoto* systems. While the opening scene privileges a certain minimalist aesthetic above others, its pedagogic function positions the film as "a social document recreating popular memory."[17] The purpose of this film's movement through various interpretations of historical truth is to implicate the spectator in the film's presentation of the extent to which politics determines artistic practices. The preferred reading of the film positions the spectator as a consumer of these authentic images which are both entertaining and very persuasive representations of the otherness of Japanese identity. It is in the spectator's embodied reactions to the intensity of psychological tension between Hideyoshi and Rikyū that the film's entertainment values are transmuted into a convincing experience of "history."

What is significant for our analysis of the ideological work performed by the film's storytelling is the degree of interpenetration between the art of tea and its political applications in the life of the nation. In the film, aesthetic preferences assume political resonance, changes in the codes and conventions of tea are understood as signifiers of historical changes, and icons of tea history are reconfigured as mileposts in the narrative of the nation.

A sequence of several scenes establishes the dominance of the military sphere over the aesthetic early in the film. Following the morning glory scene comes the film's title sequence, which features a globe that is used to identify the route taken by Portuguese merchants to Japan; the globe is presented to the first great warlord of the sixteenth century, Oda Nobunaga. A flashback sequence foregrounds how the martial might of Nobunaga enables the practices of merchant tea masters, including Rikyū. Following negotiations with Portuguese gun runners and a display of their improved efficiency, Nobunaga's entourage retires for tea, and for the first time Hideyoshi is invited to participate. In a following scene, Stefano, a young Christian and student of tea, visits Rikyū's residence and relates how Nobunaga killed himself in his tea room. Stefano presents Rikyū with Nobunaga's final present, the globe that prompted Nobunaga's earlier remark to the Portuguese, "I trust this globe. Land has no end. Nothing invisible can exist."[18] This scene is followed by the use of superimposed titles in a fire sequence that assembles burning masonry and an arrow among the crumbling wreck of a building, and finishes with a slow pan to a close-up image of a tea kettle among the blazing ruins. This explains the 1582 attack on Nobunaga:

> To avenge his master Shogun Oda
> Hideyoshi attacks the rebellious Akechi
> and, in a great battle, causes his death.[19]

This exposition naturalizes the authority of Nobunaga and elevates the loyalty and military prowess of Hideyoshi. It supplies the necessary background information to make intelligible the later scenes where Rikyū tries to warn Hideyoshi of the fundamental difference between his victory over Akechi and his international ambitions in Korea and China. The scene in a merchant's store that follows gives more information about the rise of Hideyoshi "the monkey" and a negative assessment of his unpolished manners as inappropriate for a ruler. In the next scene this is contrasted with the absolute authority he has assumed. In an official assembly of his generals and aides, he tells the Portuguese missionaries that he needs a good fleet of sturdy warships and that he will make the Koreans and

Chinese become Christians. After displaying his gold riches to his foreign guests, he takes Rikyū aside and tells him to construct a golden tea room.

In contrast to Tanaka's 1962 depiction of the golden tea room as Hideyoshi's seduction pit, where Ogin dampens Hideyoshi's ardor and raises his wrath by mentioning Takayama Ukon, Teshigahara shows the golden tea room as an implement of national consolidation. Rikyū is silent in the background as Hideyoshi serves tea to the Emperor, witnessed by other members of the imperial court. The presence of the diegetic audience emphasizes that this tea act is more than merely personal. Hideyoshi's tea service exceeds its private meaning by being inscribed with imperial authority, and the residue of this authority became important as Hideyoshi displayed the golden tea room as a seductive and coercive demonstration of the legitimacy of his hegemony.[20]

Given Teshigahara's concern with the relationship of mutual constitution between politics and art, it is thematically significant that the idea for the golden tea room comes from Hideyoshi, not Rikyū.[21] This may imply that their relationship had a collaborative element, but it also suggests the primacy of the political. In the case of the rustic Taian tea room, Hideyoshi's dialogue suggests that Rikyū built it to celebrate Hideyoshi's national unification. Teshigahara's Hideyoshi clearly states that it is "their" space and Rikyū can do anything to Hideyoshi there. This tension between the politicizing of tea room spaces like the golden tea room and the dissolving of status differences when Hideyoshi and Rikyū are together in Taian implies that the art–politics distinction established in the opening titles is a false binary. As the death of Yamanoue Sōji demonstrates the extent to which politics penetrates art, this binary is deliberately deconstructed throughout Teshigahara's film.

Yamanoue Sōji's argument for the status of black Raku as the embodiment of *wabi* enrages Hideyoshi and he is banished for a second time. The English subtitles ignore Chōjirō by anticipating the historic formation of the Raku category and flatten the gruffness of Hideyoshi's preference for red rather than black ware ("Yahari Chōjirō wa aka . . . kuro ga sukan"). When Sōji secretly returns to make a final visit to Rikyū, the latter insists that Sōji also meet Hideyoshi. Hideyoshi is in the final stages of a successful siege against Hōjō Ujimasa at Odawara Castle when Sōji refuses his offer of re-employment as a tea teacher because of Sōji's promise to teach tea to Ujimasa. Enraged at the insult of Sōji's misplaced loyalty, Hideyoshi orders his guards to behead Sōji and to slice off his nose and ears. Here the problematic status of *wabi* as a strategic attempt to shift power away from warrior tea practices centering on imported objects is directly responsible for Sōji's banishment but not his death. Teshigahara's representation of Sōji's death contrasts strongly with Kumai's depiction of Sōji's self-destructive resoluteness as he insists on using rustic utensils to serve Hideyoshi. In Kumai's film, Sōji's tea procedure is interrupted as he is seized and dragged outside. He deftly steals a dagger from a soldier, kills him, and then laughingly commits suicide in front of Hideyoshi. Kumai's Sōji assertively demonstrates and reinforces the limits of political power.

## Tea film, tea practice: voice-over as critique

It is an emancipating moment when Teshigahara uses the disembodied voice-over to push the viewers out of their willing suspension of disbelief. It allows students of tea to sense something of the cost of institutionalization to tea's core values. Rikyū's disembodied voice accompanies a sequence of five shots that together constitute two scenes. Visually, the film distances itself from its principal concerns with tea rooms and the court with a transition shot of a stream. It then cuts to a close-up of the young Catholic priest Stefano before panning away to a midshot of Rikyū and his assistant as they walk through a sparse scrub of small trees. In the next shot, all three are walking slowly, inspecting trees which Rikyū rejects as inappropriate. In the last shot of the first scene, all three descend to drink water from a stream and Rikyū washes the perspiration from his face.

In contrast to the sunlit shots of actors moving through the landscape, the second scene is much less dynamic in terms of on-screen and camera movement. It is one static long shot of a much darker forest scene marked by the monumental presence of a mature stand of trees. Amidst this epic silhouette, the movement of three almost insignificant figures, the last one carrying a tree trunk, is barely discernible. These two scenes are the visual background for the following dialogue between Stefano, Rikyū, and his assistant, and the second scene starts with Stefano's comment about the spiritual content of tea.

STEFANO:  What does it mean "A fine horse tied to a straw house?"
RIKYŪ:  How would you interpret it, Stefano?
STEFANO:  Straw houses represent poverty
    But tea-ware is expensive.
    So it's a bit like a luxurious game.
RIKYŪ:  Not at all.
    The richness is not in the humble tea-house
    But in the spirits of those who sit there.
    That's what it means.
STEFANO:  So what we are talking about is richness of the spirit.
RIKYŪ:  A narrow mind cannot open the door to tea.
STEFANO:  The tea ceremony was a great spiritual adventure for me.
RIKYŪ:'S ASSISTANT:  Will you continue it back home?
STEFANO:  Yes, but the ceremony is difficult.
RIKYŪ:  Don't take it too seriously.
    It is good to let things happen.
    The true way of tea is without expectation.[22]

It is significant that Rikyū is discussing the meaning of tea's precepts with a foreigner because this dialogue's explicitly pedagogical content naturalizes the culturally chauvinistic idea that certain cultural practices privilege those with a particular birthright. Stefano's ethnicity also raises the issue of tea's international commodification and its self-presentation as the quintessential Japanese practice. As an emancipatory moment, this dialogue equips tea practitioners with several criteria with which to assess their participation in the codification and commodification of tea practice. Given that the most informative English language tea scholarship has been privileged by a personal relationship with the Urasenke *iemoto* through the Midori Kai, an intensive program of tea instruction in Kyoto generously offered to non-Japanese,[23] the following readings of the film may be criticized as an instrumental imposition of a rather particular perspective upon the integrity of Teshigahara's film. Using the insights offered by critical pedagogy, I intend to reflect on my experience of being a low intermediate student learning tea in the manner more typical to Japanese students of tea removed from Kyoto, the knowledge production and distribution center of tea's constellation. The fundamental point to be emphasized in this section is the tendency of tea discourse to colonize the lifeworld of practitioners.

The first point is the contrast between the aesthetic of rusticity that cherishes the well worn, and the market premium that such pieces command. Given that the modern re-emergence of tea was funded by industrialist tea men like Masuda Takashi and Matsunaga Jian,[24] whose economic might was generally leveraged by imperial expansion into China or the development of Japanese infrastructure, this rhetoric of paucity appears especially ironic. The film's dialogue seems to reassert the centrality of practitioner intention, while devaluing the provenance fetish and the *iemoto*'s lucrative practice of writing certification inscriptions (*hakogaki*), the principal mechanism for maintaining and increasing the value of tea utensils.

The second point concerns the commodification of tea practice. The dialogue's metaphor of tea's open door can be extended to argue that the institutionalization of tea into a neatly codified curriculum has changed that door into a toll road. Progress is mediated by the licensing system with progressively higher fees for more advanced levels of practice. One of the responsibilities of an *iemoto* is to ensure the continuity of the tradition. As currently constituted, this demands a notion of the purity of the teachings. This is achieved by using his power of incomplete transmission to protect the integrity of advanced secret teachings and authoritatively ruling on what practices and which practitioners and combinations of utensils are appropriate for official tea displays.

The third point concerns the difficulty of tea practice referred to by Stefano. Because it is distanced by the voice-over device that steps out of the narrative, the film is addressing tea practitioners. Stefano's remark can be understood as referring to more than his sixteenth-century study of tea.

It transparently suggests the attention to perfect form and increasingly rigid control of higher levels of tea practice now common in institutionalized tea pedagogy out in the provinces away from the Kyoto metropole.

More than the merely technical difficulty referred to by Stefano is the deeper issue of how the autonomy of tea students is compromised by the success of tea's transmission. Given the fact that tea students tend to assess tea performances by the orthodox standards of their tea classrooms, end users might like to be able to enjoy the tea moment without the intrusion of the official model validating their experience. The interests of consumers of tea knowledge are discounted against those of the tradition's producer, and this is a consequence of the professionalization of tea discourse.[25]

The fourth point concerns the place of spontaneity in tea practice. If the real way of tea relies on absence of expectation as the means to advance, then the paralyzing insistence on orthodox tea practice that is currently its pedagogical foundation represents a considerable obstacle to students graduating from endless cycles of formulaic repetition. Spontaneity is the prerogative of the *iemoto*. For others elsewhere, there is a choice between following the official guidelines or facing the possibility of being denied the honor and learning experience of performing at official tea displays.

Tea pedagogy aims to naturalize certain behavioral norms: orthodox ways of acting, reacting, constructing experience and valuing utensils. "Remember with the body" (*karada de oboeru*) is a central tenet of tea pedagogy. When received uncritically, this exhortation enlivens the desire of the student to become the embodiment of the tea tradition. By directing students' attention to their bodies, the guardians of the tradition ensure that a range of practices that naturalize their authority to determine what is considered authentic are valorized. The end result of tea pedagogy is a student who has internalized an extremely mannered way of experiencing the four seasons of the world and can perform this embodied knowledge in an apparently unrehearsed way.[26]

If the true way of tea is without expectation, as Rikyū's film comment asserts, the question then arises: how is this state of being to be embodied? Given the global rhetoric of the "Peacefulness through a Bowl of Tea" campaign,[27] it is ironic that the right attitude can only be achieved by following Urasenke rules. Being able to perform the expected behavior of acting spontaneously is the product of intensive self-fashioning along the lines of certain conventions. These conventions are not innocent commonplaces, but are part of a systematic world-view that divides people into those who have been taught how to act spontaneously (according to Urasenke codes) and those who have not. The co-existence of the hospitality impulse with this division of the world into us and them is sustained by the orthodox notion of "proper form."[28] This corporeal emphasis in tea pedagogy requires the willing suspension of skepticism toward discourses of authority. It is precisely the repetitive insistence of "remembering with the body" that produces a lack of spontaneity at weekly tea practice and the official tea displays known as study sessions (*benkyō kai*) that appear to be competitive displays of orthodoxy. Given that the apparent robustness of the tradition evident in these public exhibitions requires a certain psychology[29] and a particular learning style,[30] the claim to universality of this codification of the hospitality impulse does appear to be problematic.

Of the four issues raised by the voice-over dialogue, this final point has the most substantial merit as a critical assessment of current tea practice and the Sen attempt to depoliticize, codify, and commodify the aesthetic sphere. It is appropriate that this point is made in the second scene when the camera is firmly anchored in the dark depths of the forest, safely removed from the corridors of power.

## Kumai's postmodern distance: anecdotes as discourse

In *The Death of a Tea Master* [*Sen no Rikyū: Honkakubō ibun*] the director points audience attention toward anecdotes as discourse, and the oral tradition as a constructor of history: the dead Rikyū is constantly resurrected as a spoken fiction of the present. The prevalence of embedded flashbacks and the use of multiple narrators position anecdotes not as a mere structural device, but as a consistent form of discourse.

The discursive use of anecdotes is one meta-historical function of the film, and is stylistically consistent with Kumai's (1975) combination of voice-over narration and flashbacks in *Sandakan Brothel Number 8*. In addition to this stylistic unity between these two films, within Kumai's body of work there is a thematic coherence of questions relating to the role of history in the construction of modern Japanese subjectivity.[31] Further support for this meta-historical reading comes from Sato's positioning of *Sun Over the Kurobe Gorge* [*Kurobe no taiyō*] (1968) as Kumai's criticism of the government's rhetorical call for individual subordination to national progress. The company has replaced the nation as the institution requiring the absolute sacrifice and there is a disturbing continuity of individual annihilation in this peacetime national service: the job of

> workers from a small sub-contracting company ... is little different from what the Koreans had been forced to do, and even resembles the suicidal missions given to *kamikaze* pilots ... [Their] sacrifices themselves inevitably became the result of a fanatical desire for economic development pursued "militaristically," and the upholding of the double structure of the Japanese economy.[32]

Kumai's concern with the continuing persistence of nationalist values illustrates how he addresses the costs and dangers of modern Japanese citizenship within the conventions of his Rikyū historical drama. The film comments on Rikyū's utility to the dominant interests of the state. It can be read as Kumai's considered response to the state's ideological application of the aesthetic sphere.

Pressing the aesthetic into political service includes institutional programs creating a fatalistic Japanese identity through coercive Meiji interpretations of *The Tale of Genji* that linked beauty, death, and the duties of citizenship.[33] Underpinning tea's discursive creation of the four seasons is a slippage between the natural and the social, and cherry blossoms function as wartime signifiers of the necessity of inevitable youthful sacrifices. Kumai uses cherry blossoms to accommodate the Sen aversion to a graphic re-enactment of Rikyū's suicide. It is in the film's linkage of blossoms and suicide that Rikyū's death assumes an iconic status supporting a thanacratic discourse of the nation. While the formation of the modern citizen is an ongoing process, this linking of death and beauty gave political elites a powerful vocabulary that again served to collapse the distinction between the natural and the national.

In Kumai's film, it is Honkakubō the disciple who continues to converse with the deceased Rikyū. His narration frames other accounts of past events. Honkakubō's use of the past tense is a reminder of the slippery distances between event, second-hand experience, and myth, as he glides between those conversations with his master and the obsessive questions of Oda Uraku (1547–1621). Honkakubō smoothly integrates accounts of tea gatherings at which he was present with events about which he can, at best, only have second-hand knowledge. In one example of the latter, Kumai uses a long shot of Rikyū's expulsion from Kyoto and his one-way boat ride to establish the absence of Honkakubō from the incident that has immortalized the riverside presence of Hosokawa Sansai (1563–1646) and Furuta Oribe (1544–1615).

The director's foregrounding of the absence of Honkakubō demonstrates how the distinction between first-hand experience and hearsay are glossed over by the narrative. With Kumai's cinematography having made this collapse apparent, the ease with which sentimentalized accounts come to serve the vested interests of the custodians of tea's grand narrative also becomes visible. The embedded flashback structure reinforces the status of Honkakubō as the omniscient narrator who is the authoritative chief repository of Rikyū folklore. His status is constructed and confirmed by the persistent questioning about the manner of Rikyū's death by Uraku, Rikyū's grandson Sōtan, and Furuta Oribe. The Rikyū legend is primarily determined by Uraku's pathological fascination with the suicide of Rikyū, Yamanoue Sōji, and Furuta Oribe, and the role of ritual suicide as the ultimate signifier of an authentic tea practitioner. It is in the shadow of this obsession that the ramifications of the ideological use of *The Tale of Genji* to establish a lethal link between death, beauty, and service to a national ideal resonate with the film's examination of the Rikyū legend in terms of the connection between suicide and the ideological use of the four seasons.

It is significant that Kumai compresses Rikyū's frenetic activities recorded in the *One Hundred Gatherings of Rikyū* [*Rikyū Hyakkai ki*] into the climactic sequence of Uraku's deathbed identification with Rikyū. The candlelit parade of guests gathering for Rikyū's final tea is an image of the social diversity of tea's community: monks, tea masters, merchants, and warriors. Uraku imagines he is the representative of that assembled throng, gathered to celebrate tea's position as an integral part of nationally unifying culture of the sixteenth century and to acknowledge Rikyū's authority as the officially designated First Practitioner. Shots of Honkakubō watching Uraku mime the drinking of tea prepared by Rikyū emphasize that Uraku's membership in this mythical community is illusory. This unity in the camaraderie of tea is merely Uraku's preparation for his hallucinatory entrance to the authentic life of a tea practitioner: death by ritual suicide.

Naoki Sakai has raised the importance of the ethics of philosopher Watsuji Tetsurō (1889–1960) for understanding the mechanics of an aesthetic death in the name of the nation. His analysis suggests a similarity between Rikyū's resoluteness toward his own death and the sacrifice demanded of wartime Japanese citizens.

> There is no doubt that, during the fifteen-year war (1931–1945), "dissolving into the whole" immediately suggested the physical erasure of the self, which could mean one's own death. The slogan "the total suicidal death of one hundred million" (*ichioku gyokusai*) – another version of "the final solution" – was propagated all over Japanese territories toward the end of the Second World War, and, in view of the manner in which Watsuji conceptualized authenticity in his ethics, it was no coincidence that the final moment of the total suicidal death was imagined as the aesthetic experience of ultimate communion. Death was appropriated into an experience in which one dissolved and was integrated into the body of the nation. Death was transformed into the imagined experience of togetherness and camaraderie. Resoluteness toward one's own death was translated into resoluteness toward identification with the totality. Death was consequently aestheticized so that it could mediate and assimilate one's personal identity into national identity. Finally, the nation was turned into the community of destiny (*unmei kyodotai*) toward death. To use Watsuji's vocabulary, absolute negativity equals absolute totality and was internalized into the finite totality of the nation-state. In this sense, the absolute totality lost its transcendence and infinity and became "expressible." Watsuji's ethics of being on good terms (*nakayoshi*) transformed itself into the ethics of the total suicidal death of one hundred million.[34]

This reading of the collapse of Watsuji's ethics of good companionship into a nationalized aesthetic death implies that the global "Peacefulness through a Bowl of Tea" campaign repositions the sorts of coercive discourses of the nation that reigned in Japan during the early twentieth century. Tea room camaraderie, with its vicarious participation in questions surrounding Rikyū's annihilation, reads as a metaphor for embracing the nation. In the film, ritual suicide denotes the authentic death for the tea practitioner; for spectators, the use of cherry blossoms as a substitute for Rikyū's suicide signifies the cost of wartime citizenship. With Rikyū's death actually taking place before cherry trees were in bloom, this sequence refers to the tendency of seasons to be manipulated and staged in discourses of consumption.[35] This symbolic convergence allows nature to be consumed as a commodity free from the vagaries of Japan's four seasons. In the same way, institutionalized tea practices tend not be directly experienced by Japanese who do not study tea because now the dominant use value of tea is as an icon of the nation.

In the film's flashback to the final tea of Rikyū and Hideyoshi, Rikyū rejects Hideyoshi's denial that Rikyū's suicide is necessary. When Hideyoshi requests another bowl of tea, Rikyū refuses the request and thanks Hideyoshi for the gift of ritual suicide as an opportunity to understand the real meaning of being a tea practitioner. In contrast to Rikyū's embrace of suicide as a Pyrrhic retort to the escalation of events beyond his control, Uraku's anxiety about his inadequacy as a tea practitioner centers on his untimely failure to achieve an authentic death. Rather than living an individual sense of tea values, Uraku is convinced that authenticity is mediated by the external authority of tradition. The film scrutinizes the notion that ritual suicide was the rite of entry into this community of ultimate aesthetes; we can also understand Uraku's experience of Rikyū's death as his incorporation into the history of tea and the nation.

Implicit in this argument for reading Kumai's film in light of early twentieth-century discourses of the nation is the claim that Meiji period literature, as well as modern tea practices, constitute a set of intertexts because of their collective celebration of transience as an essentially Japanese destiny. In addition, these texts are examples of how "propagandists [have used] pretended traditionalism to legitimate and mystify a thoroughly contemporary centralized and bureaucratic state."[36] This is not to imply that Kumai has responded to specific works of Meiji period literature or other social practices implicated in nation-building. Rather, we find "an intertextuality that does not require a specific familiarity with the singular texts involved, but is a reading that occurs between texts."[37]

## Resurrection by structure: Rikyū is dead, legendary Rikyū lives

What is not initially apparent from reading the scenario of Kumai's film[38] is how a four-level structure charts the distance between experience, verbal transcriptions of events, and myth. This structure emphasizes the central role anecdotes have played in the construction of the Rikyū myth and their corresponding depoliticization of Japanese culture. The four structural elements are: Rikyū as legendary dream; Rikyū the living legend, Honkakubō's "present"; and the series of flashbacks with its multiple narrators. These four levels are unified in Honkakubō's subjectivity, and the first two levels are musically marked by similar theme music.

Borrowing Baron's analysis of *The Player* as a strong version of the postmodern film narrative, I would like to suggest that the complexity of these four structural elements allows us to categorize it as a relatively weaker but definitely postmodern film. Particularly important are the embedded flashbacks that are occasionally introduced and concluded by different narrators, and the film's meta-historical concerns. Even as a moderate example of the postmodern film narrative, Kumai's film

> requires us to reconsider existing conceptions of suture, for it generates a type of postmodern pleasure that does not arise from identification with characters, the camera, or a reality present elsewhere, but instead occurs in the course of making one's way through continually shifting levels of fiction.[39]

The salient transitions are between the four levels of structure, and these movements blur the distinctions between the legendary Rikyū and the series of embedded flashbacks that seek to stabilize beliefs about Rikyū. This postmodern suture foregrounds the ideological work of anecdotes as they present themselves as authoritative historical sources of Rikyū's tea practice, oblivious to the reality that "the substance of that practice is essentially unknowable."[40]

There are three appearances of Rikyū as legendary dream. The opening titles of the film consist of almost monochrome shots of Daitokuji Daisenin lightly dusted with snow that implicate Zen in the cherry blossom myth. The story then starts with a dream that frames the rest of the film. The first dream segment is a black-and-white image of the elusiveness and impossibility of attaining the ideal of Rikyū. The rock garden of the title sequence has become a barren riverside where Honkakubō sees Rikyū ahead in the mist. Despite Rikyū's dismissive wave and imperative to return home, Honkakubō runs after his master in slow motion. The sound of his voice and his physical movements lose their synchronicity before he tumbles down and out of the frame.

The second appearance of Rikyū as legendary dream occurs during Honkakubō's account of his final tea with Rikyū and is a variation of the image of Rikyū dissuading Honkakubō from following him. With this visual repetition of Rikyū dismissing Honkakubō the impression is no longer the futility of attempting to mimic the unachievable mastery of Rikyū. These images of Rikyū dismissing others from following him reiterate the dialogue where Rikyū insists that his tea method is a cold and

lonely road. The cumulative effect of these scenes is to suggest how the
*iemoto* system has hollowed out tea's self-image as aesthetically iconoclastic. While certain anecdotes represent tea as intuitive freedom, the institutionalization of tea pedagogy has tended toward clearly structured
curricula supported by rules governing when students could learn and
observe more advanced serving procedures. The film's representation of
Rikyū's rejection of Honkakubō's diligent devotion suggests a harsh judgment of the descent into the reductive orthodoxy of tea.

The final dream collapses the division between the opening titles and
the impossible goal of attaining "Rikyūhood." Honkakubō's resolute
movement alone off into the mist as the titles roll down the screen can be
read as a rejection of the constraints of institutionalized tea. This is the
film's closing image. In the course of attending to his pastoral duties
Honkakubō has found his own way beyond the anxious concerns of others
for authenticity. His self-confident exit emphasizes the importance of faith-
fully seeking the spirit of tea over merely reproducing its external form as
defined by the predetermined horizons of the tradition's gatekeepers.

The second structural element is Rikyū the living legend, which appears
in the film three times. The first appearance is in response to the devotional
rites and questions of Honkakubō after Uraku interrogates him regarding
Rikyū's suicide. Rikyū's appearance as living legend is heralded by what
might be called the Rikyū theme music, and he appears first as a disembodied voice in the candlelit altar. The funeral tablet then dissolves into
the material form of Rikyū's torso. Rikyū proceeds to scold Honkakubō
for asking questions about the details of the suffering that consumed
Rikyū's life. The second time Rikyū the living legend appears he is seated,
waiting for Honkakubō to return after saying farewell to Uraku, and they
both adjourn to the tea room where Rikyū outlines the decline of tea's
history. The final appearance of Rikyū the living legend occurs during
Uraku's deathbed scene. Honkakubō notices the sudden appearance of
Rikyū and the next shot is a flashback. Rikyū is resplendent in white as he
prepares to commit suicide.

The third structural element is Honkakubō's "present," which serves as
the junction point for the anecdotes of the film. Honkakubō has sole
access to Rikyū the legendary dream and Rikyū the living legend. He also
curates the collection of stories comprising the Rikyū legend and has
absolute authority on questions of Rikyū's tea, life, and death. As the cus-
todian of the oral tradition of Rikyū parables he is questioned by other tea
men about Rikyū's death.

Honkakubō's "present" frames the embedded flashback structure, creating a postmodern conception of the past as the present's fiction. Cinematic time is constructed of interrelated non-linear, cyclical, and linear
elements. The episodic construction of flashbacks is non-linear, and the
presence of the spectacle of Rikyū rejecting the attempts of his disciple to
follow him at the beginning and near the end of the film suggests a circular

arrangement. At the same time, the changing seasons mark the passage of time, and as Uraku incrementally learns more about Rikyū's final justification there is a sense of moving toward understanding the reasons for Rikyū's suicide. This linear sense is reinforced by the aging of Honkakubō, from the earnest 28-year-old washing radishes in the crisp whiteness of the early spring morning to his final exit through the swirling mist of that rocky, dry riverbed.

Kumai's Rikyū transcends his past mortality and is immortalized because narrated anecdotes re-enact his life. In these nostalgic recollections his identity is attached to holy relics that he once owned or inscribed and to a set of preferences now institutionalized by the Sen schools. The Houses of Sen possess significant tea utensils associated with Rikyū and the pedagogical use of anecdotes reinforces their cultural capital as the legitimate transmitters of tea knowledge.

## Cherry blossoms as suicide: tea in the national fable

Hara Kazuo has explained that the Sen tea schools did not unconditionally cooperate in the making of his film.[41] Their request to avoid a realistic depiction of Rikyū's suicide, while negating the value of the meeting between actor Mifune and an unnamed suicide researcher, resulted in the film gaining an additional metahistorical significance. The film's concerns expand from issues of what constitutes the authentic and questions of cultural transmission in the context of tea. The expressionist use of the almost monochrome cherry blossom sequence breaks the film out of its discourse of tea anecdotes into the fable of the nation. The role of Uraku, particularly his concern with an authentic death, brings the relationship between the rulers and the ruled into view.

Kumai and Hara made the decision to respect the wishes of the Sen schools, and leave out a realistic depiction of Rikyū's suicide.[42] Their decision to replace it with images of falling blossoms linked cherry blossoms and suicide and gave the film contemporary resonance for post-war audiences. Although cherry blossoms could also function as symbols of peace, this was by no means the first linkage of suicide and cherry blossoms. The connection has frequently been made in militarist discourses of the nation, as we will see below.

The Cherry Group (Sakura Kai) was established in October 1930 with the expressed purpose of reconstructing the nation (*kokka*). This group openly advocated the violent use of force.[43] From 1933 to 1940 elementary school textbooks began with the phrase "it has blossomed, it has blossomed, the cherry tree has blossomed" (*saita, saita, sakura ga saita*) and was followed by text such as "advance, advance, soldier advance" (*susume, susume, heitai susume*) and "hinomaru flag, hurrah, hurrah" (*hinomaru hata, banzai banzai*).[44] The cherry blossom motif also appeared in the suicide-related activities of the Let's Die Group (Shinō Dan). Ritual suicide was used as a protest against government oppression of the Nichiren Group, which was established in 1928. One prominent member changed his given name to include the cherry blossom character. Certain members of Shinō Dan formed a specialist group and took up the cry "Let's die for our country! Let's die for our policy! Let's die for our religion! Let's die for our associates!" (*Waga sokoku no tame ni shinou! Waga shugi no tame ni shinou! Waga shūkyō no tame ni shinou! Waga dōshi no tame ni shinou!*).[45]

Flowering cherry was taken as a name by a special attack unit group[46] and the phrase made appearances in military communications:

> "Declining morale" was a meaningless concept to the doomed defenders of Peleliu, to whom the Emperor sent an unprecedented total of eleven telegrams of thanks before, abandoned by the High Command, they died to a single man, their last signal reading "Sakura! Sakura!"[47]

The cherry motif also appeared in a range of military hardware designed to facilitate self-destruction in the service of the Emperor:

> The Third Phase of the War Preparation Programme drawn up in late 1943 added 22 "special duty ships" for construction in 1944 and another 24 for construction in 1945. These ships were the *Kaiten* "human torpedo" and *Shinyou* ("ocean shaker"), both intended to be launched from shore at close range to enemy ships.... Special attack aircraft, likewise, were under development, primarily the Ooka ("cherry blossom") manned flying bomb (best known to history by its American nickname, the "Baka [stupid] Bomb").[48]

These linkages of cherry and death continue to reverberate in Japanese society. One month before Prime Minister Mori made his problematic "divine nation" remarks in May 2000,[49] a calendar used the cherry blossoms of Yasukuni Shrine in a photomontage with a sculpture of a "suicide squad" (*tokkōtai*) pilot against the background of the rising sun. Published by The Group Answering the Glorious Spirits of the War Dead (Eirei ni Kotaeru Kai), the March–April page of this Heisei 12 calendar also combined a photograph of a pilot who died a seasonally authentic death in early April 1945, a photograph of his military issue hat (a sacramentalizing of relics, similar to the treatment given Rikyū's tea utensils) and text detailing his final telephone conversation with his family. The cherry blossom motif is abstractedly repeated behind the text as a pink moire.

These examples are historically important because of their contemporary persistence in nationalist discourse. Kumai's cherry blossom sequence brings into view these uses of the cherry blossom motif during the 1930s and 1940s and its continual presence today. It is also useful to explore the extent to which Kumai's use of the cherry blossom motif is itself implicated in the militiarist discourses it seeks to criticize. This reading is most convincingly sustained by a narrow focus on Rikyū. In so far as the film portrays the pleasures of officially sanctified death, it is implicated in those totalitarian denials of the value of individuals not integrated into the edifice of the state. However, Kumai gives viewers ample means to resist comprehending the film in the dominant terms of nationalist discourse. The combination of the stylistic disruption of the almost monochrome sequence and the structure of embedded flashbacks offers viewers some critical perspective on the reported spectacle of ritual suicide. The cherry blossom sequence reinforces the distanced sense of seeing an account of Rikyū's death. Interrupting the visual grammar of the linked anecdotes allows a reflective space to open between the collage of tea room stories. More than pure aesthetic experience, the stylistic dissimilarity highlights the central role played by Uraku's insistence on knowing the unknowable: What did Rikyū finally say and do? Uraku's questions are reiterated by Soji and Oribe and this repetition emphasizes that the film is concerned with the power of an authentic culture to shape individual desire. It should not be forgotten that these elements of state domination remain a sonorous part of public life in Japan.

## Reading history from film: tea for war, tea for peace

Films that purport to represent national culture attempt to construct an imagined community. Attention to the ways idealized images of material culture attempt to fix the fluidities of plural cultures and identities by assigning the spectator a range of viewing positions reveals how film increasingly functions as a substitute for historical memory. As entertainment performs an educational role, these flows from the individual to the national give private pleasures a public significance.

Kumai's film answers the question that is suppressed by Teshigahara, and Teshigahara's film ends with the assertion that Rikyū's way of tea influenced the nation forever. Let us examine the critical stance of each film and how the idea of "Rikyū's tea" continues to shape Japanese subjectivity. The fifteenth Urasenke *iemoto* commented that his "Peacefulness through a Bowl of Tea" campaign resulted from reflection on the nature of wartime experience, and more specifically from serving tea to other special attack unit squad members and then hearing their final radio signals.[50] Historicizing this privileging of the individual subjectivity of one *iemoto* requires examining tea's role in the 1930s' creation of a sense of Japanese identity and solidarity.

After the Meiji Restoration, the tea schools went through a period of hardship when they had few patrons or students. They re-emerged with two large public gatherings: the Shōwa Grand Kitano Memorial Public Tea Gathering (held October 8–12, 1936) commemorating the three hundred and fiftieth anniversary of the Grand Kitano Tea Gathering

(1587); and the Rikyū 350th Commemorative Tea Gathering (April 21–23, 1940) honoring the three hundred and fiftieth anniversary of Rikyū's death in 1591.[51]

While it is convenient to assert that the original Grand Kitano Tea Gathering was a national convention of rustic tea,[52] it is important to remember the extent to which that event was redolent with the exercise of power. The gathering was ostensibly a display of cultural authority embodied in masterpieces associated with the Ashikaga Shogun or historically significant tea practitioners; it also included tea wares that had been confiscated or "donated." Hideyoshi used tea as a persuasive supplement to naked military might. Representing the event as egalitarian requires reading Hideyoshi's order as an invitation, and reproduces tea's image of itself as a purely aesthetic practice devoid of political and commercial concerns. Hideyoshi's coercive use of tea included compulsory attendance for all tea practitioners and bans on the private preparation by those who failed to attend that extended to their guests.

The discourse of the nation served as the context for the three hundred and fiftieth anniversaries of the Grand Kitano Tea Gathering and Rikyū's death. These events are examples of how history was marshaled in the cause of creating new identities: "Between 1936 and 1941, there were strenuous efforts made to express, and define, what makes Japanese people and life so Japanese."[53] Reports of the gathering of four thousand people in the 1936 event used the jingoistic tone of the day. The production and reception of prescriptive mass media texts were officially manipulated to express the sacramental Japanese identity. Honoring the national convention of rustic tea became part of an ultranationalist didactic trope that claimed to be concerned with the transmission of "warrior values" to all Japanese men, women, and children.

In the same way that the 1930s' popularity of Okakura's argument for the aesthetic unity of Asia assumed a political dimension in the expansionist rhetoric supporting the Greater East-Asian Co-Prosperity, the wartime commemoration of Rikyū's suicide gave militarists an ideological text that could be appropriated to justify the divine right of Japan to unify East Asia. Rikyū was no longer merely a historical man of tea conjured in anecdotes, a legendary embodiment of tea values, and a set of aesthetic preferences present in the tea rooms of modern tea practitioners; his legacy of tea values was to be subsumed into the larger narrative of the Japanese empire. The historical existence of practices like ritual suicide was used to legitimate the naval and air force special attack squads of which the fifteenth Urasenke *iemoto* was a member. English-language tea scholarship is silent on the extent to which tea's popularity was fueled by a deliberate courtship of patriotic sentiment. However, tea's appreciation of the instant appears to operate as an aesthetic extension of military regulations that demanded individual sacrifice in the name of the nation.

Cultural practices became a front line of conflict as political elites used their power to instrumentally define a nationalized cultural canon. Successive governments created the imaginary community of Japan by weaving aesthetic elements together into a series of intertextual relationships that endorsed the exercise of explicit state power against the interests of individuals. Significant changes in education and military regulations buttressed the aestheticization of the inevitability of death to make possible Greater East Asian War demands for absolute loyalty to the state.

The canonical *Tale of Genji* was instrumentally used to create a Japanese nation more palatable for international consumption in the same period. Sassa Seisetsu, for example, sought in 1911 to placate "yellow peril" anxieties about Japan's military success in the 1904–1905 Russo-Japanese War by deliberately othering the national self: "The *true* Japanese is a lover of beauty, a person of gentility and feeling, in other words, a latter-day Heian courtier."[54] According to Sassa's essentialized notion of Japanese identity, the role model for modern citizens was an upper-class aesthete who spoke a language unintelligible to most of the population. This othering of the national self occurred precisely when warfare was an arena for the performance of loyalty to the nation, and when military codes were being revised. The front-line diligence of Japanese Christian soldiers during the 1894–1895 Sino-Japanese War and Russo-Japanese War led to government recognition of "Christianity as one of the 'Three Religions' of Japan ... by the end of the Meiji Era in 1912."[55] The delicate sensibilities of early twentieth-century Heian courtiers were subject to appeals to " 'the attack spirit,' 'confidence in certain victory,' 'loyalty to the emperor,' 'love of country,' 'absolute sincerity,' and 'sacrifice one's life to the country, absolute obedience to superiors' "[56] by the Infantry Manual of 1909, the Army Education Regulation of 1913 and the Field Regulations of 1916.

Given the number of participants in the Shōwa Grand Kitano Memorial Public Tea Gathering and the Rikyū 350th Commemorative Tea Gathering, magnified by newspaper coverage and thematically related radio programming, and considering the government regulation of the cultural sphere through the Japanese Literature Patriotic Association (Dai-Nippon Bungaku Hōkokukai) and the Japanese Journalism Patriotic Association (Dai-Nippon Genron Hōkokukai), it can be argued that the mass culture aspects of tea's transmission constructed individual identity as something enhanced by membership of a national community. This is popular consumption of the ultranationalist sacrament of tea, and the reporting practices of the newspapers of the day helped consolidate the connection between a distinctive national culture and war as an expression of those values.

In 1936, *The Kyoto Newspaper* reported on a ceremony commemorating military deaths immediately above an account of the forthcoming Kitano Offertory Tea.[57] The thematic connection of these two items was textually and visually reinforced. The seasonal discourse common to classical literature and tea provided a reference for the headline commemorating those who died in the Manchurian invasion, and the visual dominance of the photograph of the cavalry parade with crossed flags points to the omnipresence of patriotic sentiments in daily life. The headline reads: "As autumn deepens, at Okazaki Gentō, a devotional offering to the Glorious Spirits of the War Dead." The thematic power of this visual element underlines the problematic nature of the intelligentsia's retreat into the nostalgic innocence of culture.

The central dilemma posed to these resistant acts was how to maintain the integrity of culture as a neutral territory when individual autonomy was increasingly subject to state intervention. "Once created, this imaginary space, increasingly absorbed by the interests of the state, might be filled with any aesthetic, ethical, or spiritual values implied by the term 'culture.'"[58] As tea positioned itself as the sacrament of the state, individual retreats from intrusive social control into nationally distinctive cultural practices were reduced to futile acts of resistance that resulted in receiving an aesthetic caress of state power. Governmental control sought to define the parameters of popular culture, and cultural practices were codified, commodified, and nationalized as authentic modes of citizenship. The power of the state was affirmed in the intersection of discourses of consumption and play, and authentic Japanese identity itself even now continues to be the commodity underlying these "traditional" leisure activities.

After the war, we see a significant shift from the existence of a nationally distinctive culture as a basis for regional expansion to tea being positioned as a message for peace. This vision of tea's post-war utility is more than the private insight of one *iemoto*. This apparent reversal of position, from tea as a jingoistic instrument of the militarist state, to tea as the beverage of choice among pacifist internationalists, is parallel to the strategy adopted by the Urasenke *iemoto* Gengensai (Sen Sōshitsu XI, 1810–1877) in his petition to the new Meiji government in 1872, in which he argued that tea should be understood as the expression of the nation. Shimizu Ikutaro observed in 1950 that pre-war patriotism was unconnected to democracy, and argued that

> the world-historical transformation that occurred after the war, caused by the advent of nuclear weapons, called urgently for the "completion of democracy." Therefore, "peace" and "democracy" had to be intimately connected to any rebirth of patriotism that might occur in postwar Japan.[59]

While tea profited from its representation as the embodiment of Japanese material culture during the 1930s and 1940s, Shimizu's analysis suggests that the post-war shift from a nationalist rhetoric to the possibility of a global market for tea knowledge, utensils, and practices was almost inevitable. This positioning of tea as the epitome of the reconstructed Japan involved erasing tea's complicity in stitching the aesthetic response of individuals into the fabric of the militarist arsenal. Consider how the optimistic fervor of an introduction to a book of *ukiyoe* prints assigns the cultural to the position of an outcome, and not a domestic means of achieving that goal: "On that glorious day when we have triumphed in the Greater East Asia War, when America and England have been conquered, and the radiant splendor of Japanese culture shines throughout the world, Japanese arts will illuminate the universe."[60] The post-war coupling of tea and peace recalls Sassa's 1911 representation of modern Japanese agents of expansion as refined Heian aesthetes. Culture as nationalism asserts its neutral inevitability while structuring its position in the foreground of the national identity.

Moving the focus away from the tea practices of Kyoto which have generally been positioned as the metropole in English tea scholarship reveals an explicitly military application of tea. Between 1941 and 1945 in Fukuoka's Hakozaki Hachimangu, there were tea ceremonies that sought divine assistance for victory. These gatherings (known as *senshō kigan kencha*) were prayers for victory in the Pacific War. These offertory tea practices are not connected to Sen offertory practices commemorating Rikyū and his descendants, but their existence as military sacraments supports an argument that accounts for tea's politicized position in the Japanese cultural landscape.[61]

## Film, power, and the transmission of tea

Reading these tea films as comments on sixteenth-century power, particularly the relationship between those who govern and those who are governed, highlights tea's central but contradictory positions in discourses of authority then and now. While being shown as a privileged social practice for elites and a contested arena where historic struggles of political, social and aesthetic legitimacy were enacted, cinematic embellishments of the Rikyū legend also comment on current debates about mass culture's formation of an imagined national community. The ideological work of tea films is to consolidate fifteen generations of tea tradition. This apparent continuity sustains an essentialist view of Japanese culture that underpins the perception of the nation as a stable entity.

Tanaka's 1962 film foregrounds the silenced Japanese Christian tradition. This argument for social diversity positions tea as both part of official high culture and the lived family practices of Rikyū. The romance of Ogin and the Christian warlord Ukon establishes the theme of their gendered and principled resistance to the naked might of Hideyoshi, and reference to the beauty of a Christian woman being transported to her execution links resistance with an aestheticized death. When Ogin's escape from Hideyoshi is impossible, Rikyū's domestic performance of tea is reconfigured as the equivalent of a warrior death rite. While the material comfort of Rikyū and his family depends on his ability to function as an element of Hideyoshi's display of power, tea as the culmination of Ogin's life is preparation for her ultimate act of explicit resistance to Hideyoshi. As the final expository titles offer no comment beyond merely recording the fact of Rikyū's suicide, Tanaka's film works as a preface to the later works of Teshigahara and Kumai.

Teshigahara's 1989 film categorically sets the politics of Hideyoshi against the art of Rikyū. This false binary is deliberately collapsed to demonstrate the mutual constitution of these two spheres and the inevitability of power. The flashback from the opening scene documents that Rikyū's distinctive tea practices were made possible by Hideyoshi's embrace of Portuguese guns and ships. Hideyoshi's military consolidation of sixteenth-century Japan was celebrated by Rikyū's construction of that intimate space, the Taian tea room. We see that Rikyū's desire not to have lived an unprincipled life explains his defiant reluctance to accept the mediation offered to his wife by Hideyoshi's wife as the final opportunity to delay his inevitable consumption.

The postmodern attention to the telling of the tale in Kumai's 1989 film points to the invention of tea's Rikyū mythology by the custodians of the tradition and by extension the myth of the nation. As a cautionary tale about the corrosive power of authority to consume its subjects, the film refers to significant shifts in the lived experience of citizenship.

Taken together, these tea films demonstrate the power of cinema to create and sustain the myth of the nation. Tea films are commodities themselves, and the pleasures of their consumption in cinemas or on video across the globe by culturally diverse audiences are not limited to an appreciation for a distinctive national culture that has been neatly packaged for the screen. The aesthetic sphere played a central role in Japan's movement from nationalism to imperialism,[62] and the films point to consumerism as the dominant ideological frame for understanding the iconic value of tea for Japanese advertisers, producers and consumers.

Cinema, like other forms of mass communication, functions as an element of national cultural production that aspires to be "integral, integrating and integrated."[63] Tea incorporates elements selected from diverse material practices and synthesizes them into commodified social practice; tea's claim for representative status is predicated on its reputation as an integral part of Japanese material culture. Institutionalized tea pedagogy may be privately experienced by individual practitioners as deeply integrating,[64] but students of tea are themselves integrated into dynamic sets of social relationships as gendered consumers of knowledge, embodied practices, and products bought on the basis of learned aesthetic preferences. To the extent that practitioners internalize orthodox aesthetic values and officially sanctioned taste, they become transmitters of social practices. Material and social practices are then integrated into consumerist discourses of an authentic national identity. This construction of authenticity becomes crucial as tea assumes an iconic value for a nation of non-practitioners. Cinema's convenient repackaging of tea culture as commodity operates within a cluster of seasonal discourses and permits an othering of the contemporary urban Japanese self.

For students of tea, the sense of progress that comes from moving through the hierarchical curriculum and mastering advanced serving procedures has the potential to reinforce the doctrine of the lifetime consumption of tea knowledge: personal achievement becomes something that is best defined by the limits of what can be certified inside the *iemoto* system. One issue to be individually resolved by tea practitioners is the question of how they benefit from the complexity of practices such as the Seven Exercises (*shichiji shiki*). This curriculum was invented in the eighteenth century as part of the formation of the *iemoto* system in the Sen tea schools. One of the pleasures of participating in this performance of advanced tea knowledge is the sense of dipping into an aestheticized history, before the walls erected to protect tea schools started to function as divisions amongst tea practitioners. While competent performance of these exercises gives a strong validation of one's status as a member of the tea family, the drills are an enticing element of a systematic pedagogy designed to support the doctrine of lifetime study.

The professionalization of tea discourse is a keystone in a complex of practices to ensure the successful transmission of orthodox tea knowledge:

> There is a great deal of consensus among tea practitioners on the way things "ought to be." The *iemoto* sets the standards and students uniformly recognize deviations from the norm. Doing something different makes a statement. This is not to say that guests react to originality in a critical manner. (Though – human nature being what it is – some do.) Most tea people appreciate a little variety, but the truth is that tea people have internalised Tea's symbolic structure: they cannot avoid employing the cognitive system with which they have been so thoroughly inculcated, and they are most comfortable with variations that fit into familiar patterns. In fact, when an important symbolic element is lacking, practitioners often intuitively correct for their [sic] absence – supplying missing features though [sic] their imaginations with the subliminal intent of creating a coherent illusion.[65]

It does appear that Urasenke's pedagogical success in establishing this consensus of orthodoxy results in a contradiction of its values espousing the primacy of individual experience. This undermines attempts to distinguish the knowledge production activities of the *iemoto* system from Japan's new religions. If tea practitioners are the epitome of rationality, how do individual students of tea come to intuitively supply those details which confirm to orthodox versions of tea practice? How do the aesthetic preferences of one man come to be so powerfully internalized that practitioners do not see what they see, but instead see what they have been taught to see? Tea students inside the *iemoto* system internalize the official precepts of their tea school. The rationality of tea practitioners distinguishes them from religious cult members, and yet that exercise of rationality is directed toward the formation of a group identity that rests on acceptance of a pre-scribed range of spiritual and aesthetic values.

Responses to unorthodox or alternative tea practices include gentle and/or refreshing aesthetic surprises. Unorthodox combinations of utensils or innovations in tea-serving procedures are perceived as explicit challenges to the authority of the *iemoto* to commodify and codify tea instruction and practices. By providing guests with an unconventional delight, hosts are also presenting themselves as individuals who have at least temporarily distanced themselves from the comfort of group membership provided by orthodoxy.

The construction of this critical response to originality is an inevitable consequence of the institutionalization of tea orthodoxy. The demonstration of being a true believer is mediated through a seniority system of sequential membership numbers, hierarchical relationships between teachers that produce competition inside and between practice groups and are displayed through authoritative mastery of official school taste. This explains why most practitioners are comfortable with established variations. Staying within the official aesthetic parameters naturalizes the established patterns of authority, and negates any necessity to critically assess how the relationship with one's teacher implicates participants in discourses of power. By extension, it brackets off any disturbing questions of the historical consequences of worshipping a nationally distinctive culture. It also places boundaries on what one is expected to aesthetically know. Instead of the expectation that tea practitioners have a systematic knowledge of all tea utensils, it is assumed that practitioners are familiar with the types of work created by the artisans and artists validated by the *iemoto*, particularly through the practice of signing the lid of a tea utensil box to designate it as a noteworthy example of "authentic" taste. This practice is performed by the *iemoto* for a fee paid by the artist or by the owner of the utensil, and results in the price of the object increasing substantially. It is not uncommon to hear tea room gossip about individuals who have forcefully insisted on receiving this validation. Among true believers, these conversations tend to conclude with expressions of sympathy for the difficulty of the *iemoto*'s position.

## A coda for practitioners: the hard reflexivity of future tea

The following proposals for the future development of tea are tempered by the realization that "we are part of what we oppose: we are historically, socially, and emotionally entailed in it, and we can only come to terms with that entailment if we first recognize it. This is a hard reflexivity."[66]

Students of tea may feel tension between the ambition to perform their "own" tea and the institutionalized pedagogy which serves its own interests by using a discourse of lifelong study to prevent students from "graduating." This tension is most apparent in two curriculum-related points.

First, the discursive primacy of the four seasons in Japan is used to justify the teaching of certain tea procedures (*temae*) only during their appropriate seasons. This arrangement of the tea curriculum requires years of practice before a student feels confident enough to perform procedures more suited to cherishing the seasonal here and now. The discourse of lifelong study is used to justify this pedagogical convention.

> Nothing is taught out of the season in which it is actually performed. This means that the time for practicing a certain variation may pass before the student has mastered it – frustrating to beginners, but logical seen in the context of a lifetime study.[67]

This is also a system organized to perpetuate its own authority, relative to those who receive its imprimatur. Implicit in the idea of lifetime study is an immutable hierarchy of those that teach and those that listen. This reinforcement of the indelible nature of those status differences inside the *iemoto* system pervasively mediates the experience of being a tea practitioner.

A more systemic example of the lifelong study discourse is the exhortation to return to the most basic tea procedures to once again learn the whole sequence of tea practice. If students have passed through the various levels of accreditation, they have presumably mastered the fundamental grammar of tea practice. In a pedagogical system more orientated to equipping students with the means to make a productive contribution to tea life, one might expect a less stringent emphasis on merely reproducing the established vocabulary of the *iemoto*. It is this failure by generations of tea administrators to delegate to individual practitioners the means to walk down their own path of tea that produces criticisms of tea's ossification.

It is commendable that it is possible to receive uniform tea instruction throughout Japan and beyond its national borders. However, the degree of curriculum control necessary to sustain this institutionalization does seem to occasionally deny the possibility of other ways of being a tea practitioner, and serves institutional interests ahead of the needs of learners. This is a consequence of a pedagogic emphasis on form which in turn produces formulaic sensibilities which are content to remain tethered to orthodoxy.[68]

It is ironic that the spirit of a number of tea practitioners (including but not limited to Rikyū), whose collective efforts established the roots of what we can now conveniently call rustic tea, can be located in disregarding the sedimentary formalization of tea orthodoxy. My experience as a provincial consumer of tea knowledge suggests that the challenge facing the international transmission of tea values is more fundamental than a structural concern with the hierarchical relationship pattern within the *iemoto* system.[69] Current tea pedagogy has been very successful in inculcating fundamental tea values, patterns, and preferences. What is needed now is a more self-confident administration that encourages tea life without the paralyzing insistence on orthodoxy, and a more curatorial selection and combination by private practitioners from the diverse offerings of *chanoyu* and *sencha* custodians. This rejection of tea brand loyalty will provide participants with the focus necessary to remain in the moment without constantly mediating their experience through the authoritative filters of *iemoto* orthodoxy. To reassert the primacy of personal experience, it is first necessary, going beyond the manner of Teshigahara's *Rikyū*, to acknowledge the inevitability of power/knowledge.

## Notes

1  William Johnson, "Kinuyo Tanaka," *Film Comment* 30:1 (1994): 18–25.
2  This section is a summary drawn from Teshigahara's official website: http://teshigaharahiroshi.com/english/profile/02.shtml. For an assessment of the significance of these details please refer to Dore Ashton, *The Delicate Thread: Teshigahara's Life in Art* (Kodansha, 1997).
3  Sato Tadashi, *Currents in Japanese Cinema* (Kodansha, 1982), p. 164.
4  See Chapter 1 by Watsky in this volume for more information on Sōkyū.
5  Teshigahara Hiroshi, *Rikyū* (Capitol, 1991).
6  Alternative modes of tea history include Dale Slusser's attention to the field of cultural production in Chapter 2 in this volume, or Robert Kramer, "The Tea Cult in History" (Ph.D. diss., University of Chicago, 1985).
7  This interpretation is avoided in Hiroichi Tsutsui, "The Role of Anecdotes in the Transmission of Tea Traditions," *Chanoyu Quarterly* 29 (1981): 44–49. Tetsuo Yamaori, "Anecdotes about Sen Rikyū," *Chanoyu Quarterly* 65 (1991): 43–51.
8  Joan W. Scott, "The Evidence of Experience," in James Chandler, Arnold I. Davidson, and Harry Harootunian (eds), *Questions of Evidence: Proof, Practice, and Persuasion Across the Disciplines* (University of Chicago Press, 1994), p. 369.
9  Dore Ashton, *The Delicate Thread: Teshigahara's Life in Art* (Kodansha, 1997), p. 158.
10  Hara Kazuo, "Urakusai ni gyōshuku shita Kumai Kei kantoku no aru omoi," *Kinema Junpo* 1018 (1989): 94–97.
11  See A.L. Sadler, *Cha-no-yu: The Japanese Tea Ceremony* (Charles E. Tuttle, 1998), p. 117.
12  One alternative to the *iemoto* model is the Nambō Ryū school of tea, based in Fukuoka. While aligning itself with Rikyū through the *Nampōroku* text "discovered" by Tachibana Jitsuzan (1655–1708), it is governed by a board of directors.
13  See Teshigahara, *Rikyū*.
14  See Sadler, *Cha-no-yu*, pp. 102–103 for variations of this anecdote.
15  Darrell William Davis, *Picturing Japaneseness: Monumental Style, National Identity, Japanese Film* (Columbia University Press, 1996), p. 249.
16  Pamela J. Asquith and Arne Kalland (eds), *Japanese Images of Nature: Cultural Perspectives* (Curzon Press, 1997), p. 17.
17  D. Bell, "Centre and Periphery Down Under: Australian National Cinema and the Global Information Order," *UTS Review*, 5:2 (1999): 200.

18 In the NHK teledrama *Hideyoshi*, Rikyū shares Nobunaga's parting gift, tea made from hot water boiled by burning ruins of Nobunaga's castle.

19 Oda was never made Shogun. While all English quotations for Teshigahara's *Rikyū* come from the 1991 subtitled version, released by Capitol, the remaining extracts are my translations.

20 For an example of Hideyoshi's usage of the golden tea room, see Beatrice M. Bodart, "Tea and Counsel: The Political Role of Sen Rikyū," *Monumenta Nipponica* 32:1 (1977): 49–74.

21 Murai Yasuhiko, "A Biography of Sen Rikyū," *Chanoyu Quarterly* 61 (1990): 39. Citing Luis Frois (1532–1597), Murai notes that "the man who actually made the tea room was a poverty-stricken goldsmith of Sakai ... whether Rikyū played a role remains a question."

22 Teshigahara, *Rikyū*.

23 Both Anderson and Mori acknowledge the support of Sen Sōshitsu XV.

24 Christine Guth, *Art, Tea and Industry: Masuda Takashi and the Mitsui Circle* (Princeton University Press, 1993). Ozaki Naotō, *Matsunaga Jian Collection* (Fukuoka Municipal Art Museum, 2001).

25 As the courtroom experience of Rodney King confirms, "[w]hen experts voice their version, the dialogue becomes asymmetrical in the sense that those unacquainted with these professionally crafted versions will get marginalized." Britt-Louise Gunnarsson, Per Linell and Bengt Nordberg, *The Construction of Professional Discourse* (Longman, 1997), p. 4.

26 Asquith and Kalland, *Japanese Images of Nature*, p. 12:

> There is a contradiction between the requirement of expected behaviour and spontaneity (in Japanese culture as in most other cultures), but this contradiction is solved by training to behave "spontaneously" (without thinking) according to expectations. For human beings this means that s/he must be thoroughly socialized, that is instructed or cultivated, so that the expected behaviour can be performed seemingly devoid of artificiality.

27 Personal correspondence with Gretchen Mittwer, International Division, Chado Urasenke Tankokai, Inc., August 16, 2001:

> The phrase *"ichiwan kara piisufurrunesu o"* was composed by Sen Sōshitsu XV as the theme or motto for the Third National Chadō Urasenke Tankōkai Seinenbu (Youth Division) Convention, held in Kyoto in July, 1973. Ever since then it has been the *iemoto*'s and Urasenke's common motto. Often, it is rendered into English as "Peacefulness from a Bowl of Tea," but "Peacefulness through a Bowl of Tea" is the preferred rendition.

28 Dorinne Kondo, "The Way of Tea: A Symbolic Analysis," *Man* 20 (1985): 288, 301:

> The theory is that mere good intentions are insufficient; one must know the proper form in order to express one's feelings of hospitality effectively ... [I]t is important to note the representation of a mental state by an action, and the performative aspect involved: performing these actions is as good as having the right attitude, for it should induce the right attitude.

29 Kramer, "The Tea Cult in History," p. 189. The "majority of practitioners are members of a group who derive pleasure and meaning from membership in a social organization."

30 Jennifer L. Anderson, "Japanese Tea Ritual: Religion in Practice," *Man* 22 (1987): 476. An "ideal student is born to the world of Tea with only a willingness to learn and an unquestioning respect for the authority of the teacher."

31 Shiota Nakakazu, *Nihon eiga gojunen shi 1941–91 nen* (Fujiwara Shoten 1992).

32 Sato, *Currents in Japanese Cinema*, pp. 170–171.

33 G.G. Rowley, "Literary Canon and National Identity: *The Tale of Genji* in Meiji Japan," *Japan Forum* 9:1 (1997): 2.

34 Naoki Sakai, *Translation and Subjectivity: On "Japan" and Cultural Nationalism* (University of Minnesota Press, 1997), pp. 101–102.

35 Brian Moeran and Lise Skov, "Mount Fuji and the Cherry Blossoms: A View from Afar," in Asquith and Kalland, *Japanese Images of Nature*.

36 Robert Ellwood, "Review of Joan R. Piggot, *The Emergence of Japanese Kingship*," *History of Religions* 39:2 (1999): 208.

37 M. Kraidy, "Intertextual Maneuvers around the Subaltern: Aladdin as a Postmodern Text," Cristina Degli-Esposti (ed.), *Postmodernism in the Cinema* (Blackwell, 1998), p. 56.

38 "Sen no Rikyū: Honkakubō Ibun," *Kinema Junpo* 1018 (1989): 98–111.

39 C. Baron, "*The Player*'s Parody of Hollywood: A Different Kind of Suture," Cristina Degli-Esposti (ed.), *Postmodernism in the Cinema* (Blackwell, 1998), p. 22.

40 Kramer, "The Tea Cult in History," p. 183.

41 Hara, pp. 94–95.

42 NHK's made-for-television drama, *Hideyoshi*, used the image of a pure white camellia twirling as it dropped to represent the death of Rikyū.

43 Hayashi Kentarō, *Jitsuroku Shōwa shi: Gekidō no kiseki* (Gyōsei, 1987), pp. 70–71.

44 Ibid., p. 110.

45 Hayashi Kentaro, *Jitsuroku Shōwa shi: Gekidō no kiseki*, vol. 2 (Gyōsei, 1987), pp. 39, 47–49.

46 Iguchi Rikihei and Nakajima Tadashi, *Kamikaze tokubetsu kōgekitai* (Nihon Shuppan Kyodo Kabushikigaisha, 1951), pp. 272–276.

47 Meirion Harries and Susie Harries, *Soldiers of the Sun: The Rise and Fall of the Imperial Japanese Army* (Random House, 1991).

48 Arthur J. Marder, Mark Jacobsen and John Horsfield, *Old Friends, New Enemies: The Royal Navy and the Imperial Japanese Navy, 1942–1945* (Oxford University Press, 1990), p. 398.

49 "'Divine Nation' Remark: Opposition Parties Prepare Demand for Prime Minister's Resignation" [my translation], *Asahi Shinbun* (May 17 2000). See also the Prime Minister's remark to the Shinto Federation of Diet Members Group: "The Japanese nation is a divine nation centered on the Emperor" [translation by author].

50 *Asahi Shinbun* August 15 1980, and serialized in *Nihon Keizei Shinbun* 1986–1987 and *Chanoyu Quarterly*.

51 Kumakura Isao, "The History of Chanoyu in Early-Modern Japan," *Chanoyu Quarterly* 75 (1994): 18–20.

52 Hisamatsu S., "The Way of Tea and Buddhism," *Chanoyu Quarterly* 73 (1994): 23.

53 Davis, *Picturing Japaneseness*, p. 2.

54 Rowley, "Literary Canon and National Identity," p. 9.

55 Edwin Reischauer, "Japanese Religion in the Meiji Era" [review article], *Harvard Journal of Asiatic Studies* 20 (1957): 361.

56 Ienaga Saburo (trans. Frank Baldwin), *The Pacific War, 1931–1945: A Critical Perspective on Japan's Role in World War II* (Pantheon, 1978), pp. 47–48.

57 *Kyoto Shinbun* (August 10 1936): 2.
58 Leslie Pincus, *Authenticating Culture in Imperial Japan: Kuki Shuzo and the Rise of National Aesthetics* (University of California Press, 1996), p. 221.
59 J. Victor Koschmann, *Revolution and Subjectivity in Postwar Japan* (University of Chicago Press, 1996), p. 219.
60 Ienaga, *The Pacific War*, p. 123.
61 Tim Cross, "Tea for War: The *senshō kigan kencha* of Fukuoka's Hakozaki Hachimangu," forthcoming.
62

> Historians have scrutinized the political discourses surrounding the [1894 Sino-Japanese] war, but the fact that that aesthetic discourses were the motivating moment has been ignored ... Okakura appreciated crafts as art, and by applying the same measure to all Asian nations, he confirmed the oneness of Asia within an art historical context ... His books began to be read in Japan in the 1930's, at the time when Japan began to move towards the "Great East-Asian Co-Prosperity." And it was from this moment on that the oneness of Asia, which he had discovered through his aesthetic thinking, came to function as an ideology that added the flourish to Japan's domination of Asia.
> (From Kojin Karatani, "Uses of Aesthetics: After Orientalism," *boundary 2* 25:2 (1998): 154, 155, 156)

63 Phillip Schlesinger, "On National Identity: Some Conceptions and Misconceptions Criticised," *Social Science Information* 26:2 (1987): 225.
64

> Display of the public self in Japan takes place to only a limited degree through objects (fashion, cars) given the general conservatism in these regards; but the private self can be constructed and verified through relationships to things that are affective and aesthetic as well as practical. Here, the "audience" is the self itself. What is important is not the viewing of the objects by others, but the sense of personal empowerment that comes from the possession and contemplation of things.
> (John Clammer, "The Global and the Local: Gender, Class and the Internationalisation of Consumption in a Tokyo Neighbourhood," in Michael Ashkenazi and John Clammer (eds), *Consumption and Material Culture in Contemporary Japan* (Kegan Paul, 2000), p. 263)

65 Anderson, "Japanese Tea Ritual," p. 136.
66 Michael Herzfeld, "The Taming of Revolution: Intense Paradoxes of the Self," in Deborah E. Reed-Danahay (ed.), *Auto/Ethnography: Rewriting the Self and the Social* (Berg, 1997), p. 182.
67 Anderson, *An Introduction to the Japanese Way of Tea* (State University of New York, 1991), p. 229.
68

> For a small minority of dedicated performers, the tea room is an infinitely malleable environment where they can produce quite magical events. The magic that is all but absent from the rule bound forms of the institutional practice still resides in the dedicated practice that destroys or abandons conventions even while conforming to their basic outlines.
> (Kramer, "The Tea Cult in History," p. 189)

69 Barbara Lynne Rowland Mori, *Americans Studying the Traditional Japanese Art of the Tea Ceremony: The Internationalizing of a Traditional Art* (Mellen Research University Press, 1992), pp. 162–168.

# 8 Tea records

## *Kaiki* and *oboegaki* in contemporary Japanese tea practice

*James-Henry Holland*

## Introduction

The records made of tea gatherings (*kaiki*) constitute a genre that has not been well documented. These records exist for private purposes as well as for public ones. This chapter will describe, contextualize, and interpret the functions of such texts, as well as those of an associated genre, the memorandum (*oboegaki*). Though these records are extremely stark, they reflect a creative process undertaken by the host of the tea gathering. We will examine the record of one particular gathering, fleshing out both its obvious and secret parts. This explication will also demonstrate some of the ways participants talk about tea utensils. It will be argued that tea culture as practiced by elites is in part an intellectual, symbolic, and aesthetic "game" that makes various use of written records.

What is an ethnographic study doing in this collection of essays on the history of tea? In spending time with elite practitioners, it is hard to escape the observation that many of their memories are organized around particular tea utensils. Thus, the discussion of particular tea records can be used to provoke rich narratives from informants when collecting personal histories. Also, old tea records are often used in historical research, and a close examination of some contemporary records may aid our understanding of their historical production and consumption.

## *Kaiki*

As I have argued elsewhere, a distinction can be made between novice tea practitioners, who see tea as a performing art, and elite tea practitioners, who see it as an art or game of allusion-making and -reading.[1] From the vantage point of a teacher, the students perform, but the teacher creates. The more frequently an elite teacher is involved in the creation of these elaborate webs of allusion, the more practice she gets at this art, and the more likely she is to achieve higher status among her peers.[2]

Allusions range in type, including seasonal, historical, and geographic, but also range in difficulty. A chrysanthemum-shaped sweet, for example, is a seasonal allusion that even a beginner can understand. More abstract allusions are also common, as will be discussed further below. Allusions are often of a public nature, accessible to perfect strangers who have learned the symbolic conventions of the art, or they can be private and personal, understood only by a particular audience. Research on tea culture has tended to focus on the more accessible public allusions, but private ones are just as important to tea practitioners.

The tools of allusion-making are the multiple utensils, decorations, and sweets that the host chooses for a particular tea gathering. This intentional selection process (and its result) are referred to as "selecting and combining" (*toriawase*). While the performance aspects of the ritual leave comparatively little room for creativity, the *toriawase* is an exciting challenge, and in many ways the key to the art.

> The enjoyment of tea is to be found in *toriawase*. No piece of tea art comes to life but through this process. Neither host nor guest are worthy of their position but that they understand this. Knowing *toriawase* is the basic requirement of a tea practitioner.[3]

The host's selection is often recorded in a written genre called *kaiki*, literally "records of a gathering," but often translated into English as "tea diaries." These records have public and private aspects as well, and I will begin by describing the private *kaiki* and why they are created.

Teachers who notice a student becoming more proficient and more deeply involved in tea circles will often suggest that the student begin to keep records of utensils seen used in gatherings. This might include the weekly lessons, but certainly would include periodic "public gatherings" (*ōyose chakai*) that the students attend, as well as any "high teas" (*chaji*).

Some teachers also instruct their students to begin using memo books for tea practitioners (*chajin techō*). These booklets include much reference information to assist users in identifying and contextualizing pieces of tea art they are likely to come upon, often supplying the vocabulary needed to make concise records of a tea event.[4] Memo books may include as many as ninety pages of empty forms listing about twenty-five main types of utensils likely to be used in a tea gathering.[5] The user of the booklet is encouraged to fill out a form for each gathering she attends, and to use the available blank space on the forms to make sketches, or to add notes about other less frequently encountered utensils. In the case of a high tea, the names of the small group of guests is also recorded. Students, in making such records, often say that they cannot recall everything they have seen in the gathering, but their teachers counsel patience and simply encourage them to do their best.

This exercise of creating records trains students to carefully observe and remember utensils they have seen. Many tea professionals say that they were given this task at some point in their training, and that they gradually began to realize that this was the key to the more advanced stages of their art. Most confess that after time, they became less careful in their record-keeping, making written notes very casually on the special pads of white paper used for handling sweets (*kaishi*), and later failing to organize those notes. Still, by this point, practitioners have internalized the habit of careful observation, and often have very sharp memories of specific utensils they have seen before, as well as a connoisseur's eye for discerning patterns in the use of utensils.

In addition to such records kept by advanced students or professionals in their role as guests, they might also keep records of the utensils that they, as hosts, have assembled for gatherings. Many teachers simply are able to remember which utensils have been used in lessons (*keiko*), and are likewise casual about the records of any "auxiliary teas" (*soegama*) they might have been asked to host, since most of the utensils in such cases are taken from the exhibit the tea service accompanies. The two occasions of which a professional is most likely to keep records, therefore, are the public gatherings and the high teas they host. These records help the host recall what she has "said" with her art collection in the past, and also help keep track of which guests have seen which utensils.

Thus, private records of the selections and combinations of tea utensils are kept by guests and by hosts. Such records made by guests might be part of an extended training effort, and those written by hosts for their own use help them in planning future utensil selections.

These records of utensil selections, *kaiki*, can have public functions as well. Handwritten records might be displayed at a public gathering or copied for distribution to guests, or even published in books and tea magazines. The hand-written *kaiki* is often seen at public gatherings. The head-guest might have asked about a few of the utensils, but, realizing a need to end soon, might ask if the host has a *kaiki* for inspection instead. The host generally apologizes that her *kaiki* is not really good enough to show off, but hands it to the head-guest. After a hasty perusal, the head-guest might ask another question or two based on what she sees written. Meanwhile, the list is passed around the room for the other guests to inspect in twos and threes. Guests often murmur appreciation of the host's fine handwriting. The head-guest might ask that the ritual inspection of the utensils be abbreviated; the host consents and offers to leave the records and some of the main utensils out for the guests to look at for a minute or so before they leave. Here, the *kaiki* helps facilitate the tight schedule of most public gatherings, where large numbers of guests are served in the course of a day.

In such public gatherings, some hosts are more comfortable than others in talking about their utensils with their guests. If the host enjoys a lecture-like approach, it might become obvious to the guests that there is no need to look at the *kaiki*. Some hosts, on the other hand, say that they feel nervous about talking in public, or that they feel embarrassed talking about their own utensils, lest it look as if they are bragging. Such hosts often depend more heavily on the written record to convey details to the guests.

The preparation and distribution of printed *kaiki* to each guest is a relatively new practice, practically unheard of before the 1970s. Such records consist of the host's own handwriting, mass-copied on attractive and durable paper (though not necessarily hand-made Japanese paper). Guests might receive these printed records when they first arrive at the gathering and hand over their admission tickets, perhaps receiving a *kaiki* for more than one room. In other cases, the records might be distributed to guests waiting in line for the next serving in that particular room. Reading the *kaiki* in advance can assist a guest in spotting items of special interest in the room, and might help the head-guest in asking more particular questions of the host. While some also consider the distribution of printed records as a useful memory aid, others say that it diminishes the guests' chance to look at the utensils without intervening preconceptions, while still others say that it is an immodest advertising of the strength of the room's utensils. Ideally, these utensils belong to the host or her circle, but sometimes the utensils are straight from a dealer's showroom, in which case the printed records might be considered too overtly commercial.

Some records are also professionally published. If the gathering is hosted by the head of the school (*iemoto*) or his retainers (*sōshō* or *gyōtei*), records serve as a conduit of authorized teaching, a model for all students in that tradition. Such records regularly appear in magazines put out by the various schools, such as Omotesenke's *Magazine of the Way of Tea* [*Sadō zasshi*] or Urasenke's *Tankō*. Books have also been written on the subject of selecting and combining utensils, in which we also find published records of gatherings. Also included are fairly detailed explications of the public significance of the utensils, though these might be abstract examples rather than records of actual gatherings.[6] Tea-school-sponsored magazines also report the records of certain elite public gatherings backed by the school's local associations. While these records might be taken as models of how to select and combine utensils, they also create fame for both the host of that room as well as for the group that sponsored the gathering.

*Kaiki* can thus exist as both private and public records. Some hosts also create an *oboegaki*, literally a "memory writing" or memorandum of the utensils used in a particular gathering. This is usually more detailed, and includes utensils intentionally omitted from the public record. Such a list may simply serve as a reference guide in the backstage area (*mizuya*), or a thoughtful teacher might distribute these notes for her students to help them develop a keener appreciation of the utensils they will handle at a public gathering, adding basic details aimed at the beginner, or more elaborate notes for the advanced students.

## Social context of research

Before examining the actual *kaiki* that is the core of this chapter, I should present the circumstances by which I possess it. I first met my key informant, Mrs. Konno, at her home in Western Tokyo in 1977.[7] I was visiting Japan for a month as an undergraduate student, and had befriended her son, Hiroshi. When my new friend learned of my interest in tea culture, he took me home to meet his mother and grandmother, both experienced teachers. I learned later that his grandmother was a "regional professor" (*chihō kyōju*) of the Omotesenke school of tea, and that his mother had also just recently achieved this status.

I moved to northern Japan in 1979, and lived there until 1983, ostensibly teaching English while the Konno family made every effort to nurture my interest in tea. I traveled frequently to Tokyo, where I was allowed to participate in the lessons taught at their home, and was invited to attend various tea gatherings, including public gatherings and a high tea. In the course of things, I met several of Mrs. Konno's closest tea associates, including her best friend, Mrs. Nakazawa.

From 1991 to 1993, I was living in Japan again, this time doing dissertation research. Mrs. Konno and her friends became my primary informants. While they all belonged to the Omotesenke school, I also worked with informants from Urasenke, Edo Senke, the Sekishū school, and the Enshū school, as well as with several dealers of tea and tea utensils.

In January 1993, Mrs. Konno told me that she had rather suddenly been asked to host a room (*seki*) at a monthly tea gathering (*tsukigama*) in which she had long been involved. This public gathering would be on the second Sunday of March, at the public hall of a shrine in Western Tokyo. She invited me to attend that gathering, also suggesting that I stay the entire day to get a better sense of the workings of the event. I knew that this monthly gathering was established by a tea dealer in 1950, and that its board (made up of the tea dealer and a number of tea teachers from various schools) scheduled hosts for four rooms per month, eleven months of the year (August being the month of rest). Mrs. Konno's teacher, Mrs. Baba, had been with this group since its inception, and as a matter of course, Mrs. Konno and her co-students were also deeply involved.

In late February, I attended a lesson taught at Mrs. Konno's home, and learned that the lesson was, in part, a trial run of the upcoming public gathering. The room had been arranged to simulate the unusual configuration of the room in which the students would be performing. I was told, however, that the utensils were different, since, if I were to see the utensils before the day of the gathering, part of the fun would be lost.

On the day of the gathering, I arrived at 8:00 a.m. at the public hall of the shrine, rented every month for the event. Mrs. Konno and the other students were there, setting up the tea room and the backstage area. I attended all four of the rooms at the gathering that day, but also had a chance to help backstage and to talk at leisure with the friends of Mrs. Konno who were also attending. I left at 5:00 p.m., joining Mrs. Konno's students at a coffee-shop, where they shared tales of the day.

That morning, I sat in line for the first of ten servings (*seki*) Mrs. Konno would host that day, and I was joined by an old friend of Mrs. Konno, Mrs. Fukui. Mrs. Fukui was a board member of this monthly gathering, and was known to be a friend of Mrs. Konno, so when she entered the room and sat the two of us in a hierarchically low position, a clamor arose among the other guests asking that she become the head-guest. She modestly declined, but finally, Mrs. Konno entered the room to ask her friend to be head-guest, and she consented, taking me with her as the second guest. She immediately saw another old friend of Mrs. Konno entering the room, Mrs. Gotō, and suggested that she join us as the third guest. This particular configuration of guests may have been anticipated by Mrs. Konno in her planning of that day's selection of utensils, as will be described further below.

Also in attendance that day was Mrs. Baba (Mrs. Konno's teacher), as well as Mrs. Konno's best friend, Mrs. Nakazawa. I observed that at the third serving that morning, Mrs. Baba was the head-guest, with Mrs. Nakazawa at her side as the second guest.

Two days after this gathering, I met with Mrs. Konno to interview her about the events of that day. At this meeting, she gave me a photocopy of the *kaiki* that she had shown guests that day, as well as the *oboegaki* that she had given her students. She went through these two texts with me, making sure I understood the notations, and adding other comments she thought might be of interest. I gleaned related information about Mrs. Konno's selection of utensils that same week from Mrs. Nakazawa, who had obviously heard other details during the planning stage.

I began this chapter long after the unexpected death of Mrs. Konno in 1997, and when I realized I needed to check certain details, I conducted telephone interviews in July 2000 with three people: Mrs. Nakazawa; Mr. Saida, the tea dealer who still hosts the monthly gatherings, who was also a co-student with Mrs. Konno; and my old friend, Konno Hiroshi, Mrs. Konno's son, who resumed his studies of tea after his mother's death. Thus, this chapter incorporates information from Mrs. Konno, her son, and two of her co-practitioners, in addition to my own observations.

## Case study: record of a tea gathering, March 14, 1993, held in the Tsuki-no-Ma Room, at the Shrine Hall of Iwaka Shrine [Western Tokyo]. Host: Konno Sōen

The items listed below in bold type correspond to the record shown to guests at the gathering. I have numbered the items for ease of reference, and have enclosed in square brackets the family names of artists and geographic locations originally provided only in the students' *oboegaki*. I have also included the four utensils intentionally omitted from the *kaiki*, but included in the *oboegaki*, marking these items with an asterisk after the number. Each item is followed by commentary.

**1. Hanging calligraphy (*kakemono*): "Shinka Sei-ei," The flower of the heart thrives in purity. Written by the 236th head-priest of Kenchō-ji [of Kamakura], Donge.**

This is a piece of calligraphy by a Zen priest, in this case written by the head-priest of a temple of considerable importance. Many tea practitioners say that they allow the calligraphy to set the theme and/or tone of the gathering. Perhaps some guests wondered what significance to attach to this piece.

　The *oboegaki* explains that this was written by Donge at his 88th birthday celebration, and Mrs. Konno explained this detail to her guests throughout the day. Mrs. Konno did not mention, however, that her teacher, Mrs. Baba, had turned 88 that year, and that the celebratory motifs of this gathering were in recognition of this occasion. In the first serving, Mrs. Fukui, the head-guest, also a student of Mrs. Baba, would have made this connection easily. In the third serving, Mrs. Baba herself was the head-guest.

**2. Flower vase (*hanaire*): Old Bizen ceramics, from the mid-Edo period.**

This quiet, antique piece belonged to the teacher who had turned 88, Mrs. Baba, and Mrs. Konno had borrowed it for this occasion. While it is considered ideal to only use pieces from one's own collection in the selection, it is actually not unusual for close friends and associates to borrow utensils from each other. Friends often know each other's art collections well, and are able to conceptualize their intent by thinking with their friend's utensils as part of their own expressive vocabulary. In this case, the noticeable age of the vase might have been the desired touch.

**3. Flower (*hana*): camellia variety, "Daybreak," with branches of Oily Gum.**

Most guests would have looked at this flower and the leaves as simply constituting a seasonally appropriate arrangement, but regular participants in this monthly gathering would have understood it in a different perspective. The tea-dealer who hosts these gatherings, Mr. Saida, has a garden of flowers and grasses appropriate for use in the tea room. At each of these gatherings, he supplies the hosts with a large assortment of seasonal materials he has cut from his garden, allowing these women to select and arrange them to their taste. This is considered unusual, but regular participants in the gathering say that it not only reflects Mr. Saida's generous spirit, but also his personal knowledge of and involvement in the art of tea.

**4. Incense container (*kōgō*): Makuzu ceramics, clam-shell shape. By [Miya-gawa] Kōzan.**

Paired clam shells (*hamaguri*), are said to fit together uniquely, thus no two un-matched shells will ever fit together properly. This became the basis of a game in which players searched for matching pairs of shells. Later, these shells came to be adorned with poems and pictures painted inside the shell halves. This game is associated with New Year and the Doll Festival, and the imagery of the matched shells is also alluded to in wedding celebrations. Thus, guests seeing the incense container in this shape should have realized that some kind of celebration was underway.

Inside of this pair of "shells" was an underglaze painting of the Palace of the Dragon King (Ryūgū-jō), a fabled undersea paradise, again a felicitous symbol. The theme of this painting was noted in the *oboegaki*, but not the *kaiki*, though any well-versed guest might have recognized this conventionalized motif.

The Makuzu ceramic tradition split into two halves in the Meiji era, an older brother moving to Yokohama, the younger remaining in Kyoto. This incense container is by the Yokohama branch of the family, and the *oboe-gaki* notes that this artist was the second generation master of that tradition.[8]

**5. Kettle (*kama*): Flat Spider (*hira-gumo*) type. By [Hata] Shunsai.**

This is a popular, easily recognized type of kettle. It has a flattened profile, and this particular kettle had flanges that rested on the ledge inside the hearth, thus suspending the kettle over the fire, rather than resting on andirons (*gotoku*).

This kettle also was borrowed from Mrs. Baba's collection. Like the flower vase above, this may have been borrowed to fill in a gap in Mrs. Konno's selection of utensils, but another interpretation seems likely: by using pieces from her teacher's collection, Mrs. Konno honored her teacher. The negotiations involved in borrowing such pieces would also give Mrs. Konno a way of involving her teacher more deeply in this event.

**6. Hearth-edge (*robuchi*): Wajima lacquer, plain black. By [Wakashima] Takao.**

The room assigned to Mrs. Konno for the gathering is anomalous, according to Mr. Saida: while the other rooms were built to accommodate their use as tea rooms, with an entrance for guests, an entrance for the host, a back-stage area, and a decorative alcove (*tokonoma*), this is a much larger room that requires a tall room-divider. The divider creates a six-mat room with a standard-sized decorative alcove, an entrance for the host, and a back-stage area behind the screen. Normally, there are certain aesthetic conventions considered appropriate for large rooms (*hiroma*) or small rooms (*koma*). The four-and-a-half-mat room, being considered neither large nor small, is the size that can make use of either set of conventions. Mr. Saida said, however, that even though this room is a six-mat size, the improvised conditions often lead hosts to apply some of the conventions of a small room here as well, emphasizing informality or intimacy. This, he suggests, might explain Mrs. Konno's decision to use a plain black lacquered hearth-edge, something normally used only in smaller rooms.

**7.\* Screen behind hearth (*fūro-saki*): picture of Mount Fuji with inscription, created together by Sokuchūsai and Jimyōsai-Sōin.**

Sokuchūsai was the thirteenth generation head of Omotesenke, the tea school to which Mrs. Konno, and, of course, her teacher belong. His son, Jimyōsai, became the fourteenth generation master upon his father's death. This screen had a picture of Mt Fuji drawn by the son, with an inscription by the father. The designation "Sōin" after Jimyōsai's name indicates that he made this work before succeeding his father. Mrs. Konno described this work as "by the brush of both" (*ryō-hitsu*), as well as a "joint work" (*gassaku*).

This screen was not listed on the public record, but did appear on the students' memorandum. Mrs. Nakazawa explained that the screen wasn't the real thing, but a printed reproduction of the original. As such, it wasn't really a piece worthy to be listed on the *kaiki*. Still, she said, this was useful information to share with her students, so it was included in the *oboegaki*.

**8. Shelf (*tana*): "Paradise" (Hōrai-joku), based on design by Sokuchūsai. By [Suzuki] Kōnyū.**

The *oboegaki* elaborates that this kind of shelf was designed by Sokuchūsai for the celebration of a 61st birthday. The two shelves, the base and the top, are both hexagons, a shape associated with celebration in Japan. The shelf's name is also auspicious, and any well-versed guest might realize that the shelf was associated with old-age celebrations.

Mrs. Konno told me that she bought this shelf when Mrs. Baba turned 70, and had used it in a celebratory gathering then. She hadn't used it since, but felt proud to be able to use it 18 years later, to again celebrate her teacher. She also mentioned that some of her older students remembered the shelf from its first use and thus were excited to see it.

**9. Fresh-water container (*mizusashi*): Takatori ceramics, with two "ears." Box inscribed by Sokuchūsai. By [Kamei] Miraku.**

The *kaiki* refers to the wooden box in which this utensil is stored, indicating that it has an inscription (*hakogaki*) by Sokuchūsai recording that he considered the utensil to be of special merit. The ceramic jar has a black lacquer lid, under which is a red-lacquered mark, the stylized signature, or cipher (*kaō*), of Sokuchūsai. The use of pieces so closely connected to the head of a school raises the status of the gathering.

It seems this jar was also selected because it was the right size. When using a shelf, the fresh-water container should be proportionally appropriate for use with that particular shelf.

**10. Tea container (*chaki*): Negoro lacquer, "Seven Treasures" design. Box inscribed by Jingyūsai. By [Hatsusegawa] Ryūan.**

The "seven treasures" (*shippō*) pattern is another auspicious design, widely recognized as such even outside tea circles. The exact set of "treasures" depicted varies, but is taken from a set of about a dozen graphic motifs, including items such as a gemstone, mallet of luck, sacred key, cloak of invisibility, or bale of rice.[9]

In the case of this container, six of the treasures were represented in *makie* lacquered pictures inside the lid, with the seventh drawn on the inside lip of the container. On the lid, in the midst of the six figures, was the cipher of Jingyūsai, a member of the Hisada house, a family historically important to both the Omotesenke and Urasenke lineages. Here again, while the record notes the inscription by Jingyūsai on the storage box of this utensil, the record could have instead described the piece as "*zaihan*" because of the lacquered cipher on the utensil itself.

**11. Tea bowl (*chawan*): Yagoto Kiln. Wave-pattern drawn directly by Sokuchūsai. By [Nakamura] Dōnen.**

This Raku tea bowl was made at the Yagoto Kiln in Nagoya. On the face of the bowl are several nested semi-circles, of the blue sea wave (*seikaiha*) pattern, another design associated with celebrations. This pattern was drawn onto the bowl by Sokuchūsai, and was then realized in glaze by the ceramic artist. The cipher of Sokuchūsai also appears to the lower left of this design. It is said that without the patronage of Omotesenke after World War II, this kiln would not have survived. The *oboegaki* notes that the artist, Dōnen, is the kiln's third generation master.

Mrs. Nakazawa comments that while the celebratory motif and the connection with Sokuchūsai are certainly enough to justify the selection of this bowl, Mrs. Konno also seemed to have a special fondness for this piece, and used it often.

**12. Secondary tea bowl (*kae*): Hagi ceramics, by [Saka] Kōraizaemon.**

This bowl is of the rough style of Hagi ceramics called Demon Hagi (*Oni Hagi*), and is an impressive example of the work of the eleventh generation Kōraizaemon. Mrs. Konno bought this bowl in the late 1970s, around the time when I met the artist and traveled with him and a group of tea professionals. Soon after meeting him, I bought one of his sake cups (*guinomi*) in this Oni Hagi style. When Mrs. Konno and I realized that we had both acquired similar pieces, we showed them to each other and afterwards spoke of them often, talking about how the famed Hagi patina (*Hagi no nana-bake*) was developing on each of our pieces. When this piece appeared in the tea room, I instantly recognized it as that "sibling" to my own small piece, even though I had not seen it for about thirteen years. As I was the second guest at this gathering, this bowl was the one in which I was served.

Talking with Mrs. Konno after that day's gathering, I mentioned my gratification at seeing this bowl, and she said she was pleased I had enjoyed it. She, of course, had known that I would be a guest at that gathering, and also knew that it would be one of the last tea gatherings I would attend for a long while (as I was about to return to the United States), so she had clearly decided to use this bowl for my particular enjoyment. She may have also anticipated that I would be second guest, attending her room along with an old friend of hers.

**13.\* Secondary tea bowl (*kae*): reproduction of a piece by Nonomura Ninsei, with a picture of bamboo grass. By Miura Chikuken.**

As summarized above, when I attended Mrs. Konno's room, Mrs. Fukui was the head-guest, I was the second guest, and Mrs. Gotō was invited to be the third. The first bowl of tea was ritually prepared in the tea room by one of Mrs. Konno's students and served immediately to Mrs. Fukui. The student began making the second bowl of tea for me, but in the meantime, bowls of tea prepared back-stage were served to the remaining guests, beginning with the fourth guest. These bowls were the matched tea bowls listed below as item 14. My bowl of tea was served to me, and then the third guest, Mrs. Gotō, was also served a bowl of tea prepared in the back, but in another special tea bowl, a unique piece. This was the tea bowl listed here as item 13.

Ideally, the conversation in a tea room at a public gathering is limited to the head-guest and the host, but occasionally this rule is bent. Mrs. Gotō asked, after drinking her tea, if her tea bowl wasn't the one used "that time, with the four of us." Mrs. Konno smiled and nodded in agreement, then continued discussing the artworks in the room.

I later asked Mrs. Konno what Mrs. Gotō had meant by her elliptic question. Mrs. Konno explained that she had achieved the rank of Regional Professor (*chihō kyōjū*) in 1977, at the same time as Mrs.

Nakazawa, Mrs. Gotō, and one other friend. All four of them had originally been students of Mrs. Abe, and when she died, they switched to Mrs. Baba. It was unusual for a group of friends to achieve this rank at the same time, and they decided to celebrate by co-hosting a room at this same monthly tea gathering. They consulted, of course, with their teacher, Mrs. Baba, who helped them decide upon the utensils they would use, and who also suggested that they visit the grave of their old teacher in Gumma Prefecture to "report" their progress. The four of them made this grave-visit together, taking with them the main utensils they had selected to use in the upcoming gathering. This tea bowl, Mrs. Konno explained to me, was the main tea bowl they had used at that gathering fifteen years before. When Mrs. Gotō saw it, she recognized it and made her remark to indicate that she had understood the bowl's significance.

This bowl was listed only on the *oboegaki*. When I asked why, Mrs. Nakazawa explained that normally you only list a main bowl and one secondary bowl on the public record. Anything more might look pretentious. Even so, she added, hosts often have an extra bowl with them in case there are more than two "special guests" in the room, so that they can mark their recognition of a third honored guest. This extra bowl, she said, is also of artistic interest, and would merit mention on the gathering record if only it weren't the third bowl. Also, she continued, this third bowl will not be used in every group of guests, and depending on circumstances, it might not be used at all, so it makes sense to leave this piece off the *kaiki*. Still, I note, Mrs. Konno included it on the *oboegaki*, and had perhaps anticipated using it to serve Mrs. Gotō.

The artist, Miura Chikuken, active in Kyoto, was the third son of the founder of the Chikusen line.[10]

**14.\* Matched tea bowls (*kazu-jawan*): Tsunashima Kiln, by Kamiya Hōsai.**

Discussed above, under item 13, sets of matched bowls are considered relatively minor, and often go unmentioned in the *kaiki*. The *oboegaki* indicates that the kiln was in Yokohama, but is now defunct.

**15. Tea scoop (*chashaku*): named, "Mount Miwa." Made with bamboo used in the "Shunie" ritual in the Nigatsu-do Hall of Tōdai-ji [in Nara]. By the 209th head-priest of the Nigatsu-do Hall, Gyōkai. The inscriptions on the accompanying box and tube are also by this priest.**

This was the first utensil Mrs. Fukui asked about, and she asked about it in a peculiar fashion: "What is the name of the priest who made the tea scoop?" The host answered "Gyōkai," and Mrs. Fukui replied, "Oh! The head-priest of Nigatsu-do Hall!" Mrs. Konno smiled in assent, and Mrs. Gotō began asking about other utensils.

Mrs. Fukui had probably recognized that the tea scoop had been made by a priest because of an unusual mark on the underside of the tip of the scoop, a Sanskrit character written in red lacquer. Mrs. Konno later told me that it was the letter "kya," which carries the celebratory meaning of "eternal blessings" (*kitchō jōjū*).

It seems likely that Mrs. Fukui recognized the name of the priest, Gyōkai, because he was a friend of another tea-practitioner in Tokyo, Mr. Endō, who was close to Mrs. Konno's circle. When Mrs. Fukui announced the priest's institutional affiliation to the room, she was dropping a loud hint to the rest of us: Nigatsu-do Hall is the site of a well-known annual rite of spring called Omizutori (also called Shunie). Surely many of the guests realized that this famous ritual would conclude that very day, March 14. Thus, the use of this tea scoop not only alluded to the start of spring heralded by this ritual, but also, more specifically, to the very dates of the ritual. These, too, are seasonal allusions, though not of an immediately apparent sort.

There was, however, an additional level to this allusion: I had traveled to that famous event ten years before with Mrs. Konno's son, Hiroshi, and we had been among the hundred or so guests allowed to see the very unusual rituals that follow the famed public ceremony and last until dawn. This had been made possible by a letter of introduction written for us by the priest's friend, Mr. Endō. In effect, this personal allusion was Mrs. Konno's way of saying to me, "Do you remember that trip with my son?"

**16. Waste-water jar (*kensui*): Kanagawa ceramics, water-bird pattern. By [Inoue] Ryōsai.**

When elaborating on this *kaiki*, Mrs. Konno did not say anything about this entry, nor were my other informants able to say anything in particular about it. Still, it elicited special attention from the woman celebrated that day, Mrs. Baba. I was back-stage when Mrs. Baba was being served. After drinking the tea, when the conversation about the utensils began, she apparently asked Mrs. Konno if she could be shown the waste-water jar. Since this genre does not normally receive much attention, this request was unexpected. The utensil had already been removed from the room, so Mrs. Konno relayed the request to her students in the back stage area, who rinsed it, patted it dry, and handed it out to their teacher.[11]

**17. Lid-rest (*futaoki*): Makuzu ceramics, pine-seedling illustration. By [Miyagawa] Kōsai.**

Pine-seedlings are often associated with New Year, which is traditionally symbolic of early spring. They are also used to signify the more literal coming of spring in March. Mr. Saida pointed out that the selection of this piece reinforced the theme of spring suggested by the use of the tea scoop described above.

This lid-rest was made by the Kyoto branch of the Makuzu house. The Kyoto branch remained active under the head name "Kōsai" after the main tradition, the one headed by "Kōzan," moved to Yokohama.

**18. Sweets platter (*kashi-bachi*): red line drawing of a mythical lion grasping a jewel. By first generation, [Miura] Chikusen.**

This platter's decoration is another of the auspicious symbols used in this gathering. The artist, Chikusen, was the father of the maker of item 13, Chikuken.

**19.* Secondary sweets platter (*kae*): reproduction of a Dutch piece, made by Tsunohazu Kiln. Original is in the collection of [Kazue] Hyōnenshi.**

The secondary sweets platter is another utensil that is often not recorded on the public record, as in this case.

Over the years, while always continuing their studies under Mrs. Baba, Mrs. Konno and Mrs. Nakazawa began to supplement their study by taking on additional teachers. They not only had monthly lessons with a head teacher (*sōshō*) from Omotesenke, but also studied with a scholar of tea, Kazue Hyōnenshi, who has multivalent ties with the various schools of tea. Under Hyōnenshi, they studied how to plan and host high teas in particular. An organization of people who have studied with him sponsors tea gatherings, among other activities. Apparently, Hyōnenshi commissioned Tsunohazu Kiln to make a number of copies of a platter in his collection, and gave them as gifts to his students at a New Year's tea. Mrs. Nakazawa saw the platter and recognized it, and it may have been recognized by a number of other guests that day who had also studied under Hyōnenshi.

Historically, the Kazue house served as suppliers to the Ii house, a lineage of feudal lords. To cancel debts, parts of the art collection of the Ii house were given to the Kazue house. The original platter, upon which this copy was based, was one of those pieces once owned by the Ii house.

**20. Moist cake (*kashi*): "Spring Fields," from Taiichi Confectionery.**

The name of this sweet, "Haru no No," was, in fact, a pun. This cake was made of a light-green paste with a bright yellow swirl running through the sweet. The second "No" of the name is written with the character for "fields," yet the yellow swirl is shaped like the *hiragana* character "no" as well. Thus, the name might also mean, "The Character 'No' of Spring." A seasonal allusion, with a little word-play for those who read the *kaiki*.

**21. Dried cake (*higashi*): "Bales of Fortune," from Tsuruya Yoshinobu Confectionery.**

This was a beige-colored dry sweet that had been pressed in a detailed mold, giving it the shape of a rice-bale, one of the many "treasures" mentioned above under item 10. Small flecks of gold foil also shone from the sweet's surface. This is another celebratory symbol.

**22. Tea (*ocha*): "Verdant Clouds," from Tōkō-en Tea.**

Mrs. Konno had bought this tea from Mr. Saida, the tea merchant who is also the convener of this monthly gathering. I was told that while there was no obligation to use his tea, most hosts at these gatherings do, simply as a matter of etiquette. She reminded me that Mr. Saida is highly regarded in her circles.

### Public themes

Public themes, and the allusions that carry them, are accessible to all guests, regardless of whether or not they have personal ties to the host. Those guests with sharper eyes and keener wits will understand more of the allusions than will others, but hosts anticipate the possibility that some of their intentions might go unnoticed, and welcome unintended interpretations as well.[12]

Perhaps the theme that was most immediately obvious to the guests at the public gathering discussed above was that of the season, early spring. It is rare for a set of selected utensils to fail to allude to the season, so every beginner is able to look for this theme successfully. The flower, a camellia (item 3), and the pastel green and yellow moist sweet (20) are easily associated with early spring. The lid-rest with the pine seedlings (17) might not be as visually obvious, and might require a bit more reading, but is still very simple compared with the seasonal significance of the tea scoop (15). Mrs. Fukui, the clever and well-informed head-guest in my serving, understood the connection between the maker of the scoop with the famous sub-temple of which he was head-priest. Having mentioned the name of the temple, she made it easier for the rest of us to connect the tea scoop to the famous seasonal ritual that would conclude that very day.

It was also relatively easy to discern that the gathering was some sort of celebration. The dried sweet, both with its gold flecks and its rice-bale shape (21) was the most apparent, especially if the guest noticed the name of the sweet, "Bales of Fortune." The platter with the jewel-bearing mythological lion (18), the tea bowl with the blue sea wave pattern (11), and the lacquered tea container with the seven treasures design (10) also conveyed this theme easily. The incense container shaped as a pair of clam shells (4) required the viewer to associate paired shells with holidays to achieve the thematic association. The tea scoop (15) again provided the most difficult clue in this set, the Sanskrit character "kya" written on the back. Mrs. Konno told me this character alluded to "eternal blessings," but it is unclear if any guest that day realized this intention.

More particularly, this was a celebration of Mrs. Baba's 88th birthday. Besides the generic celebratory motifs, three items of the utensil selection alluded to old age celebrations. The calligraphy (1) was written by a Zen priest to celebrate his own 88th birthday. Mrs. Konno explained this throughout the day at each serving. It seems likely she did not write this on the *kaiki* because she intended to make this connection explicit in her own comments. The shelf (8) was designed specifically for age celebrations, and would have been recognized as such by the most knowledgeable guests. The name of the shelf ("Paradise") and the depiction of the Dragon King's Palace on the incense container (4) might have also been understood as celebratory symbols. The Dragon King's Palace was where years stood still for the fisherman Urashima Tarō in the famed folk tale, making this paradise one of agelessness.

Another theme was that of status, or prestige. While not normally acknowledged as a theme in such gatherings, practitioners certainly agree that the use of pieces associated with the heads of their school (*iemoto*) improves the status of the gathering. The main tea bowl of the day (11) was decorated by Sokuchūsai, the thirteenth generation master of Omotesenke, and had his cipher on the front of the bowl itself. The fresh-water container (9) had his cipher on its lacquered lid, and the shelf (8) was based on his design. The screen behind the hearth, while a reproduction and thus not listed on the public record, was inscribed by him and illustrated by his son (the current master of Omotesenke). The tea container (10) had the cipher of Jingyūsai of the Hisada house.

The status of a gathering can also be raised by the use of utensils made by famed artists. As in the case of the heads of schools, part of this status is based on the generational depth of the artists' traditions. In this gathering, the second tea bowl (12) by the eleventh generation Kōraizaemon would most immediately draw guests' attention. Other objects by famous artists include the calligraphy (1) by the 236th head-priest of a famous Zen temple and the tea scoop (15) by the 209th head-priest of another famous sub-temple. The pieces from the Makuzu tradition (4 and 17) and from the Chikusen lineage (13 and 18) also represent some generational depth. The use of the reproduction of the historical piece from the Ii collection (19) gives the set of selected utensils a further degree of status derived from historic rootedness.

The incessant allusion to buoyant celebration, gold flecks and all, was probably balanced by the gravity of the references to the school-heads and other artistic lineages. Three other pieces seem also to point the selection of utensils in a quieter direction. The hanging scroll (1) consists of calligraphy by a Zen master, which aside from its generational depth represents a selection typical of a quiet, intimate gathering. The hearth-edge of plain black lacquer (6), typical of smaller tea rooms, and the obviously antique flower vase (2) might also have been selected to help subdue the tone of the celebration.

The last public theme is one of hierarchical or inter-generational pairs. Mrs. Nakazawa reported that this theme had not been immediately obvious to her, if even intended by Mrs. Konno. Mrs. Nakazawa also admitted that Mrs. Konno thought carefully about her allusions, often planning some to levels of depth not necessarily understood quickly by her guests. Perhaps most importantly, Mrs. Nakazawa seemed to enjoy this interpretation, which might be its best claim to legitimacy.

The hearth-screen (7) was the creation of a father and son team, and the incense container (4) was in the shape of a pair of clam shells. The main tea bowl (11) represented the patron/client relation of the Omotesenke *iemoto* with Yagoto Kiln. The Makuzu ceramic tradition is represented by the incense container from the main branch of the family in Yokohama (4) and the lid-rest by the "sibling" branch in Kyoto (17). Similarly, the Chikusen lineage is represented by the main sweet platter (18), made by the father, and the third tea bowl (13) made by his son. The Makuzu and Chikusen examples are especially noteworthy because of the general tendency to avoid the use of allusions that make the same point by means of the same symbolic convention (*daburu*). Mrs. Konno may have selected these sets of pairs to highlight the teacher/student relation that existed between Mrs. Baba and her students, and to represent those students as her successors. The lid-rest (17), with its design of pine seedlings might reinforce this interpretation.

These suggestions help to explain why nineteen of the twenty-two pieces listed on the *kaiki* and *obaoegaki* might have been selected for the tea gathering. These allusions were all publicly accessible, though ranging in difficulty. The expectation that, at this type of tea gathering, the guests will include rank beginners mandates the use of some very simple allusions, but other, more complex allusions are included for the enjoyment of more proficient guests. As I have discussed elsewhere,[13] the game-like play of allusion-reading is very enjoyable to life-long students of tea, and the ethos requires an openness to the indeterminacy of the interpretations of these allusions.

## Personal allusions

Besides these interpretations that can be arrived at by anybody who has studied enough, there are also allusions aimed at particular members of the anticipated audience. Aside from the references to her birthday celebration, Mrs. Baba was referred to obliquely in the day's selection of utensils at least three times. Two items, the vase (2) and the kettle (5) were borrowed from Mrs. Baba, and other students of Mrs. Baba in attendance that day surely recognized these pieces. Mrs. Konno had bought the shelf (8) eighteen years before to celebrate Mrs. Baba's 70th birthday, and this connection was understood by at least some of the guests.

Two of the allusions seem to have been made for my sake, as a kind of farewell to me at the end of my research stay in Japan. Both the Kōraizaemon tea bowl (12) and the tea scoop (15) referred to my shared personal history with Mrs. Konno.[14]

Mrs. Fukui, the head-guest in my serving, was given a chance to show off her ability to connect the name of the priest who made the tea scoop (15) with the name of the temple, made possible by her connections with Mr. Endō, a friend of that priest. Mrs. Gotō, the third-guest in my serving, was served with a bowl (13) that she had used together with Mrs. Konno and Mrs. Nakazawa sixteen years before. I am sure it was heartening to Mrs. Konno that Mrs. Gotō recognized the bowl and announced her recognition, but also exciting for Mrs. Gotō, who must have felt flattered to be remembered in this way in the planning of the utensils.

Mr. Saida, the tea dealer who organizes this monthly gathering, was referred to twice, in the use of the flowers he had grown (3) and in the use of the tea (22) from his shop. Both of these allusions would have been understood by any teacher regularly involved in the monthly gathering.

The use of the second sweet platter (19) would probably be recognized by peers of Mrs. Konno who also studied with Hyōnenshi.

Mrs. Konno said that some of her older students recognized the shelf (8) as the one that had been used eighteen years before to celebrate Mrs. Baba. Whether or not this was an intended allusion on the part of Mrs. Konno, it sounds from her description of the students' recognition as if they were pleased at their own ability to recognize it.

In addition to the publicly accessible allusions described above, we therefore find personal allusions in at least nine other utensils. Considerable overlap exists between the public list and the personal list, as well as among personal references: the tea scoop, for example, seems to have had at least two discrete personal meanings. These pieces of art are multi-vocal symbols, intended to convey different things to different people.

Personal allusions can only be attempted by the host, or understood by the guest, because of long, intertwined personal histories. My ability to comment on these personal allusions is based on my understanding of some of the personal relationships that existed among Mrs. Konno and that day's assembled guests. My perspective is of course limited, and other pieces may have carried personal significance to other guests that day as well. General discussions of the selection and combination of utensils[15] tend to focus on the public themes of gatherings because the personal allusions are not of general interest. Nonetheless, when individuals read an allusion that involves them personally, this recognition by the host is considered a compliment, and may also be emotionally moving.

Hosts often incorporate utensils received as gifts from guests into the selection of utensils in order to make personal allusions.[16] The fact that no such gifts were apparent in the gathering described above makes me suspect that I simply do not know the personal histories of the assembled utensils well enough. It is also possible, however, that at gatherings of this sort, where most of the guests are strangers, more attention is paid to the publicly accessible themes and less to the personal allusions. Perhaps it is in the intimacy of a high tea enjoyed among friends that the most elaborate personal allusions are made.

## Conclusion

At this point, we can reconsider the various types of *kaiki* in light of the elite practice of interpreting the selection and combination of utensils. Promising students are set the task of creating records of gatherings they attend. Their teachers hope that by this practice, the students will transcend a performance-oriented view of tea ceremony and arrive at an experiential understanding of the symbolic manipulations involved in understanding a host's selection of objects. Once a student begins to make such records, the patternedness of the selection is often quickly apparent. The longer the student has been involved in a particular tea circle, the more likely it is that shared history with other practitioners will become the basis of personal allusions. By the time the student has fallen out of the habit of regularly keeping records, the skill of careful observation and interpretation has become ingrained. This can serve as the basis for the social reproduction of teachers who are able to expressively create meaningful tea utensil selections.

The *kaiki* kept by a host, we can now see, serves as a record of the various allusions made. The host can look at previous records to verify the last time a particular piece was used. In the case of a high tea, the host can confirm who has seen which parts of the collection to date. This assists in planning future gatherings, as an element of surprise is required for the elaborate game to work. The *kaiki* written as something to be displayed or even distributed at a public gathering, besides serving as a memory aid or time-saver, might also be seen as a sheet of hints for those guests looking for the significance of the utensil selection.

*Kaiki* serve as training tasks, skeletal records, and hints, but they are never full accounts: These records reflect the particular kind of guessing game that animates contemporary tea practice.

## Notes

1  James-Henry Holland, "Allusion, Performance, and Status: The Social and Aesthetic World of Elite Practitioners of the Japanese Tea Ceremony" (Ph.D. diss., Cornell University, 1997); James-Henry Holland, "A Public Tea Gathering: Theater and Ritual in the Japanese Tea Ceremony," *Journal of Ritual Studies* 14:1 (2000): 32–44.

2 The female generic referent is used in this article because the overwhelming majority of current practitioners are female.
3 Sasaki Sanmi, *Ocha no toriawase* (Kōbunsha, 1949), p. 1.
4 See, for example, Murai Yasuhiko, Tsutsui Hiroichi, and Akanuma Taka (eds), *Chadō bijutsu techō* (Tankōsha, 1987).
5 See Sasaki Sanmi (ed.), *Chajin techō* (Kawahara Shoten, 1952; revised 1992).
6 See, for example, Sasaki, *Ocha no toriawase*; Mita Tomiko, *Toriawase no kufū* (Tankōsha, 1981); or Awata Tensei, *Chanoyu shiki no toriawase* (Muramatsu Shokan, 1982).
7 With my informants' consent, I have changed the names and a very few identifying characteristics of those whose names are not normally part of public discourse.
8 For information on the two Makuzu lines, see Kōgei Shuppan (eds), *Saishin gendai tōgei sakka jiten* (Kōgei Shuppan, 1987), p. 536; Edward S. Morse, *Catalogue of the Morse Collection of Japanese Pottery* (Charles E. Tuttle Company, 1979), p. 280; and Katō Tōkurō (ed.), *Genshoku tōki daijiten* (Tankōsha, 1972), pp. 326–327 and 928–929.
9 Concerning this pattern, see Toraya Bunko (eds), *Fukusa to wagashi ten* (Toraya Bunko, 1992), p. 25; and Tankōsha Henshūkyoku (eds), *Cha no kireji nyūmon* (Tankōsha, 1997), pp. 34–35.
10 For information on the Chikusen and Chikuken lineages of the Miura house, see Kōgei Shuppan (eds), *Saishin gendai tōgei sakka*, p. 523.
11 I am unable to say whether Mrs. Baba made this unusual request simply out of an abstract interest in the waste-water jar, or whether the utensil held some personal significance for her, an allusion to which I am not privy.
12 Holland, "Allusion, Performance, and Status," pp. 172–174.
13 Ibid, pp. 168–169 and 172–174.
14 This article has focused on explicating the written record of this gathering, and in so doing, has failed to consider other opportunities Mrs. Konno might have used to make allusions. In particular, I should report that I was served lunch at this gathering in Mrs. Konno's room for receiving special guests (*settai shitsu*) along with some of her friends. Rice-crackers were set out on the table in some small lacquered plates which I had given her some ten years before. See Holland, "Allusion, Performance, and Status," p. 78.
15 Such as Sasaki, *Ocha no toriawase*; Mita, *Toriawase no kufū*; or Awata, *Chanoyu shiki no toriawase*.
16 Holland, "Allusion, Performance, and Status," pp. 116 and 190.

# Select bibliography

Adami, Norbert R. "Tee-Zeremonie in Japan oder Form und Inhalt," *Münchner japanischer Anzeiger: Eine Vierteljahrsschrift* 4 (1993).

Akanuma Taka. "Wabi no chaki – shikisai no hensen," *Tankō* 8 (1993).

Anderson, Jennifer L. "Japanese Tea Ritual: Religion in Practice," *Man* 22:3 (1987).

Anderson, Jennifer L. *An Introduction to the Japanese Way of Tea*. State University of New York Press, 1991.

Andō Seiichi. "Tokugawa Yorinobu no nyūkoku to han taisei no kakuritsu," in Wakayama Kenshi Hensan Iinkai (eds), *Kinsei*. Unnumbered volume. *Wakayama kenshi*. 1990.

Asao Naohiro. "Shokuhōki no Sakai daikan," in *Akamatsu Toshihide kyōju taikan kinen kokushi ronshū*. Bunkōsha, 1972.

Asao Naohiro. "The Sixteenth-century Unification," in John Whitney Hall (ed.), *The Cambridge History of Japan*, vol. 4. Cambridge University Press, 1991.

Ashkenazi, Michael. "The Can-nonization of Nature in Japanese Culture," in Pamela J. Asquith and Arne Kalland (eds), *Japanese Images of Nature: Cultural Perspectives*. Curzon, 1997.

Ashton, Dore. *The Delicate Thread: Teshigahara's Life in Art*. Kodansha, 1997.

Asquith, Pamela J. and Kalland, Arne (eds), *Japanese Images of Nature: Cultural Perspectives*. Curzon Press, 1997.

Awata Tensei. *Chanoyu shiki no toriawase*. Muramatsu Shokan, 1982.

Baron, C. "*The Player*'s Parody of Hollywood: A Different Kind of Suture," in Cristina Degli-Esposti (ed.), *Postmodernism in the Cinema*. Blackwell, 1998.

Bartlett, Christy Allison. "The *Tennōjiya kai-ki*: The Formative Years of Chanoyu" (MA thesis, University of California at Berkeley, 1993).

Bell, D. "Centre and Periphery Down Under: Australian National Cinema and the Global Information Order," *UTS Review* 5:2 (1999).

Benjamin, Walter. "The Storyteller," in Walter Benjamin. *Illuminations*. Schocken Books, 1968.

Berry, Mary Elizabeth. *Hideyoshi*. Harvard University Press, 1982.

Berry, Mary Elizabeth. *The Culture of Civil War in Kyoto*. University of California Press, 1994.

Bodart, Beatrice M. "Tea and Counsel: The Political Role of Sen Rikyū," *Monumenta Nipponica* 32:1 (1977).

Bodart-Bailey, Beatrice M. "Tea and Politics in Late-Sixteenth-Century Japan," *Chanoyu Quarterly* 41 (1985).

Bourdieu, Pierre. *Distinction: A Social Critique of the Judgment of Taste*. Harvard University Press, 1984.

Bourdieu, Pierre. *Language and Symbolic Power*. Harvard University Press, 1990a.

Bourdieu, Pierre. *The Logic of Practice*. Stanford University Press, 1990b.

Bourdieu, Pierre. *The Field of Cultural Production*. Columbia University Press, 1993.

Breen, H. "The Meanings of Things: Interpreting the Consumer Economy in the Eighteenth Century," in John Brewer and Roy Porter (eds), *Consumption and the World of Goods*. Routledge, 1993.

Castile, Rand. *The Way of Tea*. Weatherhill, 1971.

Chadō Shiryōkan. *Kōchi kōgō – Fukenshō shutsudo ibutsu to Nihon denseihin*. Chadō Shiryōkan and MOA Bijutsukan, 1998.

Chikamatsu, Shigemori. *Stories from a Tearoom Window*. Charles E. Tuttle Company, 1982.

Clammer, John. "The Global and the Local: Gender, Class and the Internationalisation of Consumption in a Tokyo Neighbourhood," in Michael Ashkenazi and John Clammer (eds), *Consumption and Material Culture in Contemporary Japan*. Kegan Paul, 2000.

Clarence-Smith, William Gervase. *Cocoa and Chocolate, 1765–1914*. Routledge, 2000.

Cort, Louise Allison. *Shigaraki, Potters' Valley*. Kodansha, 1979, reprint 2000.

Cort, Louise Allison. "The Grand Kitano Tea Gathering," *Chanoyu Quarterly* 31 (1982a).

Cort, Louise Allison. "Gen'ya's Devil Bucket," *Chanoyu Quarterly* 30 (1982b).

Cort, Louise Allison. *Seto and Mino Ceramics*. Freer Gallery of Art, 1992.

Cort, Louise Allison. "Vietnamese Ceramics in Japanese Contexts," in John Stevenson and John Guy (eds), *Vietnamese Ceramics: A Separate Tradition*. Art Media Resources with Avery Press, 1997.

Cross, Tim. "Tea for War: The *senshō kigan kencha* of Fukuoka's Hakozaki Hachimangu," forthcoming.

Davis, Darrell William. *Picturing Japaneseness: Monumental Style, National Identity, Japanese Film*. Columbia University Press, 1996.

Doi Tsugiyoshi. *Kinsei Nihon kaiga no kenkyū*. Bijutsu Shuppan, 1970.

Edo Senke Chanoyu Kenkyūjo (ed.), *Fuhaku hikki*. Chanoyu Kenkyūjo, 1987.

Ehmcke, Franziska. *Der japanische Tee-Weg: Bewusstseinsschulung und Gesamtkunstwerk*. Cologne: DuMont, 1991.

Elisonas, Jurgis. "Christianity and the Daimyo," in John Whitney Hall (ed.), *Early Modern Japan*. Vol. 4 of *The Cambridge History of Japan*. Cambridge University Press, 1991a.

Elisonas, Jurgis. "The Inseparable Treaty: Japan's Relations with China and Korea," in John Whitney Hall (ed.), *Early Modern Japan*. Vol. 4 of *The Cambridge History of Japan*. Cambridge University Press, 1991b.

Ellwood, Robert. "Review of Joan R. Piggot. *The Emergence of Japanese Kingship*," *History of Religions* 39:2 (1999).

Elyot, Thomas. *The Boke Named Governour*. First edition by Henry Herbert Stephen Croft, 1531; originally published in London, 1883. Reprinted in New York, Burt Franklin, 1967.

Faure, Bernard. *Chan Insight and Oversight: An Epistemological Critique of the Chan Tradition*. Princeton University Press, 1993.

Fieve, Nicolas, Sylvie Guichard-Anguis, Michèle Pirazzoli-t'Serstevens, *et al. Les arts de la cérémonie du thé*. Faton, 1996.

Fischer, Felice (ed.), *The Arts of Hon'ami Kōetsu, Japanese Renaissance Master*. Philadelphia Museum of Art, 2000.

Frois, Luis. *Historia de Japam*. 5 volumes. Biblioteca Nacional, Lisbon, 1976–1983.

Fujiansheng Bowuguan. *Zhangzhou yao*. Fujian Renmin Chubanshe, 1997.

Fujioka, Ryoichi. *Tea Ceremony Utensils*. Weatherhill, 1973.

Fukimoto Seijirō, Kasahara Masao, and Hiromoto Mitsuru. "Nōgyōson shihai no kakuritsu," in Wakayama Shishi Hensan Iinkai (eds), *Kinsei*. Vol. 2 of *Wakayama shishi*. Wakayama shi, 1989.

Fukuoka-shi Hakubutsukan (ed.), *Sakai to Hakata ten – yomigaeru ōgon no hibi*. Fukuoka-shi Hakubutsukan, 1992.

Gotō Bijutsukan. *Yamanoue Sōjiki*. Gotō Bijutsukan, 1995.

Gotō Yōichi. "Asano Nagaakira," *Kokushi daijiten*. Vol. 1. Yoshikawa Kōbunkan, 1979.

Graham, Patricia J. "*Yamamoto Baiitsu no Chūgokuga kenkyū*," *Kobijutsu* 80 (Fall 1986).

Graham, Patricia J. *Tea of the Sages: The Art of Sencha*. University of Hawai'i Press, 1998.

Graham, Patricia J. "The Appreciation of Chinese Flower Baskets in Premodern Japan," in Joseph N. Newland (ed.), *Japanese Bamboo Baskets: Masterworks of Form and Texture*. Cotsen Occasional Press, 1999.

Gunnarsson, Britt-Louise, Linell, Per and Nordberg, Bengt. *The Construction of Professional Discourse*. Longman, 1997.

Guth, Christine. *Art, Tea, and Industry: Masuda Takashi and the Mitsui Circle*. Princeton University Press, 1993.

Haga Kōshirō *et al.* (eds), *Daitokuji to chadō*. Tankōsha, 1972.

Haga Kōshirō. "The *Wabi* Aesthetic through the Ages," in Paul Varley and Kumakura Isao (eds), *Tea in Japan: Essays on the History of Chanoyu*. University of Hawai'i Press, 1989.

Hammad, Manar. *L'architecture du thé*. Paris: Groupe de recherches semio-linguistiques, École des hautes études en sciences sociales, Centre nationale de la recherche scientifique, 1987.

Hara Kazuo. "Urakusai ni gyōshuku shita Kumai Kei kantoku no aru omoi," *Kinema Junpo* 1018 (1989).

Harada Kinjirō (ed.), *Shina meiga hō kan*. Otsuka Kogeisha, 1936.

Harada Tomohiko. *Sadō bunkashi*. Vol. 3 of *Harada Tomohiko chosakushū*. Shibunkaku, 1981.

Harries, Meirion and Harries, Susie. *Soldiers of the Sun: The Rise and Fall of the Imperial Japanese Army*. Random House, 1991.

Hattox, Ralph S. *Coffee and Coffeehouses: The Origins of a Social Beverage in the Medieval Near East*. University of Washington Press, 1985.

Hayakawa Junzaburō (ed.), *Tokitsugu Kyō ki*. Vol. 4. Kokusho Kankōkai, 1914–1915.

Hayashi Kentarō (ed.), *Jitsuroku Shōwa shi: Gekidō no kiseki*. Gyōsei, 1987.

Hayashiya Seizo *et al. Chinese Ceramics from Japanese Collections: T'ang Through Ming Dynasties*. The Asia Society, 1977.

Hayashiya Seizō. "Kōshin chakaiki ni miru chagu," in Sen Sōsa (ed.), *Kōshin Sōsa chasho*. Shufu no Tomosha, 1998.

Hayashiya Tatsusaburō *et al.* (eds), *Kadokawa chadō daijiten*. Kadokawa Shoten, 1991.

Hayashiya, T., Nakamura, M. and Hayashiya, S. *Japanese Arts and the Tea Ceremony*. Weatherhill, 1974.

Hennemann, Horst Siegfried. *Cha-no-yu: die Tee-Kultur Japans*. Nachrichten der Gesellschaft für Natur- und Völkerkunde Ostasiens, Hamburg. Otto Harrassowitz, 1980.

Hennemann, Horst Siegfried. *Chasho: Geist und Geschichte der Theorien japanischer Teekunst*. Harrassowitz, 1994.

Herzfeld, Michael. "The Taming of Revolution: Intense Paradoxes of the Self," in Deborah E. Reed-Danahay (ed.), *Auto/Ethnography: Rewriting the Self and the Social*. Berg, 1997.

Hirota, Dennis. "Heart's Mastery: *Kokoro no fumi*, The Letter of Murata Shukō to His Disciple Choin," *Chanoyu Quarterly* 22 (1979).

Hirota, Dennis. *Wind in the Pines: Classic Writings of the Way of Tea as a Buddhist Path*. Asian Humanities Press, 1995.

Hisada Sōya. "Hisada ke no daidai," in Iguchi Kaisen *et al.* (eds), *Kyō no chake*. Bokusui Shobō, 1969.

Hisada Sōya. "Dōan to Shōan," in Kumakura Isao (ed.), *Oribe, Enshū, Sōtan*. Vol. 4 of *Chadō shūkin*. Shogakkan, 1983.

Hisamatsu, S. "The Way of Tea and Buddhism," *Chanoyu Quarterly* 73 (1994).

Hisashi Fujiki with George Elison. "The Political Posture of Oda Nobunaga," in John Whitney Hall, Keiji Nagahara, and Kozo Yamamura (eds), *Japan Before Tokugawa: Political Consolidation and Economic Growth, 1500–1650*. Princeton University Press, 1981.

Holland, James-Henry. "Allusion, Performance, and Status: The Social and Aesthetic World of Elite Practitioners of the Japanese Tea Ceremony," Ph.D. diss., Cornell University, 1997.

Holland, James-Henry. "A Public Tea Gathering: Theater and Ritual in the Japanese Tea Ceremony," *Journal of Ritual Studies* 14:1 (2000).

Honjō Sōsen (ed.), *Ishikawa Hōten Izumigusa*. Rōsokusha, 1965.

Hora Tomio. *Teppō denrai to sono eikyō: Tanegashimajū zōhoban*. Azekura, 1959.

Horinouchi Sōkan. "Sōtan no Zen," in Sen Sōsa (ed.), *Gempaku Sōtan monjo*. Chatobisha, 1971.

Horinouchi Sōkan. "Sōtan no chafū," in Kumakura Isao (ed.), *Oribe, Enshū, Sōtan*. Vol. 4 of *Chadō shūkin*. Shogakkan, 1983.

Horinouchi Sōkan. "Senke jisshoku," in Murai Yasuhiko (ed.), *Chanoyu no tenkai*. Vol. 5 of *Chadō shūkin*. Shogakkan, 1985.

Horiuchi Shin (ed.), *Nanki Tokugawa shi*. Vol. 1. Nanki Tokugawashi Kankokai, 1930–1933; Seibundō, 1989 reprint.

Ignatovich, Aleksandr Nikolaevich. *Filosofskie, istoricheskie i esteticheskie aspekty sinkretizma*. Moscow: Russkoe fenomenologicheskoe obshchestvo, 1997.

Iguchi Rikihei and Nakajima Tadashi. *Kamikaze tokubetsu kōgekitai*. Nihon Shuppan Kyodo Kabushikigaisha, 1951.

Ii Masahiro and Kurasawa Yukihiro (eds), *Ichigo ichie*. Toei Sha, 1989.

Ikeda Hyōa. "Take kago no hanaire," in Nakamura Masao *et al.* (eds), *Chadōgu I*. Vol. 10 of *Chadō shūkin*. Shogakkan, 1986.

Imai Shizuo (sup. ed.), Toki-shi Mino Tōji Rekishikan (ed.), *Momoyama no hana – Osaka shutsudo no Momoyama tōji*. Toki: Oribe no hi jikkō iinkai, 1993.

Ishii Shirō (ed.), *Kinsei buke shisō*. Iwanami Shoten, 1974.

Itō Teiji. "Sen Rikyū and Taian," *Chanoyu Quarterly* 15:9, (1976).

Ivy, Marilyn. *Discourses of the Vanishing: Modernity, Phantasm, Japan*. The University of Chicago Press, 1995.

Jobst, Christlieb. "Befriedigung aus Tee und Blumen: Traditionelle Formen der Selbstverwirklichung," in Gebhard Hielscher (ed.), *Die Frau in Japan*. Vol. 1. OAG-Reihe Japan modern, 1984.

Johnson, William. "Kinuyo Tanaka," *Film Comment* 30:1 (1994).

Kane, Melissa Marie. "Communicating Tea: An Ethnography of Social Interaction and Relationship Construction in the Japanese Tea Ritual," Ph.D. diss., University of Washington, 1998.

Kanematsu Romon. *Chikutō to Baiitsu*. Gahōsha, 1910.

Karatani, Kojin. "Uses of Aesthetics: After Orientalism," trans. Sabu Kohso. *boundary 2* 25:2 (1998).

Karavan, Dani. *Tè: la cerimonia del tè*. Gliori-Fattoria di Celle, 2000.

Kato, Etsuko. "Bodies Representing the Past: Japanese Women and the Tea Ceremony after World War II," Ph.D. diss., University of Toronto, 2001.

Katō Tōkurō (ed.), *Genshoku tōki daijiten*. Tankōsha, 1972.

Kawahara Masahiko. "Kyōyaki ni tsuite no oboegaki," *Bunkazaihō* 40 (1983).

Kawasaki Kikuko. "Oda seikenka no Sakai: Matsui Yūkan no yakuwari ni tsuite," *Hisutoria* 92 (1981).

Kazue Kazuichi. "Sōtan no chichi oya," in Sen Sōsa (ed.), *Gempaku Sōtan monjo*. Chatobisha, 1971.

Kita, Brigitte. *Tee und Zen – der gleiche Weg*. Erd, 1993.

Kōgei Shuppan (eds), *Saishin gendai tōgei sakka jiten*. Kōgei Shuppan, 1987.

Komatsu Shigemi. *Kohitsu*. Kōdansha, 1972.

Komatsu Shigemi. *Rikyū no tegami*. Shōgakukan, 1985.

Kondo, Dorinne. "The Way of Tea: A Symbolic Analysis," *Man* 20 (1985).

Kon'ishi Jinichi. "Michi and Medieval Writing," in Earl Miner (ed.), *Principles of Classical Japanese Literature*. Princeton University Press, 1985.

Kornicki, Peter. *The Book in Japan: A Cultural History from the Beginnings to the Nineteenth Century*. Brill, 1998.

Koschmann, J. Victor. *Revolution and Subjectivity in Postwar Japan*. University of Chicago Press, 1996.

Koyama Yoshiki and Isao, Mitsuo. "Tokugawa Yorinobu no Kishū nyūkoku," in Wakayama Shishi Hensan Iinkai (eds), *Kinsei*. Vol. 2 of *Wakayama shishi*. Wakayama shi, 1989.

Kraidy, M. "Intertextual Maneuvers around the Subaltern: Aladdin as a Postmodern Text," in Cristina Degli-Esposti (ed.), *Postmodernism in the Cinema*. Blackwell, 1998.

Kramer, Robert. "The Tea Cult in History," Ph.D. diss., University of Chicago, 1985.

Kumakura Isao (ed.), *Shidai chakaiki*. Vol. 3 of *Chanoyu no koten*. Sekai Bunkasha, 1984.

Kumakura Isao. "Kan'ei Culture and *Chanoyu*," in Paul Varley and Kumakura Isao (eds), *Tea in Japan: Essays on the History of Chanoyu*. University of Hawai'i Press, 1989a.

Kumakura Isao. "Sen no Rikyū: Inquiries into his Life and Tea," in Paul Varley and Kumakura Isao (eds), *Tea in Japan: Essays on the History of Chanoyu*. University of Hawai'i Press, 1989b.

Kumakura Isao. *Gomizuno'o tennō*. Iwanami Shoten, 1994a. Published by Asahi Shinbunsha in 1982 as *Gomizuno'o*.

Kumakura Isao. "The History of Chanoyu in Early-Modern Japan," *Chanoyu Quarterly* 75 (1994b).

Kumakura Isao *et al.* (eds), *Shiryō ni yoru chanoyu no rekishi*. Vol. 2. Shufu no Tomosha, 1995.

Kumakura Isao. "Kōshin Sōsa chasho no naka no Sen no Rikyū," in Sen Sōsa (ed.), *Kōshin Sōsa chasho*. Shufu no Tomosha, 1998.

Kumakura Isao. *Bunka to shite no manaa*. Iwanami Shoten, 2000.

Kuwata Tadachika (ed.), *Sengoku shiryō sōsho*. Vol. 2. Jinbutsu Ōraisha, 1965.

Kyoto Kokuritsu Hakubutsukan. *Tanyū shukuzu*. Kyoto Kokuritsu Hakubutsukan, 1980–1981.

Kyoto Kokuritsu Hakubutsukan (ed.), *Nihonjin ga kononda Chūgoku tōji*. Kyoto Kokuritsu Hakubutsukan, 1991.

Kyoto-shi Maizō Bunkazai Kenkyūjo. *Kyoto-shi maizō bunkazai hakkutsu chōsa gaiyō*. Kyoto-shi Maizō Bunkazai Kenkyūjo, 1987.

Lawton, Thomas. "Yamanaka Sadajirō: Advocate for Asian Art," *Orientations* 26/1 (January 1995).

Lawton, Thomas. "Chinese Ritual Bronzes: Collections and Catalogues Outside Japan," in Steven D. Owyoung. *Ancient Chinese Bronzes in the Saint Louis Art Museum*. Saint Louis Art Museum, 1997.

Levine, Greg. "Jukōin: Art, Architecture, and Mortuary Culture at a Japanese Zen Buddhist Temple," Ph.D. diss., Princeton University, 1997.

Lillehoj, Elizabeth. "Flowers of the Capital: Imperial Sponsorship of Art in Seventeenth Century Kyoto," *Orientations* 27:8 (September, 1996).

Ludwig, Theodore M. "The Way of Tea: A Religio-Aesthetic Mode of Life," *History of Religions* 14 (1974).

Ludwig, Theodore M. "Before Rikyū: Religious and Aesthetic Influences in the Early History of the Tea Ceremony," *Monumenta Nipponica* 36 (1981).

Ludwig, Theodore M. "*Chanoyu* and Momoyama: Conflict and Transformation in Rikyū's Art," in Paul Varley and Kumakura Isao (eds), *Tea in Japan: Essays on the History of Chanoyu*. University of Hawai'i Press, 1989.

Marder, Arthur J., Jacobsen, Mark and Horsfield, John. *Old Friends, New Enemies: The Royal Navy and the Imperial Japanese Navy, 1942–1945*. Oxford University Press, 1990.

Maske, Andrew. "New Advances in Tea Ceramic History: Recent Excavations of Tea Wares from Consumer Sites," *Chanoyu Quarterly* 70 (1992).

Matsudairake Henshūkai (eds), *Matsudaira Fumai den*. Keibundo Shoten, 1917.

Mew, James and Ashton, John. *Drinks of the World*. Charles Scribner's Sons, 1892.

Mita Tomiko. *Toriawase no kufū*. Tankōsha, 1981.

Mittwer, Henry. *The Art of Chabana: Flowers for the Tea Ceremony*. Charles E. Tuttle Company, 1974.

Miura Hiroyuki (ed.), *Sakai-shi shi*. 8 vols. Sakai Shiyakusho, Sakai, 1929–1931.

Miyazaki Noriko. "Nihon kindai no naka no Chūgoku kaigashi kenkyū," in Tōkyō Kokuritsu Bunkazai Kenkyūjo (ed.), *Ima, Nihon no bijutsushi gaku o furikaeru*. Tōkyō Kokuritsu Bunkazai Kenkyūjo, 1999.

Moeran, Brian and Skov, Lise. "Mount Fuji and the Cherry Blossoms: A View from Afar," in Pamela J. Asquith and Arne Kalland (eds), *Japanese Images of Nature: Cultural Perspectives*. Curzon, 1997.

Montreal Museum of Fine Arts (ed.), *The Tokugawa Collection: Japan of the Shoguns.* Montreal Museum of Fine Arts, 1989.

Mori, Barbara Lynne Rowland. "The Tea Ceremony: A Transformed Japanese Ritual," *Gender and Society* 5 (1991).

Mori, Barbara Lynne Rowland. *Americans Studying the Traditional Japanese Art of the Tea Ceremony: The Internationalizing of a Traditional Art.* Mellen Research University Press, 1992.

Morimoto Asako. "On the Vietnamese Trade Ceramics Excavated in Japan and Their Production Places," *Tōyō tōji* 23–24 (1993–1995).

Morimura Ken'ichi. "Jūroku-jūnana seiki shotō no Sakai Kangō Toshi iseki shut-sudo no Tai shijikō," *Bōeki tōji kenkyū* 9 (1989).

Moriya Takeshi. "The Mountain Dwelling Within the City," *Chanoyu Quarterly* 56 (1988).

Morris, V. Dixon. "Sakai: The History of a City in Medieval Japan," Ph.D. diss., University of Washington, 1970.

Morris, V. Dixon. "The City of Sakai and Urban Autonomy," in George Elison and Bardwell L. Smith (eds), *Warlords, Artists, and Commoners: Japan in the Sixteenth Century.* University of Hawai'i Press, 1981.

Morse, Edward S. *Catalogue of the Morse Collection of Japanese Pottery.* Charles E. Tuttle Company, 1979.

Murai Yasuhiko, Tsutsui Hiroichi, and Akanuma Taka (eds), *Chadō bijutsu techō.* Tankōsha, 1987.

Murai Yasuhiko. "The Development of Chanoyu: Before Rikyū," in Paul Varley and Kumakura Isao (eds), *Tea in Japan: Essays on the History of Chanoyu.* University of Hawai'i Press, 1989.

Murai Yasuhiko. "A Biography of Sen Rikyū," *Chanoyu Quarterly* 61 (1990).

Nagashima Fukutarō. "Oda Nobunaga no Tajima keiryaku to Imai Sōkyū: Tsuke-tari Ikuno Ginzan no keiei," *Kansei Gakuin shigaku* 5 (1959).

Nakamura Katsumaro (ed.), *Ii tairo sadō dan.* Tokyo Daigaku Shuppankai, 1978 reprint, 1917 original print.

Nakamura Masao. *Chashitsu to roji.* Shōgakkan, 1972.

Nakamura Toshinori. "Early History of the Teahouse," *Chanoyu Quarterly.* Part 1, 69; Part 2, 70 (1992).

Nakano-Holmes, Julia. "Furuta Oribe: Iconoclastic Guardian of Chanoyu Tradition," Ph.D. diss., University of Hawai'i, 1995.

Narasaki Shōichi. "Mino Momoyama-tō no seiritsu," *Seto-shi Maizō Bunkazai Sentaa kenkyū kiyō* 7 (1999).

Nezu Bijutsukan (ed.), *Momoyama no chatō.* Nezu Institute of Fine Arts, 1989.

Nezu Bijutsukan Gakugeibu. *Kanan no yakimono: Kiseto, Oribe, Aode Kokutani no genryū o motomete.* Kanshō seriizu I. Nezu Institute of Fine Arts, 1998.

Nishiyama Matsunosuke. "Yamada ke," in Sen Sōsa *et al.* (eds), *Rekishihen.* Vol. 1 of *Chadō no genryū.* Tankōsha, 1983.

Nishiyama Matsunosuke (ed.), *Nampōroku.* Iwanami Shoten, 1986.

Noguchi Zuiten (ed.), *Teihon Sekishū ryū.* Vol. 2. Mitumura Suiko Shoten, 1985.

Nomura Zuiten. *Enshū ryū: rekishi to keifu.* Mitsumura Suiko Shoin, *n.d.*

Nomura Zuiten. *Sōhen ryū: rekishi to keifu.* Mitsumura Suiko Shoin, 1987.

Oka Yoshiko. "*Kakumeiki* ni miru karamonoyatachi – kinsei shotō no tōjiki ryūtsū," *Shisō* 48 (1991).

Oka Yoshiko. "Kan'ei bunka no chanoyu," in Oka Yoshiko *et al.*, *Kan'ei bunka no nettowaaku: "Kakumeiki" no sekai*. Shibunkaku Shuppan, 1998a.

Oka Yoshiko. "Karamonoya oboegaki – Ōhira Gohei to Katsuyama Chōji," in Oka Yoshiko *et al.*, *Kan'ei bunka no nettowaaku: "Kakumeiki" no sekai*. Shibunkaku Shuppan, 1998b.

Okuno Takahiro (ed.), *Zōtei Oda Nobunaga monjo no kenkyū*. Yoshikawa, 1988.

Ooms, Herman. *Tokugawa Ideology: Early Constructs, 1570–1680*. Princeton University Press, 1985.

Ozaki Naotō. *Matsunaga Jian Collection*. Fukuoka Municipal Art Museum, 2001.

Pincus, Leslie. *Authenticating Culture in Imperial Japan: Kuki Shuzo and the Rise of National Aesthetics*. University of California Press, 1996.

Pitelka, Morgan. "Raku Ceramics: Tradition and Cultural Reproduction in Japanese Tea Practice, 1574–1942," Ph.D. diss., Princeton University, 2001.

Pitelka, Morgan. "Yūgei bunka to dentō," in Kumakura Isao (ed.), *Nihonshi ni okeru yūgei no shoos*. Yoshikawa Kobunkan, forthcoming.

Plutschow, Herbert E. *Historical Chanoyu*. The Japan Times, Ltd, 1986.

Plutschow, Herbert. "An Anthropological Perspective on the Japanese Tea Ceremony," *Anthropoetics* 1:5 (Spring/Summer 1999).

Raab, Bernadette. *Das Wunder der Teestunde: Teegeniesser erzählen eigene Erlebnisse*. Aufl. – Ottensheim: Lilanitya, 1997.

Reischauer, Edwin. "Japanese Religion in the Meiji Era," Review article. *Harvard Journal of Asiatic Studies* 20 (1957).

Rowley, G.G. "Literary Canon and National Identity: *The Tale of Genji* in Meiji Japan," *Japan Forum* 9:1 (1997).

Sadler, A.L. *Cha-no-yu: The Japanese Tea Ceremony*. J.L. Thompson & Co., 1934, Charles E. Tuttle Company, reprint 1962.

Saiki Kazuma and Yoshihiko Iwasawa (eds), *Tokugawa shoke keifu*. Vol. 2. Zoku Gunsho Ruijū Kanseikai, 1970–1984.

Sakaguchi Yoshiyasu. "Oda Nobunaga no jōraku to Sakaishū, 2: Nobunaga to Seishō Imai Sōkyū," in *Shōkei Daigaku kenkyū kiyō* 7 (1984).

Sakai Sōga. "Yukō nikki," in Kurita Tensei (ed.), *Sakai Sōga Chakaiki*. Muramatsu Shokan, 1977.

Sakai, Naoki. *Translation and Subjectivity: On "Japan" and Cultural Nationalism*. University of Minnesota Press, 1997.

Sakai-shi Hakubutsukan. *Sakaishū – chanoyu o tsukutta hitobito*. Sakai-shi Hakubutsukan, 1989.

Sasaki Sanmi. *Ocha no toriawase*. Kōbunsha, 1949.

Sasaki Sanmi (ed.), *Chajin techō*. Kawahara Shoten, 1952; revised 1992.

Sato Tadao. *Currents in Japanese Cinema*. Kodansha, 1982.

Schama, Simon. "Perishable Commodities: Dutch Still-life Painting and the 'Empire of Things,'" in John Brewer and Roy Porter (eds), *Consumption and the World of Goods*. Routledge, 1993.

Schechner, Richard. *Between Theater and Anthropology*. University of Pennsylvania Press, 1985.

Schlesinger, Phillip. "On National Identity: Some Conceptions and Misconceptions Criticized," *Social Science Information* 26:2 (1987).

Schwalbe, Hans. *Die Teezeremonie*. Munich, 1979.

Scott, Joan W. "The Evidence of Experience," in James Chandler, Arnold I.

Davidson, and Harry Harootunian (eds), *Questions of Evidence: Proof, Practice, and Persuasion Across the Disciplines*. University of Chicago Press, 1994.

Seikadō Bunko Bijutsukan (ed.), *Seikadōzō senchagu meihin ten*. Seikadō Bunko, 1998.

Sen Sōin. "Sōtan no cha," in Sen Sōsa (ed.), *Gempaku Sōtan monjo*. Chatobisha, 1971.

Sen Sōin. "Kōshin Sōsa den," in Sen Sōsa (ed.), *Kōshin Sōsa chasho*. Shufu no Tomosha, 1998.

Sen Sōsa (ed.), *Gempaku Sōtan monjo*. Chatobisha, 1971.

Sen Sōsa (ed.), *Kōshin Sōsa chasho*. Shufu no Tomosha, 1998.

Sen Sōsa *et al.* (eds), *Rekishi hen*. Vol. 1 of *Chadō no genryū*. Tankōsha, 1983.

Sen Sōshitsu (ed.), *Kama*. Vol. 10 of *Chadō bijutsu zenshū*. Tankōsha, 1970.

Sen Sōshitsu XV. *The Japanese Way of Tea from its Origins in China to Sen Rikyū*. University of Hawai'i Press, 1998.

Sen Sōshitsu *et al.* (eds), *Chadō koten zenshū*. 12 vols. Tankō Shinsha, 1956–1962.

Sen Sōshu. "Mushanokoji Senke," in Sen Sōsa *et al.* (eds), *Rekishihen*. Vol. 1 of *Chadō no genryū*. Tankōsha, 1983.

Seseragi Toneri. "Senke jisshoku," in Sen Sōshitsu *et al.* (eds), *Chadō zenshū*. Vol. 3. Sōgensha, 1936.

Shiota Nakakazu. *Nihon eiga gojunen shi 1941–91 nen*. Fujiwara Shoten, 1992.

Shufu no Tomosha. *Gendai senchadō jiten*. Shufu no Tomosha, 1981.

Simmel, Georg. *On Individuality and Social Forms*. The University of Chicago Press, 1971.

Sokabe Yōko and Fusa, Kiyose. *Sōtan no tegami*. Kawara Shoten, 1997.

Stallybrass, Peter and White, Allon. *The Politics and Poetics of Transgression*. Cornell University Press, 1986.

Stanley-Baker, Richard. "Mid-Muromachi Paintings of the Eight Views of Hsiao and Hsiang," Ph.D. diss., Princeton University, 1979.

Stewart, Susan. *On Longing: Narratives of the Miniature, the Gigantic, the Souvenir, the Collection*. Duke University Press, 1993.

Tanaka, Sen'o. *The Tea Ceremony*. Kodansha, 1973.

Tanihata Akio (ed.), "Ii Naosuke chakaiki," *Chanoyu* 16 (1979).

Tanihata Akio. "Men of Tea: An Evaluation by Yamanoue Sōji, Part 1," *Chanoyu Quarterly* 28 (1981).

Tanihata Akio. "Daitokuji to cha no yu," in Murai Yasuhiko (ed.), *Sen Rikyū*. Vol. 3 of *Chadō Shūkin*. Shogakkan, 1983.

Tanihata Akio. "Daimyo sadō no keifu," in Murai Yasuhiko (ed.), *Chanoyu no tenkai*. Vol. 5 of *Chadō shūkin*. Shogakkan, 1985.

Tanihata Akio. "Nobunaga no meibutsugari to gochanoyu goseidō," *Tankō* 9 (1993a).

Tanihata Akio. "Tenkajin Toyotomi Hideyoshi to chanoyu no kakudai," *Tankō* 10 (1993b).

Tanihata Akio. "Wabicha no hatten to Sakai no chajintachi," *Tankō* 8 (1993c).

Tanihata Akio (ed.), "Ii Naosuke no chakaiki," *Chanoyu bunka gakkai* 3 (1996).

Tanimura Reiko. *Ii Naosuke: shūyō to shite no chanoyu*. Sobunsha, 2001.

Tankōsha Henshūkyoku (eds), *Cha no kireji nyūmon*. Tankōsha, 1997.

Teshigahara Hiroshi. *Rikyū*. Capitol, 1991.

Tokugawa Bijutsukan (ed.), *Tokugawa Bijutsukan no meihin shirizu: Daimyo chadōgu ten*. Tokugawa Bijutsukan, 1991.

Tokugawa Bijutsukan and Bijutsukan, Nezu (eds), *Chatsubo*. Tokugawa Art Museum and Nezu Institute of Fine Arts, 1981.

Tōkyō Kokuritsu Hakubutsukan. *Tokubetsu ten: Muromachi jidai no bijutsu.* Tōkyō Kokuritsu Hakubutsukan, 1989.

Tōkyō Kokuritsu Hakubutsukan (ed.), *Tōkyō Kokuritsu Hakubutsukan zuhan mokuroku Chūgoku kaiga hen.* Tōkyō Kokuritsu Hakubutsukan, 1979.

Toraya Bunko (eds), *Fukusa to wagashi ten*. Toraya Bunko, 1992.

Totman, Conrad. *Politics in the Tokugawa Bakufu, 1600–1843*. Harvard University Press, 1967.

Toyoda Takeshi. *Sakai: Shōnin no shinshutsu to toshi no jiyū*. Shibundō, 1957.

Tsutsui, Hiroichi. "The Role of Anecdotes in the Transmission of Tea Traditions," *Chanoyu Quarterly* 29 (1981).

Tsutsui Hiroichi. *Yamanoue Sōji ki o yomu*. Tankōsha, 1987.

Tsutsui Hiroichi. "Rikyū no densho," in Kumakura Isao *et al.* (eds), *Rikyū Daijite*. Tankōsha, 1989.

Varley, H. Paul. "Ashikaga Yoshimitsu and the World of Kitayama: Social Change and Shogunal Patronage in Early Modern Japan," in John Whitney Hall and Toyoda Takeshi (eds), *Japan in the Muromachi Age*. University of California Press, 1977.

Varley, H. Paul and Elison, George. "The Culture of Tea: From Its Origins to Sen no Rikyū," in George Elison and Bardwell L. Smith (eds), *Warlords, Artist and Commoners: Japan in the Sixteenth Century*. University of Hawai'i Press, 1981.

Varley, H. Paul and Kumakura Isao (eds), *Tea in Japan: Essays on the History of Chanoyu*. University of Hawai'i Press, 1989.

Wakita Osamu and Wakita Haruko. "Tokken shōnin no taitō," in Hayashiya Tatsusaburō (ed.), *Momoyama no kaika*. Vol. 4 of *Kyoto no rekishi*. Kyoto-shi Hensanjo, 1969.

Weinberg, Bennett Alan and Bealer, Bonnie K. *The World of Caffeine: The Science and Culture of the World's Most Popular Drug*. Routledge, 2001.

Wilson, Richard. "The Tea Ceremony: Art and Etiquette for the Tokugawa Era," in The Montreal Museum of Fine Arts. *The Japan of the Shoguns*. The Montreal Museum of Fine Arts, 1989.

Yamaori, Tetsuo. "Anecdotes about Sen Rikyū," *Chanoyu Quarterly* 65 (1991).

Yonehara Masayoshi. "Chanoyu," in Okamoto Ryōichi (ed.), *Oda Nobunaga jiten*. Shin Jinbutsu Oraisha, 1989.

# Index

Page numbers in *italic* refer to illustrations